From Meetinghouse to Megachurch

From Meetinghouse to Megachurch

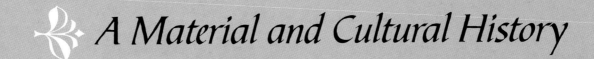 A Material and Cultural History

Anne C. Loveland and Otis B. Wheeler

University of Missouri Press
Columbia and London

Copyright © 2003 by
The Curators of the University of Missouri
University of Missouri Press, Columbia, Missouri 65201
Printed and bound in China
5 4 3 2 1   07 06 05 04 03

Library of Congress Cataloging-in-Publication Data

Loveland, Anne C., 1938–
    From meetinghouse to megachurch : a material and cultural
history / Anne C. Loveland and Otis B. Wheeler.
        p. cm.
Includes bibliographical references and index.
    ISBN 0-8262-1480-0 (alk. paper)
    1. Church architecture—United States—History.   2. Protestant
church buildings—United States—History.   3. Evangelicalism—
United States—History.   I. Wheeler, Otis B., 1921–   II. Title.
    NA4828.5.L68 2003
    726.5′0973—dc21

                                                    2003006706

⊗™ This paper meets the requirements of the
American National Standard for Permanence of Paper
for Printed Library Materials, Z39.48, 1984.

Designer: Jennifer Cropp
Typesetter: The Composing Room of Michigan, Inc.
Printer and binder: Regent Publishing Services, Ltd.
Typefaces: Palatino, Esprit, Bible Script

In Memoriam
Robert Warren Heck
Architect, Scholar, Teacher, Friend

Contents

Acknowledgments

We have been aided in many ways by many persons. To name all who have taken a friendly interest in the project would not be feasible, but those who have made our task easier in substantial ways must be noted.

Archivists and librarians included Susan G. Broome, Stuart W. Campbell, Joyce Lee, Sandra Mooney, Don Veasey, and the staff of the Interlibrary Loan Department of the Middleton Library at Louisiana State University, Baton Rouge, Louisiana. Helpful friends were Evelyn Heck, Rena Bloom, and Paul Nagel, who provided photos and/or information on possible churches for inclusion in the study; and Dale Edwards and Keuren Pinckney who gave print materials that we otherwise would not have seen. Several LSU colleagues were also very helpful. Alumni Professor Emerita Gresdna Doty provided valuable consultation on theater history and design, as did Professor Marchita Mauck on the history of religious art and architecture. Professor Gaines Foster answered numerous questions about American evangelical history and reviewed the manuscript. We profited immensely from his thoughtful assessment, as well as the suggestions he made for improving the narrative.

Graduate students Andrew Gallagher and John Sykes contributed to the research effort. We also appreciated student worker Erin Murray's intelligent and skillful word processing.

At the megachurches we visited, the pastors, building administrators, secretaries, and other staff members welcomed and assisted us in more ways than we can recount. Pastors Jim

Garlow and Stephen Strader provided valuable information about other churches that we ultimately included in the study.

Jack DeBartolo, Jr., and Kenn Sanders gave generously of their time in discussions of church architecture and church planning, the latter serving as our guide in Phoenix during our first research trip in the spring of 1996. John Vaughan directed our attention to several interesting megachurches in the Midwest, as did Philip Goff and Kate McGinn, in California.

The LSU Graphic Services division and the LSU Instructional Technology Center helped with photographic reproductions.

Our project would have been impossible without the research funds of the T. Harry Williams Professorship at Louisiana State University. We are also grateful for a grant the Louisville Institute gave us to aid in the completion of the project.

All photographs in this book are by Otis B. Wheeler, unless otherwise credited.

From Meetinghouse to Megachurch

> A building condenses a culture in one place.
> —Edward S. Casey, *Getting Back into Place* (1993)

Introduction ✤

Building the Faith

When evangelical megachurches appeared on the American landscape, journalists and religious commentators hailed them as something new under the sun—"new paradigm churches . . . changing the way Christianity looks and is experienced," or heralds of a "new reformation." Labels such as "the next church" and "a church for the 21st century" conveyed their revolutionary character. Not just their seven-day-a-week programming (religious, educational, social, and recreational) but also their architecture seemed unprecedented. "From curbside to carpeting, church architecture is being reshaped by changing lifestyles and ministry demands," declared the writer of an article entitled "So Long to Sacred Space." Like him, most observers regarded the megachurches as a product of late-twentieth-century American culture, describing them as "shopping mall" or "supermarket churches" reflecting the values and practices of a consumer-oriented society.[1]

Comparatively speaking, the number of megachurches was insignificant. In 1970, there were but ten. By the mid 1990s, they numbered about four hundred, representing slightly less than 2 percent of Protestant churches in the United States.[2] What riveted attention was their great size: they attracted an average weekend worship attendance of two thousand or more persons; their sanctuaries commonly seated three to four thousand, in a few cases as many as ten thousand; and their campuses sometimes extended to hundreds of acres. Those numbers rendered them not only impressive but seemingly unique in the history of Protestant church architecture.

We view evangelical megachurches not as something new or unique, but as an evolution. Approaching them from the standpoint of material and cultural history and focusing on their architecture, we have placed them in their larger religious and historical context in order to demonstrate how their form and function evolved from earlier religious structures built by nonliturgical Protestants.

Our study encompasses several generations of white and African American evangelical church builders: the mainline evangelicals of the nineteenth century (Presbyterians, Methodists, Congregationalists, and Baptists); the "dissenting evangelicals" (fundamentalists, holiness people, and pentecostals) of the late nineteenth and early twentieth century; and the fundamentalists, "new evangelicals," pentecostals, and neopentecostals of the late twentieth century. Notwithstanding important doctrinal and socioeconomic differences, all of these evangelicals affirmed three beliefs. They all regarded the Bible as the inerrant authority on faith and life. They all believed in salvation by faith, as a result of a conversion experience in which one surrendered one's life to Jesus Christ as Lord and Savior. And they all shared a compulsion to evangelize the unconverted and unchurched, based on the Great Commission handed down by Jesus in Matthew 28:19: "go . . . and teach all nations, baptizing them in the name of the Father, and of the Son, and of the Holy Ghost." Of the three

tenets, the commitment to evangelism exerted the greatest influence on building design.

During much of their history, regardless of their numbers, evangelicals have constituted a subculture of American society. As material historians, focusing on religious architecture, we treat evangelical religious structures not only in terms of their design and construction but also as expressions of evangelical beliefs and practices.[3] Their structures reveal their perspectives on theology, worship practices, religious art and symbolism, evangelism, and community outreach.

As cultural historians, we demonstrate how evangelical Protestants adapted their architectural forms as well as their beliefs and practices to shifting religious and social currents. Their architecture reflected and facilitated two important developments in the history of evangelical religion: the adaptation of church evangelism to changes in American culture and society, and the shift of emphasis in evangelical worship from the preaching of the Word to music and other performing arts and from a participatory to a performance-oriented service.

Chapters 1 through 6 treat the antecedents of the late-twentieth-century megachurches, beginning with the seventeenth-century meetinghouses built by the New England Puritans. Their utilitarian, plain-style structures embodied a functionalist aesthetic that became the hallmark of evangelical architecture in the nineteenth and twentieth centuries.

The second chapter discusses the revival structures used by evangelists in the late eighteenth and early nineteenth century to reach the unchurched and unconverted in frontier areas, villages, towns, and even large cities of the United States. More often than not, they held their revival meetings in nonchurch structures: open-air campgrounds, tents, and, especially in the large cities, commercial buildings, including music halls and theaters.

Chapter 3 considers the large, often sumptuous auditorium churches built by white and African American mainline evangelical congregations (Congregational, Baptist, Methodist, and Presbyterian) from the mid–nineteenth century well into the twentieth century. The fourth chapter describes the multi-purpose facilities (educational, social, recreational, community welfare) found in many of these auditorium churches.

The fundamentalists, holiness people, and pentecostals who appeared on the religious scene in the late nineteenth and early twentieth century are discussed in chapter 5. While their gospel tents and tabernacles recall the revival structures of the early-nineteenth-century evangelists, the large auditorium churches and temples they erected in Chicago, Fort Worth, Detroit, and Los Angeles were quite innovative. The sixth chapter briefly considers the "gathered churches" built during the mid-twentieth-century revolution in church architecture in the United States. Although they were mainly constructed by liberal, mainline Protestants, their architecture exerted a significant influence on the late-twentieth-century megachurches.

The remaining four chapters and the Epilogue discuss the architecture of the late-twentieth-century evangelical megachurches. Between 1996 and 2000, we visited some one hundred evangelical megachurches located throughout the United States. Our book focuses on sixty-three of those churches, including predominantly African American as well as biracial, multiethnic, and predominantly white congregations. Chapter 7 discusses the origins and development of these megachurches, paying particular attention to the key role played by strategists of the church growth movement in the 1970s, 1980s, and 1990s. The eighth chapter describes the variety of megachurch architecture. Although the media and many church growth experts regarded Willow Creek Community Church in South Barrington, Illinois, as the prototype, we found that megachurch buildings varied considerably in terms of size, architectural style, and the use of religious symbolism and art. Chapter 9 describes the myriad nonworship facilities found in the so-called full service megachurches. The tenth chapter treats the design and furnishings of the megachurch auditorium or "worship center," focusing on the influence exerted by contemporary Christian worship practices. The Epilogue presents an interpretation of evangelical megachurch architecture that draws on recent scholarship regarding the relationship between the sacred and the profane.

Our book fills a significant gap in the historiography of evangelical religion in the United States. Studies of American evangelicalism have mainly focused on its theology, social origins, political involvement, and relationship to popular culture, whereas the material culture of evangelical religion has attracted comparatively little attention. At a recent conference on evangelical worship and church architecture, Professor

Jhennifer Amundson speculated that this was because Protestant architecture has not been so "visually rich" as the architecture of Roman Catholicism or Orthodoxy.[4] But what evangelical structures may lack in visual richness they more than make up for in cultural expressiveness, communicating the beliefs, values, intentions, and practices of the people who built and worshiped in them. If only for that reason, evangelical religious structures demand our attention.

1

The Meetinghouse ❧

To prepare and repair places for the public worship . . . is but an act of obedience to him who requires worship from us . . . but the setting of these places off with a theatrical gaudiness does not savor of the spirit of a true Christian society.—Cotton Mather, *Magnalia Christi Americana* (1702)

The earliest American antecedent of the late-twentieth-century evangelical megachurches was the seventeenth-century and early-eighteenth-century meetinghouse, the "new architectural creation" devised by the English Puritans who settled Massachusetts Bay in 1630 (Fig. 1).[1] Their main contribution to the evolution of the megachurches was a functionalist aesthetic that mandated designing religious buildings to suit the purposes, beliefs, and activities of the people who used them. As dissenters in the Church of England, the Puritans designed their meetinghouses to reflect their religious beliefs and worship practices, as well as their rejection of Anglican architecture and liturgy.

In keeping with their Reformed theology, the seventeenth-century Puritans repudiated the notion of a consecrated place of worship and the idea of a church building as a sacred space. "There is no just ground from scripture to apply such a trope as church to a house for public assembly," declared the Puritan theologian Richard Mather. To the Puritans, the word "church" described not a building but a body of people who had entered into a covenant for the purpose of worshiping

Fig. 1. Elder Ballou Meeting House, Cumberland Hill, Providence County, Rhode Island (ca. 1740), pen and ink drawing. Photograph by Frank Farley, courtesy of Library of Congress, Washington, D.C., Prints and Photographs Division, Historic American Buildings Survey, Reproduction number HABS RI, 4-CUMB, 1-14.

God. And, as historian Peter Williams has explained, the Puritans contended, contrary to the traditional Catholic and Anglican view, that "the physical setting for worship was no different from any other secular space and only had to provide an appropriate setting for the preached Word." The very term *meetinghouse* implied "a neutral public space" that could be and was used for both religious and secular activities. Thus the Puritans saw nothing wrong with using their meetinghouses not only for worship but also for political functions such as town meetings, elections, and other public gatherings, or even as forts. Eventually, of course, they built other structures for secular activities and reserved the meetinghouse for religious purposes, but even then they did not regard it as an intrinsically sacred structure.[2]

The seventeenth-century Puritan meetinghouse was an unpretentious, unadorned structure built of wood and quite modest in size. The Dedham meetinghouse, for example, built in 1638, was thirty-six feet long and twenty feet wide. The Hingham "Old Ship" Meeting House, erected in 1681, was somewhat larger, fifty-five by forty-five feet. Instead of the cruciform or narrow rectangular shape characteristic of Anglican (and Roman Catholic) church buildings, the Puritans chose a boxlike form: square or, more often, rectangular, but wider than the Anglican parish churches in England and the southern English colonies. During the second half of the seventeenth century, the Puritans began adding dormers, belfries, and porches, but they retained the original form and horizontal emphasis.[3]

Like the exteriors, the interiors of the early meetinghouses were free of ornamentation—in the words of Rev. Cotton Mather, "not set off with gaudy, pompous, theatrical fineries, but suited unto the simplicity of Christian worship." The Puritans opposed the use of religious symbols and depictions of religious figures and scenes (for example, in stained-glass windows) not only on theological grounds, as idolatry, but also as a distraction and a waste of money. As followers of the Reformed theology, they made the preaching of the Word, rather than the sacraments, the central element of the worship service. The emphasis on the sermon dictated an interior arrangement different from that of Anglican or Catholic churches. The interior of the meetinghouse was an undivided space. There was no narthex; neither was there a chancel separating the priest and choir from the laity, as in the liturgical churches. Not the altar, but the pulpit became the main focus of attention during the worship service. And the placement of the pulpit differed as well. In the Anglican churches built in the southern English colonies, it was located close to the center of the long side of the sanctuary of a rectangular building or at an interior corner in a cruciform-shape building. The Puritans placed the pulpit in a central position, facing the entrance, on the narrow dimension of the structure.[4]

There has been considerable speculation as to the form of the pulpit in the seventeenth-century meetinghouse. The earliest meetinghouses may not have had any pulpit at all or perhaps only a raised platform for the minister. Charles A. Place suggested that the early-seventeenth-century pulpits were

Fig. 2. Interior, Elder Ballou Meeting House, looking toward the pulpit. Photograph by Arthur W. LeBoeuf, courtesy of Library of Congress, Washington, D.C., Prints and Photographs Division, Historic American Buildings Survey, Reproduction number HABS RI, 4-CUMB, 1-15.

fastened to uprights with a four-inch board laid flat on the top and moulded." The form soon changed, however. Peter Benes and Philip Zimmerman cited contract descriptions for mid- to late-seventeenth-century pulpits that suggested "a flattened, wall-attached structure." On the basis of other survivals, they asserted that the pulpits used throughout the eighteenth century in Puritan meetinghouses "consisted of an elevated platform fixed to the wall, a projecting front and desk supported by a base, and flanking wings that angled back and met the wall." The pulpit in the Sandown Meetinghouse in Sandown, New Hampshire (Fig. 3) illustrates that type of pulpit. Whatever their form, meetinghouse pulpits differed significantly from the freestanding capsule-type pulpits common in Anglican churches. The eighteenth-century meetinghouse pulpits were also more elaborate and of much finer design than those of the previous century, and they were often ornately decorated or carved. Like the Sandown pulpit, many were surmounted by a "canopie" or sounding board, designed to improve the acoustics as well as to accentuate the prominence of the pulpit.[5]

In the late eighteenth and early nineteenth century, the Puritans (who by that time formed the Congregationalist denomination) abandoned the plain style. As the onetime dissenters became more numerous and prosperous, they desired "an elegance and dignity of architectural expression which the simple meetinghouse could not provide." Influenced by architectural forms developed by the Anglican Church in the

similar to the "extremely simple and plain" one found in the Elder Ballou Meeting House built in Cumberland Hill, Rhode Island, around 1740 (Fig. 2). It was basically "a platform, reached by a few steps," that extended between the middle posts supporting the galleries. The front was made of "boards

Fig. 3. Interior, Sandown Meeting-house, Sandown, New Hampshire (1773–1774). Photograph by L. C. Durette, courtesy of Library of Congress, Washington, D.C., Prints and Photographs Division, Historic American Buildings Survey, Reproduction number HABS NH, 8-SAND, 1-12.

Fig. 4. Sandown Meetinghouse. Photograph by L. C. Durette, courtesy of Library of Congress, Washington, D.C., Prints and Photographs Division, Historic American Buildings Survey, Reproduction number HABS NH, 8-SAND, 1-4.

American colonies, and particularly by the designs of English architects Sir Christopher Wren and James Gibbs, they added high, standing towers and spires to the traditional meetinghouse structure. Under the influence of the neoclassical revival, they embellished their meetinghouses with classical details such as porches, pilasters, columns, capitals, entablatures, pedimented roofs, and dentil work.[6]

The Sandown Meetinghouse in New Hampshire and the First Congregational Church in Bennington, Vermont, illustrate the transition from the plain style to the more orna-

Fig. 5. First Congregational Church, Bennington, Vermont (1806).

mented meetinghouse. The Sandown Meetinghouse (Fig. 4), built in 1773–1774, featured a clapboard exterior decorated with the neoclassical detailing that became popular at that time. The First Congregational Church (Fig. 5), erected 1804–1806, exhibited the kind of towers or belfries New Englanders added to their meetinghouses in the eighteenth and early nineteenth century. Its elaborate three-stage tower featured four Palladian windows in the first stage that complemented the Palladian windows at the second story and the Palladian opening over the main entry, which was set in a broken pediment.[7]

The influence of the Puritan meetinghouse extended beyond New England Congregationalists. Other eighteenth- and early-nineteenth-century dissenters (Presbyterians, Quakers, Baptists, Methodists, and Shakers) made use of the meetinghouse form. So did African American church builders. To be sure, in the South, most slaves worshiped in biracial churches, usually in a seating area separate from the whites. However, some slaves and free blacks had their own churches that were adjunct to white churches, and, as John B. Boles has pointed out, "in most southern cities and large towns there were completely independent black churches, with black ministers, black deacons or elders, and a panoply of self-help associations connected to and supported by the church."[8] In the North, a significant number of black congregations were affiliated with predominantly white denominations, but African Americans also founded independent black denominations such as the African Methodist Episcopal (A.M.E.) and the

Fig. 6. First African Baptist Church, Boston (1806), courtesy of Library of Congress, Washington, D.C., Prints and Photographs Division, Historic American Buildings Survey, Reproduction number HABS MASS, 13-BOST, 42-3.

African Methodist Episcopal Zion (A.M.E.Z.) Churches, as well as numerous independent black Baptist churches and a much smaller number of black Protestant Episcopal, Presbyterian, and Congregational churches.

Whether by design or as a result of economic limitations, the churches African Americans built prior to the Civil War were, for the most part, boxlike frame or brick buildings in the meetinghouse style. Indeed, the first house of worship used by Richard Allen and the members of what became the Bethel African Methodist Episcopal Church (the mother church of the A.M.E. denomination) was a blacksmith shop that had been moved to Sixth and Lombard Streets in Philadelphia. The First African Baptist Church (Fig. 6) in Boston (also known as the Abolition Church) was a simple Federal-style building, constructed in 1805, that measured forty by forty-eight feet, about the size of an early Puritan meetinghouse. An 1850s renovation included the installation of arched windows in place of the original rectangular windows. The First African Baptist Church of Savannah, Georgia (Fig. 7) was also built by an independent black congregation. Erected in 1859 at a cost of twenty-six thousand dollars, it was a boxlike building constructed in the form of a Greek temple with a classical pediment; the tower and projecting base were added later.[9]

By the nineteenth century, although the meetinghouse form persisted among smaller and newly founded congregations, it had been eclipsed by other types of religious architecture. However, the functionalist aesthetic continued to exert an influence. In the late eighteenth and early nineteenth century, it

Fig. 7. First African Baptist Church, Savannah, Georgia (1859).

guided the thinking of the first generation of American evangelicals—revivalists committed to evangelizing the multitudes of unchurched people in the United States—who built or used various structures to aid them in achieving their objective.

2

Building for Revivalism

How goodly are thy tents, O Jacob, *and* thy tabernacles, O Israel!—Numbers 24:5

Just as the Puritans developed a "new architectural creation" to reflect their religious beliefs and worship practices, the revivalists of the Second Great Awakening introduced new structures for religious gatherings that helped them accomplish their main objective—converting sinners to Protestant Christianity and persuading them to become church members.[1] Their structures constituted an important link in the evolution of the late-twentieth-century megachurches because they incorporated evangelistic strategies used by later generations of evangelicals, including those associated with the megachurches.

The earliest of the new strategies was the camp meeting. Beginning in the late eighteenth century and continuing into the antebellum period, Baptist, Presbyterian, and Methodist evangelists found camp meetings to be a very effective means of reaching large numbers of unchurched people. Thousands of such meetings were held throughout the United States, in the sparsely settled regions of the West and Southwest as well as in rural areas of the eastern seaboard states. Typically they lasted several days, and many attracted thousands of participants. Whether large or small, improvised or routine, they became, in the words of Rev. B. W. Gorham, a "tremendous engine of spiritual power."[2]

The practical advantages of the camp meetings constituted their chief rationale, but evangelicals also invoked the Scriptures in defending the new practice. Thus Gorham, in his

Camp Meeting Manual, cited the Israelites' Feast of Tabernacles and the injunction in Leviticus 23:41–42, "And ye shall keep it a feast unto the Lord seven days in the year. *It shall be* a statute forever in your generations: ye shall celebrate it in the seventh month. Ye shall dwell in booths seven days; all that are Israelites born shall dwell in booths." Translating "booths" to mean "tents," Gorham contended that the passage showed God expressly instituting "a religious convocation, indentical [*sic*] with a modern Camp Meeting, in its principal or characteristic fact, namely, that the people were to leave their dwelling-houses and live in tents during the meeting." In the New Testament Gorham discovered the examples of John the Baptist and the Apostles holding "out-door meetings." In addition, he insisted, "the practice of the Saviour, in holding protracted religious meetings in places remote from the Synagogue and the Temple, and in the uninhabited portions of the country" constituted "a full sanction of the principle involved in the holding of modern Camp Meetings."[3]

The architecture of the camp meeting was more rustic than that of the seventeenth-century meetinghouse but just as simple and utilitarian. American evangelists sometimes located their camp meetings near a cabin, barn, or meetinghouse, but more frequently in a clearing in the woods shaded by large trees and close to a spring, creek, or navigable river. The campground varied in size, but usually occupied at least an acre, often more than that. Generally it was flat, with the outline in the shape of a rectangle, an open horseshoe, or a circle. In his manual, Gorham offered a diagram of a circular campground (Fig. 8), which was the most popular arrangement. The architect Benjamin Latrobe sketched the plan of a campground he saw outside of Washington, D.C., in 1809, that had the shape of a semicircle (Fig. 9). He described it as "placed on the descent of a narrow ridge," which created a kind of amphitheater, with the preaching stand near the bottom and seating arranged on the slope rising in front of it. As in Latrobe's sketch, tents sat at the edge of most campgrounds, with wagons and horses behind them. Seating for the congregation, when provided, consisted of felled logs or backless benches made from rough-hewn planks supported by tree stumps. Illumination for evening services came from candles and pine-knot torches or tall "fire altars," six-foot wooden platforms topped with packed earth on which fires burned.[4]

The focal point of the campground was the pulpit or preaching stand, as it was called, and the space between it and the area where the congregation sat or stood during the services. "Preaching stand" was a better descriptor than "pulpit" because it had a form quite different from the typical church pulpit. It was invariably an elevated structure, with the floor raised between four and eight feet above the ground. Some preaching stands were simple, open platforms set on stilts, whereas others were roofed, shedlike structures with a "canopy." The preaching stand was much more commodious than either the enclosed meetinghouse pulpit or the Anglican capsule-type pulpit. It was large enough to hold not only the preacher but also several other ministers and lay exhorters awaiting their turns to speak (Fig. 10).[5]

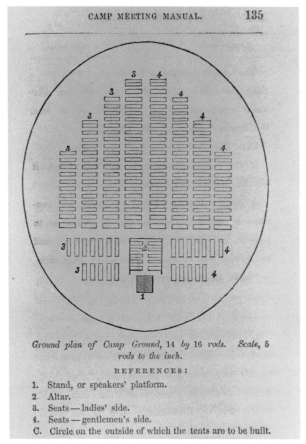

Ground plan of Camp Ground, 14 by 16 rods.   Scale, 5
rods to the inch.

REFERENCES:

1. Stand, or speakers' platform.
2. Altar.
3. Seats—ladies' side.
4. Seats—gentlemen's side.
C. Circle on the outside of which the tents are to be built.

Fig. 8. Ground plan of campground, from B. W. Gorham, *Camp Meeting Manual, a Practical Book for the Camp Ground* (Boston: H. V. Degen, 1854), 135.

Between the preaching stand and the seating or standing area was a straw-covered space, perhaps as large as twenty-five feet square, known as the altar, mourners' bench, or anxious seat. There sinners under conviction (the "mourners" or "the anxious") gathered in response to the preacher's "altar call" inviting them to come forward. Then, while the congregation sang, the minister (or ministers) stepped down from the preaching stand and mingled with the mourners, exhorting and praying with them to bring on the conversion experience. "Convert-exhorters," "good singers," and "praying persons" aided the ministers and/or encouraged and assisted the mourners. During the altar call, the gathering experienced what most of the participants believed to be the power of God, "made manifest among the people in the behavior of the mourners—in convulsive physical exercises such as jerking and barking, or in the exhibited impotence of crying and trances."[6]

The altar call was the highlight of the camp meeting because the conversion of individuals constituted the encampment's main objective—that and bringing them into church membership. Promoters of camp meetings insisted that outdoor encampments were peculiarly effective in achieving such objectives. Not only did they draw a larger number of persons than most churches were able to attract or accommodate for a single meeting but they also drew from a much more extended territory than churches did. More important, as Rev. Gorham emphasized, camp meetings, by virtue of their nov-

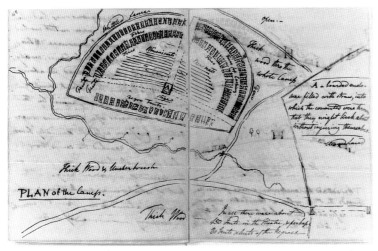

Fig. 9. "Plan of the Camp" by Benjamin Henry Latrobe, courtesy of the Maryland Historical Society, Baltimore.

elty, succeeded in evangelizing a segment of the population that churches were unable or unwilling to reach.[7]

While camp meetings proved effective in converting unchurched people in rural areas of the United States, antebellum revivalists devised other means of reaching those living in America's villages, towns, and large cities. In 1832 the *American Baptist Magazine* published an article in which Rev. Howard Malcom proposed "open-air preaching" as the best way to promote the gospel among a wide range of the unchurched—not just the poor, but "all idlers, all Sabbath-breakers of every grade, comprising apprentices, journeymen, laborers, and respectable persons who prefer the recreation of a walk abroad to the spiritual refreshments of the house of God." If they would not "come to the sanctuary," then, Malcom declared, paraphrasing Luke 12:23, they "must be sought in the highways and hedges and in the streets and lanes of the city." In case any reader thought he disparaged regular church services, Malcom conceded their utility and scriptural grounding. But, he added, "Are not Christians bound to use every honorable and practicable mode of diffusing the gospel?" Open-air preaching had the sanction of the fathers of the evangelical church, he asserted: "Calvin, not content with the duties of his theological chair, taught the inhabitants of Geneva, every week, in the open air, in a certain convenient street. Wesley went over all England and shook the slumbers of the whole population by field-preaching. . . . Whitefield preached abroad both in England and America. The Boston Common was one of his regular preaching-stations." (Rev. Gorham had offered a similar justification of camp meetings, citing John the Baptist, Jesus, and the Apostles as practitioners of "out-door meetings," as well as "the apostolic Wesley" preaching to "assembled thousands . . . on the moors and commons of England" and, in America, "the out-door preaching of Whitfield" [*sic*].[8])

In urging the resumption of open-air preaching, Malcom added a new twist. "If necessary," he suggested, "a tent, awning, or other slight accommodations could be provided,

Fig. 10. Illustration of a preaching stand. From B. W. Gorham, *Camp Meeting Manual, a Practical Book for the Camp Ground* (Boston: H. V. Degen, 1854), picture facing title page.

capable of being easily removed and placed in different situations." By the mid-1830s, if not before, other revivalists began toying with the idea of using tents for their meetings. In December 1834, the *New York Evangelist* printed excerpts of a speech by Rev. James Gallaher of Cincinnati on the subject of home missions. Like Malcom, Gallaher directed the attention of his audience to the unchurched, particularly the thousands of new settlers living in the Ohio valley. Missionaries in that "western country" were experiencing great difficulty finding structures for religious services. Churches were few and far between, and private houses proved too small. His remedy? A movable tent.[9]

How Gallaher hit upon the idea was significant. He pointed to the example of "circus men, and those who travel through the country with caravans of animals." They used "a large tent, like that of a military officer, only twenty times as large," carrying it from place to place. It contained "all their elephants, and rhinoceroses, and lions, and tigers, and ponies, and monkeys, &c &c. and five or six hundred spectators to boot." Gallaher recalled seeing such a tent in western Pennsylvania. "The people were streaming from all directions to see it. . . . I looked on the spectacle before me, and said, why cannot the friends of the gospel have a tent like that, and set it up in the neighborhood or village where there is no church, and bring the whole population at once under the preaching of the gospel." Rev. Gallaher was not unique among evangelicals in citing a secular structure as a model for a revival meeting place. What is significant is his choice of the circus, a "worldly amusement" evangelicals regarded as morally dubious. Evangelicals welcomed a wide range of "means" in the business of revivalism. That tents were used for a questionable activity did not preclude their serving as a means of spreading the gospel. The use of tents for revival meetings may also have been inspired by the camp meetings, which featured various types and sizes of tents.[10] Moreover, scriptural justification for tents could be found in passages in Exodus describing how, during their journey in the wilderness, the Israelites carried their tabernacle with them, putting it up and taking it down as the occasion required.

In publishing Gallaher's remarks, Joshua Leavitt, the editor of the *New York Evangelist,* endorsed his novel idea, urging missionaries and evangelists in the Ohio valley to "try the experiment of the GREAT TENT[.]" What began as an experiment became a staple of nineteenth- and twentieth-century revivalism. And evangelists did not limit the use of tents to rural areas or small towns. During the Revival of 1857–1858, an interdenominational organization of evangelicals in Norristown, Pennsylvania, the Union Tabernacle Association, set up a large tent at Broad and Locust Streets and chose the Philadelphia Young Men's Christian Association (YMCA) to manage it.[11]

The Union Tabernacle (Fig. 11), also called the "big tent," the "Canvas Church," and the "Movable Tent-Church," cost some two thousand dollars. It was an oblong, two-pole tent; with its sides raised and extended, it accommodated as many as three thousand persons for a service. Inside, a long, rectangular preaching platform provided space for a number of preachers and prominent laymen; a preaching desk stood on a slight projection in the middle of the platform. By means of ropes and pulleys a large curtain suspended over the platform could be lowered, thereby dividing the tent into two "departments." The one encompassing the platform area held about two hundred persons and was used for prayer meetings and the like. The one housing the "main auditory" was used for much larger meetings (Fig. 12). During the six months the tent

was in operation, the YMCA moved it to other sites within Philadelphia and then, finally, to Quakertown, about forty miles from the city.[12]

Rev. Edwin M. Long estimated the expenses of the tent during its four and a half months in Philadelphia at $1,830 and declared it "a cheap instrumentality for conveying the gospel message to multitudes who otherwise would not receive it." Like other revivalists who preceded and followed him, he discovered numerous benefits in using a tent. It was mobile, enabling revivalists to move their meetings from one place to another, much as an earlier generation had moved camp meetings around the countryside. By virtue of its novelty, it attracted people out of curiosity, if not piety. It seemed to be a very effective means of reaching "the multitudes who usually go to no stated place of worship," particularly the poor. It could be pitched in their neighborhood. It was respectable. Yet, because of its informality, it did not intimidate the poor. They did not have to "dress up" to attend the meetings. Nor did they have to pay pew rents, as most church members did. And, finally, a tent the size of the Union Tabernacle accommodated a much larger congregation than did many church buildings, even those in large cities. It also featured more services: three or four on Sundays and two on the weekdays. Long boasted that on the Sabbath "we reached as many minds as the preaching in six ordinary churches, and many of those, minds which apparently could be reached no other way."[13]

Besides campgrounds and tents, evangelists of the antebellum period often held their revival meetings in secular build-

Fig. 11. Union Tabernacle (also known as the Movable Tent-Church), as it appeared on the corner of Broad Street and Girard Avenue, Philadelphia (1858), from Edwin M. Long, *The Union Tabernacle: or, Movable Tent-Church: In Its Rise and Success a New Department of Christian Enterprise* (Philadelphia: Parry and McMillan, 1859), frontispiece.

Fig. 12. Interior, Union Tabernacle (1858), from Edwin M. Long, *Children of the Tent: The Work of God Among the Young, at the Union Tabernacle* (Philadelphia: Parry and McMillan, 1859), frontispiece.

ings. In rural areas, small villages, and towns, they obtained whatever structures seemed suitable: schoolhouses, barns, courthouses, "dining halls" in hotels or taverns.[14] Larger towns and cities, such as New York, Philadelphia, and Boston, did not lack church buildings, but often they were too small for the crowds revivalists attracted (or hoped to attract), or were not centrally located, or were inaccessible to the specific groups the evangelists targeted. Consequently, even in urban centers evangelists often appropriated secular buildings for their meetings.

In doing this, they followed a precedent established by regular pastors. Jonathan Greenleaf's mid–nineteenth-century history of the churches of New York City described newly formed or very small, usually impecunious Protestant congregations holding worship services in various types of secular buildings. They met in private homes and schoolhouses or schoolrooms, or rented vacant buildings or unused rooms in shops or other commercial structures. Or they worshiped in "halls," places that provided meeting space for military companies, working-class groups, or fraternal organizations, or that offered various types of entertainment, such as lectures, dramatic or musical productions, exhibitions, panoramas, balls, and fairs. Most halls were probably little more than large rooms, perhaps with some kind of seating. Others were much greater in size and more elaborate, featuring a stage, perhaps even a sloping floor and/or a gallery.[15]

While limited finances seem to have been the main impulse behind the use of secular buildings, another factor played an important role. Like the seventeenth-century Puritans, these congregations believed that the people, not the building per se, constituted the church. And since they did not regard the worship space as a sacred or consecrated area, any suitable setting would serve, and it could be used for both religious and secular activities.

The evangelists viewed their revival structures in much the same way. Jacob Knapp, a leading Baptist evangelist, insisted it was "a matter of discretion whether we preach in a dedicated building, an ordinary dwelling, a barn or the open field."[16] So in large towns and cities, as in rural areas, evangelists had no qualms about using secular structures. They judged schoolrooms and small buildings unsuitable, because of their limited seating capacity, but they used halls, just as some church congregations did. They also held revival meetings in theaters. Charles Grandison Finney led the way in the early 1830s by preaching in a theater that had been turned into a Presbyterian chapel.

Finney's preaching stint in a former theater constituted one very important episode during evangelicals' long and somewhat equivocal association with the theater, which influenced not only their church architecture but also their mode of worship. The association was a natural outgrowth of the historic affinities between religion and drama and the church and the theater, which reached back to the medieval period, when the Roman Catholic Church celebrated Christian feast days or festivals with performances of various types of liturgical drama. Originally written and performed by the clergy, in the church or on its grounds, the plays were presented in the vernacular rather than Latin as a means of providing religious instruction to the people. Soon the plays were performed away from the church, in the village or town, perhaps because the church building could no longer hold the crowds that assembled to see and hear the plays. In addition, control over their production passed from the clergy to laymen, who supplemented the didactic religious and moral themes with comic or farcical interludes, some of which were quite bawdy or irreverent. Almost inevitably, the development of secular drama led to tensions between the church and the theater, which lasted for centuries.[17]

The English Puritans voiced strong opposition to the theater. When the Civil War broke out, the Long Parliament closed the theaters and kept them from operating until 1660. Like their co-religionists in England, seventeenth-century New England Puritans also criticized the theater—and with a surprising intensity, given that no theaters or professional companies of actors then existed in North America. In explaining the Puritans' hostility to the theater, historian Edmund Morgan has argued that they viewed it as a rival to the church. They thought the church had a duty to persuade human beings to suppress their emotions and follow the guidance of their reason. Indeed, one of the reasons they disapproved of Roman Catholicism was because they believed its ceremonies and rituals appealed to the senses and the emotions, in contrast to their own sermons that addressed the rational faculty. Like Roman Catholicism, the theater appealed to human beings' emotions and thereby encouraged the worst kinds of sin and corruption.[18]

In the early eighteenth century, however, the evangelists of the First Great Awakening abandoned the Puritan emphasis on reason. They addressed their sermons to the "affections" or emotions. In so doing, they adopted, however unwittingly, the methods of the theater. This is clearly seen in the career of the "Great Awakener" George Whitefield, as portrayed in a recent book by Harry Stout, *The Divine Dramatist*. Although Whitefield had had a youthful infatuation with the stage, as an Anglican minister he censured the theater as intrinsically evil and the church's greatest rival. Nevertheless, his style of preaching revealed an instinct for theatrics. Stout described him as "a consummate actor" who sold religion "with all the dramatic artifice of a huckster." His "pulpit arsenal" included pathos, tears, humor, and appeals to the imagination of his audience. "His prodigious memory for characters and dialogue enabled him to transform the pulpit into a sacred theater that vitally re-presented the lives of biblical saints and sinners to his captivated listeners." Preaching extemporaneously, he acted out his message using vigorous bodily movement. "The words were the scaffolding over which the body climbed, stomped, cavorted, and kneeled, all in an attempt— as much intuitive as contrived—to startle and completely overtake his listeners." His field preaching, especially, was an artfully staged performance that drew huge crowds, much larger and more socially diverse than could be found in any church.[19]

Among Whitefield's heirs were the antebellum American evangelists. Like the "divine dramatist," the evangelists criticized the theater for its immorality and considered it a rival to the church. They agreed with many other nineteenth-century religious critics of the theater, who censured the drama as a "worldly amusement" that not only distracted attention and drained money from religion but also made "piety and virtue . . . appear contemptible, and vice, in the person of some favorite hero, . . . [seem] attractive, honourable, and triumphant." A common indictment was that "the Supreme Being is often addressed profanely" and plays were "interlarded with oaths and irreverent expressions." Costumes seemed indecorous, even scandalous, especially after the introduction of the ballet in the 1830s. As for the actors and actresses, they exemplified "a life of vanity, licentiousness and sin." Nor did the patrons of the theater escape criticism. Most antebellum theaters drew all classes of people, and religious critics frowned on not only the noisy, rambunctious rabble in the galleries but also the "middling classes" in the pit and the upper-class theatergoers in the boxes, all of whom were wasting their money and time on "tragedy, comedy, [and] farce." Especially appalling were the occupants of the "third tier" of boxes, which was traditionally reserved for prostitutes who used the theater as a place of assignation.[20]

Their anti-theater views notwithstanding, many itinerant evangelists adopted "stage techniques," either consciously or unconsciously. Like Whitefield, they preached to the heart and the emotions, not to the head and the reason. Even more than Whitefield, they engaged in "vernacular preaching"— sermons aimed at and in the language of the common people. Evangelists such as Lorenzo Dow, Peter Cartwright, and John Leland made use of not only pathos and tears but also "earthy humor" and "biting sarcasm." They jettisoned the decorum traditionally associated with the pulpit and engaged in gesturing and bodily movement that their critics described as "the very reverse of elegance." As a result, they quickly gained a reputation—among their supporters as well as their critics—for "theatrics."[21]

If the early-nineteenth-century evangelists only intuited the connection between revivalism and stage performance, Charles Grandison Finney, the most famous revivalist of the antebellum period, made it explicit. In *Lectures on Revivals of Religion* (1835), he advised fellow evangelists to look to actors as models. They could learn from them "the best method of swaying mind, of enforcing sentiment, and diffusing the warmth of burning thought over a congregation." Finney regarded the theater as immoral, but he also recognized it as a rival to the church. He warned "ministers too stiff . . . to learn even from an actor . . . that while they are thus turning away and decrying the art of the actor, and attempting to support 'the dignity of the pulpit,' the theatres can be thronged every night."[22]

Given Finney's appreciation of the affinity between stage performance and revival preaching, his acceptance of an invitation to preach in a converted theater is not surprising. The offer came in 1832 from New York businessman Lewis Tappan and his associates, all evangelicals, who were greatly concerned about rampant Sabbath-breaking, vice, and other forms of immorality in their city. Having heard of Finney's 1830–1831 revival in Rochester, New York, which had not only converted hundreds of people but also closed saloons, taverns, theaters, and other places of iniquity, they wanted the evangelist to launch a similar crusade in New York City.[23]

Like other antebellum evangelicals, Tappan and his associates also worried about the large numbers of unchurched people in New York, and they faulted the churches (including their own) for neglecting such people and catering to the middle and upper classes instead. They expressed particular concern about the pew rents charged by most churches, which they believed prevented poor people from attending worship services. To solve these problems, in 1830 they organized the First Free Presbyterian Church. Its mission, described by Tappan, was to preach the gospel to "the neglected, the poor, the emigrant, and those who, in the arrangements in the old churches, have been almost entirely overlooked."[24] The word "free" in its name indicated that it did not charge pew rents. It was the first of five "free churches" founded in New York City in the 1830s and 1840s.

Heartened by the success of the First Free Presbyterian Church, three of its elders and some thirty other members decided in 1832 to organize another free church, which met initially in a hall on Broadway and became known as the Second Free Presbyterian Church. This was the church to which Finney was called. According to his *Memoirs,* in 1832, "some earnest brethren" wrote to him "proposing to lease a theater and fit it up for a church, upon condition that I would come there and preach."[25] The theater they had in mind was the Chatham Garden Theatre on the north side of Chatham Street between Pearl and Duane Streets (Fig. 13).

Built in 1824, the Chatham was part of a pleasure garden that catered to the upper-class residents of lower Manhattan, offering light musical and dramatic entertainment. The theater accommodated about thirteen hundred people, four hundred in the pit and the rest in two circles of boxes. Its stage was

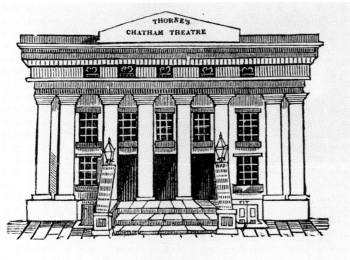

CHATHAM THEATRE.

Fig. 13. Thorne's Chatham Theatre. Woodcut in the Eno Collection, Miriam and Ira D. Wallach Division of Art, Prints and Photographs, the New York Public Library, Astor, Lenox and Tilden Foundations, New York.

thirty-two feet wide, almost thirty feet high, and about forty feet deep. The interior exhibited the gaudy decoration typical of many theaters of the time (Fig. 14). The boxes were "lined with crimson cloth" and embellished with "brass nails and fringe," and the seats had green upholstery. Gas lighting, a recent innovation in theater illumination, shed "a clear soft light over audience and stage." For a few years the Chatham ri-

valed the Park Theatre in attracting "the beauty and fashion of New York," but by 1829, the management was practically bankrupt, and the quality of the theater's entertainments and the socioeconomic level of its audience had declined markedly. Tappan and other evangelicals regarded it as "the pest of the neighborhood" and complained that it was "frequented by the lowest classes of society." Nearby was the Five Points district, an area of grog shops, dance halls, saloons, and run-down boardinghouses notorious for debauchery, crime, and riots.[26]

When Tappan wrote Finney in March 1832 about leasing the Chatham Theatre, the evangelist replied, "Is not the location too filthy for decent people to go there?" Tappan responded, "No. It is more decent than I had apprehended & can be made quite so." Thus began a remarkable exchange of views. Finney asked many more questions, and Tappan noted and answered them, one by one. Sensing the evangelist's skepticism, he presented the project in a very positive light. He proposed a most unconventional method of evangelization and reform, which he viewed with great enthusiasm precisely because it was unconventional.

Wouldn't it cost about the same to build a church as to renovate and rent the theater for several years? Finney asked. Businessman Tappan explained that it was "much easier to raise 2000 annually than to raise a capital." Besides, he added, "I am decidedly opposed to putting the funds of the church into expensive edifices. We must continue in this age, to build spiritual temples & make no heavy investments in brick &

Fig. 14. The Chatham Theatre, New York, 1825. From an original drawing by A. J. Davis, 1825, lithograph by H. A. Thomas, negative number 51371, courtesy of the Collection of the New-York Historical Society, New York.

mortar." Tappan touted the venture as much for its religious and moral impact as for its viability. It would "strike a great blow" at what Finney had referred to as one of Satan's "haunts." It would "have the effect of storming a redoubt, or taking cannon & turning them upon the enemy," Tappan asserted. Indeed, the Chatham Theatre presented an ideal opportunity. "We shall break up a place admirably located for the destruction of souls; & what is more we shall have a place equally well located for converting them," he declared. Chatham Street was "the greatest thoroughfare in the city next to Broadway, and the middling class of society, be they inhabitants or strangers pass & repass thro' this street." Moreover, taking the theater and "appropriating it for a church" would cause a "sensation," and "curiosity will be excited, in the city & out of it, to visit a place thus appropriated."[27]

Tappan and Finney knew that to convert the unchurched, it was necessary to appeal to them on their own ground—not only by locating in their neighborhood but also by inducing them to come to a worship service or revival meeting. This was particularly difficult in an urban environment. In rural areas, many people welcomed camp meetings as a diversion from the monotony of farm life; in villages and small towns, a protracted meeting might well be the only "entertainment" available. But in large cities, evangelists competed with the cheap, secular entertainments that enticed workers, immigrants, and poor people away from the church—taverns, dance halls and bawdy houses, billiard and gambling rooms, and, of course, theaters.[28]

No doubt that was why Tappan announced, early in the correspondence, "I would preserve the form of a theatre as much as possible." Both he and Finney envisioned adapting the theatrical design of the Chatham interior so as to enhance the religious meetings that would take place there. Tappan wanted to retain the circular arrangement of the orchestra and seating. He proposed to raise and cover the pit with seats and to "run the floor, over the pit, onto the stage, so that the rise will commence a few feet in front of the pulpit." He reported that Rev. Joel Parker, pastor of the First Free Presbyterian Church, who was helping to plan the renovation, had determined that the congregation would "be as near (in fact nearer) the preacher" than in most churches. "He stood on the stage & took a survey. His remark was 'if I were to build a church it should be in this form.'" Tappan also wanted to install large windows to make the place "airy" and to "admit sufficient light." Finney apparently expressed much concern about the location of the pulpit and the importance of good acoustics. Initially, Tappan planned to put the pulpit "in the middle of the stage with a large window in the rear." But a few weeks later he promised Finney that "we will take advice, & be careful," in altering the interior, not "to make it more difficult to speak in; & will wait, if possible, for you to give directions about Pulpit." Eight days later he wrote, "What you say of location of pulpit is all true. It will not be fixed until you are here. Besides, we think of having a portable pulpit."[29] Thus reassured, Finney accepted the call to preach in the newly renovated building.

Tappan and the other organizers of the Second Free Presbyterian Church spent nearly seven thousand dollars "fitting up the theatre for a house of God." The saloons were converted into lecture and Sunday school rooms; the barroom became "a room for social prayer." The pit was covered over and proper theater seats were installed there. Three galleries provided additional seating, enabling the auditorium to accommodate twenty-five hundred persons. On May 6, 1832, the Chatham Street Chapel, as it came to be known, held its first Sunday services. Reporting on the opening, a writer in the *New York Evangelist* observed that "the three galleries, and even the aisles were crowded, and great numbers were obliged to leave for want of seats." Although he complained about distracting noise caused by persons entering the chapel after the service had started, the writer noted approvingly that "the speaker's voice was distinctly heard in all parts of the house."[30]

The spatial design and facilities of the converted theater surely provided great satisfaction to Finney. The auditorium was much bigger than most of the churches he had preached in, and, as the *New York Evangelist* reporter noted, it had excellent acoustics. There was space for an anxious seat—actually, a row of seats located in front of the footlights of the stage—to which Finney invited "inquirers" during the altar call. But what must have particularly gratified him was the stage. It was much larger than a traditional church pulpit, larger even than the preaching stands and platforms evangelists used at camp meetings and in revival tents. Early in his career Finney had demonstrated his scorn for the enclosed pulpits found in most seventeenth-, eighteenth-, and early-

nineteenth-century Protestant churches. When asked to preach during his appearance before the St. Lawrence Presbytery as a candidate for ordination, he had avoided the "high, small pulpit up against the wall" and stood among the people, walking "up and down the broad aisle" of the church. As an evangelist in the villages and towns of western New York, he had claimed for himself the same freedom of movement the backwoods evangelists enjoyed in brush arbors and on camp meeting stands: the freedom to gesticulate, to walk about or pace instead of standing in one place, perhaps even to kneel in prayer when urging the conversion of a particular individual. The use of gestures, he insisted, was as important as plain and pointed language. "Mere words will never express the full meaning of the gospel," Finney declared. "The *manner* of saying it is almost every thing" [*sic*].[31] By 1832 he had become more urbane, but he still considered himself primarily an evangelist, and he still engaged in powerful and exciting preaching, using gestures and bodily movement to enforce his message. The stage of the Chatham Street Chapel provided him with a perfect opportunity to exhibit the "theatrical" style that had become his stock in trade.

Eleven years after the opening of the Chatham Street Chapel, another free church congregation turned a theater into a house of worship. Formed in 1839 by a group of antislavery Baptists who left the Charles Street Baptist Church because it discriminated against African Americans, the First Free Baptist Church of Boston met initially in a building on Tremont Street, then moved in 1840 to somewhat larger quarters, Congress Hall and, later, a hall in the Boston Museum. One of their deacons, a businessman named Timothy Gilbert, began looking for a building large enough to serve the unchurched of Boston—African Americans, poor people, immigrants, and the many young mechanics and artisans who came to the city looking for work, all of them neglected by and unwelcome in most Boston churches. To provide free seats for such a multitude would be costly, so Gilbert sought a building that could accommodate stores and offices whose rent would pay the expenses of the church and perhaps even furnish mission funds to aid the destitute at home and abroad. In the winter of 1841–1842, when the Tremont Theatre became available, he purchased it for slightly less than sixty thousand dollars.[32]

The theater was a substantial building with a marble front and solid brick walls, located on a large lot in the heart of Boston. The First Free Baptist Church congregation spent some twenty-four thousand dollars transforming it into a church with a lecture room measuring eighty-eight by ninety feet that seated more than two thousand persons. Gilbert oversaw much of the remodeling. As he had planned, offices and stores providing rental income composed part of the building, and the large lecture room, which was used for worship on Sundays, was also rented on weekdays and evenings for various meetings, concerts, political caucuses, lectures, and the like.[33]

The new Tremont Temple was dedicated on December 7, 1843; more than fifteen hundred persons attended the service.

Like the organizers of the Chatham Street Chapel, the founders of the temple relished the idea of appropriating one of Satan's "haunts." Two hymns, specially written for the occasion, celebrated the conversion of the theater into a house of worship. The first two stanzas of one composed by the pastor went as follows:

> Great God, before thy reverend name,
>   Within these ransomed walls, we bow;
> Too long abused to sin and shame,
>   To thee we consecrate them now.
>
> Satan has here held empire long,—
>   A blighting curse, a cruel reign,—
> By mimic scenes, and mirth, and song,
>   Alluring souls to endless pain.[34]

Unlike the Chatham Street Chapel, which its congregation relinquished after a few years, the Tremont Temple was intended to be and became a permanent house of worship. In 1852, when it burned to the ground, the pastor and congregation decided to rebuild on the existing site. Here was an opportunity to replace the onetime theater with a more "churchly" building—to eschew any association with worldly amusement. Instead, the Baptists built a structure that was "grander, larger, and more expensive" than the previous one. Completed in 1853 at a cost of $160,000, the new Tremont Temple (Fig. 15) was seventy-five feet in height and had a cupola on the roof that afforded a panoramic view of Boston and its

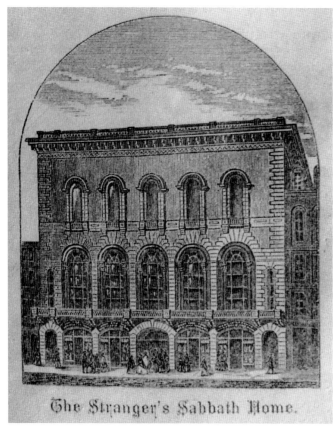

The Stranger's Sabbath Home.

Fig. 15. Tremont Temple, Boston (1853), from *The Work in Tremont Temple* (Boston: Union Temple Baptist Church, [1871?]). Photograph courtesy of and used with the permission of the American Baptist Historical Society, American Baptist-Samuel Colgate Library, Rochester, New York.

vicinity. The exterior had the same secular look as the former building, but featured a more "substantial and elegant frontage." A "bold and handsomely designed cornice," surmounted by a balustrade, ran across the top of the facade. Immediately below it were five "arched recesses or niches," and under them were the windows of "apartments" rented by the Boston YMCA for its headquarters. A balustraded balcony at the second-floor level sheltered "four fine stores" at street level. Like the YMCA apartments, the stores, as well as other rooms on the upper floors, were leased by the church as a source of income. The congregation and pastor remained determined to continue the temple as a free church, serving the young working people of Boston and visitors to the city.[35]

The interior of the new temple included a "commodious and magnificent audience-room," known as the Main Hall, measuring 120 feet long, 72 feet wide, and 50 feet high, and accommodating as many as three thousand persons. Certain features made it look more like a theater or concert hall than a church. Instead of the usual elevated, enclosed pulpit, there was a large "platform" with a "gracefully panelled, semicircular front," resembling a proscenium stage. The seating plan also mimicked that of a theater or concert hall: curved pews arranged on a sloping floor in a semicircle in front of the platform. In the galleries were banked rows of "nicely cushioned and comfortable seats" rather than pews. The audience room featured the lavish ornamentation characteristic of theaters and concert halls—at the back of the platform, on the side walls, and even the ceiling. No doubt one of the reasons for retaining the theatrical ambience of the audience room was that it would be rented for lectures and concerts on weekday evenings. But it is clear that the Baptists appreciated the way the theatrical features enhanced their worship. As pastor Justin D. Fulton observed, the seating arrangement ensured that "every face is directed toward the speaker or singer," and the sloping main floor and banked galleries afforded "every person in the hall a full and unobstructed view" of the platform.[36]

By the time of the Revival of 1857–1858, the practice of evangelizing in halls and theaters was well established. In Louisville, Kentucky, a thousand people crowded into the Masonic Hall for an early morning prayer meeting, and in Chicago twice that number filled the Metropolitan Theater daily. In Philadelphia, promoters of the revival held prayer meetings in National Hall, Handel and Hayden Hall, the American Mechanics Hall, and Jayne's Hall. The ten-story Jayne's building on Chestnut Street, near the central business district, was the largest of these structures. It had an auditorium that accommodated more than four thousand persons, with a large stage and tiers of elegantly ornamented boxes as well as galleries. For several weeks, some three thousand persons attended the meetings there each day.[37]

In New York City, a group of Chambers Street merchants working with the YMCA organized a series of noon prayer meetings at the former Burton's Chambers Street Theatre, recently leased to a minstrel group. Since the evangelicals used the building only briefly, they did not bother to convert it into a "churchlike" space. But like the Baptists at the Tremont Temple, the clergy who led the prayer meetings at Burton's exploited the symbolism of using a theater for religious purposes. Thus Rev. Theodore L. Cuyler reminded his audience of the earlier conversion of the Chatham Garden Theatre, "a haunt of obscenity, blasphemy and vice," and celebrated the current use of Burton's. "A theater has become a school of virtue, and not a school of vice—a house of prayer, and not a haunt of profanity—a spot for the real tears of penitence, and not the scene of fictitious grief over the fictitious sorrows of the stage," he asserted. "May this former habitation of the Tempter be the very habitation of God—the very gate of Heaven to souls seeking after Jesus!"[38]

Despite the precedent established by the Chatham Street Chapel, the novelty of using a place such as Burton's for religious purposes, as well as the rhetoric it inspired, provoked skepticism on the part of at least one New Yorker. "A Looker On" sent a letter to the editor of the *Tribune* questioning "the expediency of the whole Burton operation." He declared that "the 'sensation' produced by such a place takes away from the sober, real character which has been so marked in the other prayer-meetings." He worried that the revival was losing "its solemn and almost awful character" and becoming "a kind of clap-trap." A rejoinder by "One of Them" appeared the following day. "Burton's Theater was leased in behalf of the merchants in the immediate neighborhood, for the simple and only reason that no other public hall existed in the vicinity adapted to the purpose in view," he observed. To suppose "that such a place, in the absence of a better one, might not be made a means of good, is simply to deny the plainest common sense," he added.[39]

The pragmatic ethos "One of Them" detected in the Burton's Theatre prayer meetings characterized all of the revival operations Protestant evangelists mounted during the antebellum period—that and the desire to reach "the ungodly" and "the poor." Whatever facility proved suitable to their purposes, whether a campground or a tent, a theater or some other secular building, the evangelists used or adapted it to their needs. The YMCA leaders of the Union Tabernacle in Philadelphia summed up the evangelical point of view: "Wise fishermen use all the various kinds of means and appliances to catch the different kinds of fish."[40]

The revival structures evangelists used during the first half of the nineteenth century constituted an innovation as important as any of the other experiments or "new measures" associated with antebellum American revivalism. The evangelists rejected traditional notions of ecclesiastical space and designed their new structures primarily for the purpose of evangelism, making them accessible, interesting, unintimidating, and open to all persons, especially the unconverted and unchurched. And, as Paul Conkin has observed, they introduced into those structures "revival motifs," such as exhortatory sermons, altar calls, the anxious seat, and personal testimonies, that made the meetings more participatory than worship services in most churches of the time.[41]

At midcentury, evangelicals turned their efforts to consolidating the great gains they had realized from half a century of evangelistic effort.[42] In subsequent decades they continued to view religious structures as instruments of evangelism, but they also paid increasing attention to other elements of church design. Especially in the urban centers of the United States, where they served large, affluent, and socially prominent congregations, they developed a more "churchly" form of ecclesiastical architecture to appeal to that constituency. That new form was the auditorium church.

3

The Auditorium Church

The house to be built to the Lord must be exceedingly magnificent.—1 Chronicles 22:5

Beginning in the early nineteenth century and continuing into the early twentieth century, auditorium churches gained increasing popularity among the evangelical denominations of the United States. Affluent Presbyterian, Methodist, Baptist, and Congregationalist congregations in the nation's cities and large towns built hundreds of such churches. Independent black Baptist congregations and African American denominations such as the African Methodist Episcopal Church, the African Methodist Episcopal Zion Church, and the Colored Methodist Episcopal Church, whose membership increased dramatically following the Civil War, also constructed auditorium churches in both northern and southern cities. Like the meetinghouses and revival structures discussed in preceding chapters, the auditorium church represented an important innovation in religious architecture that contributed to the development of the late-twentieth-century megachurches.[1] Virtually all of the megachurches adopted some of its features, especially the arrangement of the worship space.

The originator of the auditorium church in the United States was Robert Mills of South Carolina (1781–1855), a student of Benjamin Latrobe and protégé of Thomas Jefferson. Influenced partly by Andrea Palladio's drawings of the Roman Pantheon (which he probably discovered while using Jefferson's library) and partly by James Gibbs's plans for a "round church," Mills designed several churches, including the Sansom Street Church in Philadelphia and the First Baptist Church of Baltimore, as domed, rotunda-type buildings. They were octagonal or circular in shape, rather than rectangular, a dramatic departure from the prevailing Wren-Gibbs type of church. The Sansom Street Church (Fig. 16), built for a congregation of Baptists in 1812, had a dome crowned by a "lanthorn," or cupola, which allowed sunlight and fresh air into the rotunda. Its circular audience room (Fig. 17), ninety feet in diameter, featured a baptismal pool in the center, with seating arranged in straight lines around it, and a horseshoe-shaped gallery supported on tapered columns. The auditorium seated about four thousand persons. The First Baptist Church, erected in 1818, featured a nearly seventy-seven-foot domed rotunda with straight-line seating, a horseshoe-shaped gallery, and a smaller "public gallery" constructed above the vestibule, which was reserved for black members of the church. It also accommodated about four thousand (Figs. 18, 19).[2]

Besides the rotunda shape, Mills also introduced another important feature of the auditorium church—banked, curved seating. In both the Sansom Street and First Baptist galleries, the pews were set on tiers and curved to fit the horseshoe shape. According to architectural historian William Pierson, such an arrangement had been used in theaters since the time of the ancient Greeks, but was unknown in the United States until Mills incorporated it into his auditorium churches.[3]

Pierson and Rhodri Windsor Liscombe have pointed out that Mills devised the auditorium church to accommodate the distinctive worship practices of the evangelical denomina-

Fig. 16. Sansom Street Baptist Church (also known as Staughton's Baptist Church), Philadelphia (1812). Photograph of Staughton's Baptist Church, Penrose Collection-Medium-Churches, Box 4, courtesy of the Historical Society of Pennsylvania, Philadelphia.

tions in the United States (he himself was a Presbyterian), which were growing rapidly in the early nineteenth century. He decided that the rotunda shape was better adapted than the rectangular shape to their emphasis on preaching and the need for all to hear and see the preacher. He later boasted that the acoustics of the Sansom Street auditorium rendered "the voice of the speaker, whether the room was full or empty, . . .

distinct & clear to the most distant hearer, and the speaker made no uncommon effort to speak."[4]

No doubt the rotunda-type building appealed to Charles Grandison Finney for exactly the same reason. His second New York City church, the Broadway Tabernacle, was a domed, neoclassical building like the Sansom Street Church, which he probably saw while preaching in Philadelphia in 1827. The interior of the Chatham Street Chapel may also have influenced his thinking. Whatever their source, his ideas struck the architect and builder of the tabernacle, Joseph Ditto, as quite unconventional. He declared that constructing a church according to Finney's design would injure his reputation. Finney insisted, however, and Ditto complied.[5]

The tabernacle was built for Finney by some members of the Chatham Street Chapel, who wanted to extend the free church movement in New York City. Completed in April 1836, the new structure stood one hundred feet back from Broadway between Anthony (later known as Worth) Street and Catharine Lane (Fig. 20). Located in an area of new businesses and theaters—the commercial center of the city in the 1830s—it was in a better neighborhood than the Chatham Street Chapel, but was still close enough to the slums of the lower Bowery that Finney and the members could continue their evangelistic efforts among the poor and the ungodly. An entrance on Broadway, through a double building into a yard in front of the church, made it accessible to the main thoroughfare of the city. There were also entrances on Anthony Street and Catharine Lane.[6]

Fig. 17. Auditorium, Sansom Street Baptist Church. Unfinished lithograph, Sansom Street Baptist Church, accession number Bb 13 F527, courtesy of the Historical Society of Pennsylvania, Philadelphia.

Finney himself named the new edifice. Traditionally, the word "tabernacle" had suggested a hastily constructed building designed as a temporary accommodation. After the Fire of London, in 1666, Sir Christopher Wren had erected a number of wooden shelters referred to as tabernacles, which were used as places of worship until churches could be rebuilt. In the United States, during the Second Great Awakening, revival structures were sometimes called tabernacles, and the word was also used as a synonym for a tent. Indeed, Joseph P. Thompson claimed the Broadway church was called a tabernacle because the building was "spread somewhat in the man-

Fig. 18. First Baptist Church, Baltimore (1818), courtesy of the Maryland Historical Society, Baltimore.

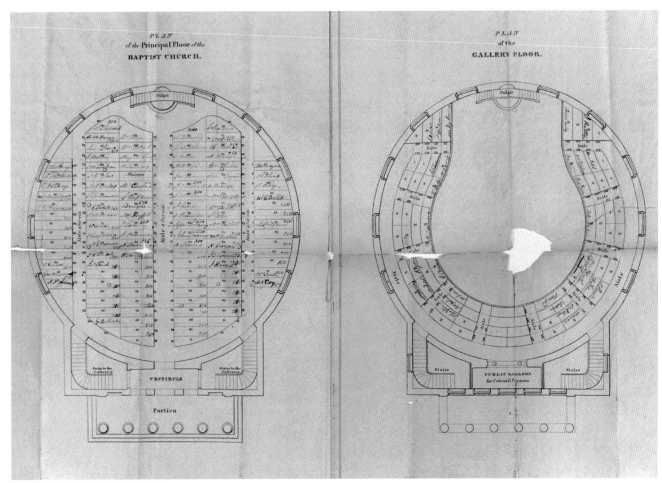

Fig. 19. Floor plan of the New Baptist Church designed by Robert Mills, Baltimore (1818). Engraving courtesy of the Maryland Historical Society, Baltimore.

Fig. 20. The Tabernacle, with entrance on Broadway, in 1836. Woodcut from *Valentine's Manual,* 1865, negative number 36360, courtesy of the Collection of the New-York Historical Society, New York.

ner of a tent."[7] Finney was probably thinking of more permanent revival structures such as Moorfields Tabernacle, built for the legendary George Whitefield in London in 1753. Finney had proposed, without success, "tabernacle" for the name of the converted Chatham Theatre, presumably to indicate its evangelistic purpose, and he wanted to communicate a similar orientation on the part of his new church.

Finney designed the interior of the Broadway Tabernacle to facilitate his evangelistic style of preaching. The auditorium seated twenty-five hundred comfortably but could accommodate nearly four thousand if crowded (Fig. 21). In accord with his wishes, and like the Sansom Street Church, it was circular in shape, with the pews arranged in a semicircle on both the ground floor and in the gallery; those in the gallery were banked so that individuals could see over the heads of persons sitting in front of them. There was also a large platform, with the orchestra, choir, and a huge organ at the back. Finney paid special attention to acoustics and sight lines. "I had observed the defects of churches in regard to sound; and was sure that I could give the plan of a church in which I could easily speak to a much larger congregation than any house would hold that I had ever seen," he wrote in his *Memoirs.* As Keith Hardman has pointed out, Finney also wanted every member of the congregation to have an unobstructed view of the pulpit platform and the preacher. Indeed, he did not just want the congregation to be able to see him. His theology of preaching, and particularly his desire to "look every auditor in the eye," to use Charles Hambrick-Stowe's phrasing, dictated that he should be able to see each one of them. The circular auditorium of the tabernacle, with curved seating surrounding the pulpit platform on three sides, not only enabled the congregation to hear and see the preacher but also placed him much closer to them than was possible in a traditional, rectangular church. (In fact, the tabernacle did not provide a totally unobstructed view of the platform, as Finney had requested, because of the six pillars Ditto had installed to support the

LITH. OF F. PALMER & CO. 96 NASSAU STREET, N.Y.

Fig. 21. Broadway Tabernacle in Anniversary Week. Lithograph from book illustration, by F. Palmer and Co., 18–?, negative number 48100, courtesy of the Collection of the New-York Historical Society, New York.

Fig. 22. Plymouth Church, Brooklyn, New York (1850), from Noyes L. Thompson, *The History of Plymouth Church. (Henry Ward Beecher) 1847–1872. Inclusive of Historical Sketches of the Bethel and the Navy Mission, and the Silver Wedding* (New York: G. W. Carleton and Co., 1873), 14.

roof.)[8] The large platform, similar to the one Finney used in the Chatham Street Chapel, also encouraged a sense of closeness, since it was not elevated high above the congregation like the traditional enclosed pulpit. And it provided the space Finney needed to exhibit the dramatic gestures and bodily movement he used to underscore his message.

Two other famous nineteenth-century evangelists, Henry Ward Beecher and T. DeWitt Talmage, also found the auditorium church to be the perfect arena for powerful and exciting preaching. Like Finney, Beecher immersed himself in the planning of his church. Plymouth Church (Fig. 22), in Brooklyn, completed in 1850, resembled a meetinghouse in certain respects. Unadorned except for a few neoclassical details, it had neither marble columns nor a tall spire. It was "plain even to bareness," the coauthors of one of Beecher's biographies observed. It could have been a bank or mercantile establishment. "One would never take it for a church at all," another of his biographers exclaimed. The auditorium was rectangular rather than circular, but it had a large platform, a "mighty organ," and choir seating for between fifty and one hundred persons at the back of the platform. Its horseshoe-shaped gallery featured banked pews and, at the far end of the audience room, two additional levels of seating (Fig. 23). The total seating capacity was about two thousand. Lyman Abbott, who succeeded Beecher as pastor, pronounced it a "perfect auditorium." The preacher standing upon the platform could be "seen by every person in the house—there are no great pillars to obstruct the view—and heard by every auditor in the

Fig. 23. Auditorium, Plymouth Church, from Lyman Abbott, *Henry Ward Beecher: A Sketch of His Career: With Analyses of His Power as a Preacher, Lecturer, Orator and Journalist, and Incidents and Reminiscences of His Life* (Hartford, Conn.: American Publishing Company, 1887), 255.

house—there is no vaulted roof in which the voice is lost, no angles to catch and to deflect it." Two of Beecher's biographers pointed out the features that brought the audience "near together and near to the speaker": the arrangement of the pews in a partial curve and the way the platform, "with no railing in front," projected "well forward toward the centre of the circle" (Fig. 24). It was "as far removed as possible from those boxes where the man must stand, cramped and stiff, while he delivers his message," so it not only enabled the preacher to address the congregation "with great ease" but

also afforded an opportunity to cultivate feelings of "homeness [*sic*] and fraternity" in the gathering.[9]

DeWitt Talmage built three auditorium churches during his twenty-five-year pastorate with the Central Presbyterian Church of Brooklyn, New York. His first tabernacle, dedicated in 1870, replaced the "cramped brick rectangle" the congregation had outgrown after only fifteen months of his preaching. He had told the architects exactly what he wanted in the new building. The audience room should hold four thousand persons on one floor. Instead of a traditional pulpit, there should be a platform; the pews "must all form semicircles converging from that platform, and must gradually rise, so as to give those far off as good a chance to see and hear as those near by." (Talmage wanted amphitheater seating, which had become popular by the 1870s.) In addition, he also urged the architects to make the building "as little like a church as possible, so the people not used to sacred edifices will feel welcome." He got his wish. One commentator described the tabernacle as "a great barn-like structure of wood and corrugated iron," with a brick exterior. A writer for the *New York Times* noted that it looked "more like a railway station than like a church," but he liked the way the iron walls, which were painted the color of lead, gave "an air of height and lightness to the entire building." The auditorium featured amphitheater seating in the shape of a horseshoe, as Talmage had requested, but it accommodated only thirty-five hundred, not four thousand. The platform Talmage had insisted upon bridged the ends of the horseshoe.[10]

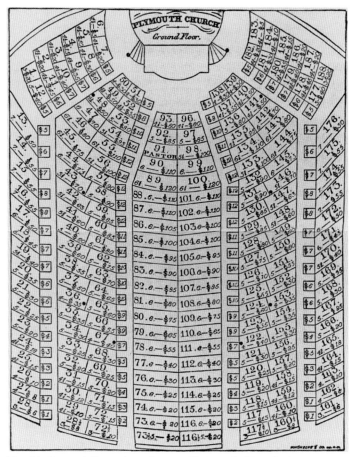

Fig. 24. Ground-floor plan of pews, Plymouth Church, from Thompson, *The History of Plymouth Church*, 236.

The second tabernacle was a neo-Gothic building, constructed of brick and stone and described as "cathedral-like above, amphitheatre-like below." The third was a more massive brick and brownstone structure in the Eclectic style popular in the late 1880s (Fig. 25). Both buildings featured the horseshoe-shaped amphitheater seating arrangement found in the first tabernacle. Talmage's specifications for the second tabernacle included "wide and spacious aisles and foyer" to give standing room for one thousand persons. When built, the structure had seats for four thousand and standing room for almost two thousand. The third tabernacle also seated four thousand, but it had two galleries rather than one (Fig. 26).[11]

Finney, Beecher, and Talmage improved upon Mills's design for the auditorium church, adding features that became standard during the late nineteenth and early twentieth century. All three men used curved seating on the main floor of their auditoriums, not just in the galleries, and Talmage had the seats placed on an inclined floor. An even more significant alteration replaced the traditional pulpit with a large platform, which provided them with the space they desired for dynamic preaching. Like Finney, both Beecher and Talmage incorporated dramatic gestures and bodily movement into their preaching and were often charged with being "theatrical," even "sensational." Beecher was described by a contemporary as moving quickly about the platform, and one of Talmage's biographers told of the evangelist striding "up and down the platform boiling with energy, pouring forth picture-

Fig. 25. DeWitt Talmage's third tabernacle, Brooklyn, New York (1891), from John Rusk, *The Authentic Life of T. DeWitt Talmage, the Greatly Beloved Divine* (n.p.: L. G. Stahl, 1902), 74.

Fig. 26. Auditorium, DeWitt Talmage's third tabernacle, from Rusk, *The Authentic Life of T. DeWitt Talmage*, 91.

painting words, brandishing his arms long enough to pull down the head of a giraffe."[12]

By adopting the design of the auditorium church, Finney, Beecher, and Talmage helped popularize it among the evangelical denominations. In addition, a small but influential group of architectural commentators promoted its construction in the late nineteenth and early twentieth century. Some of these men headed one or another of the denominational boards that provided advice on church building and supplied architectural plans to ministers and congregations. P. E. Bur-

roughs, for example, served for many years as educational secretary of the Southern Baptist Convention Sunday School Board and chief of its Department of Church Architecture. John A. Lankford, a Washington, D.C., architect, became the "supervising architect" of the African Methodist Episcopal Church in 1912. Other evangelicals who published their views on church architecture were Henry Martyn Dexter, the mid-nineteenth-century historian of Congregationalism; William Wallace Everts, pastor of the First Baptist Church in Chicago from 1859 to 1879; and W. T. Euster, a Methodist who described himself as an "editor, traveler, and preacher." Mouzon William Brabham and W. M. Patterson were Methodist preachers who also wrote books on church architecture. Architects F. E. Kidder, J. E. Greene, and George W. Kramer published books containing architectural plans and renderings to be used by building committees and local architects and builders throughout the United States.[13] Other architects contributed letters or essays on church architecture to the *American Architect and Building News*.

These churchmen and architects thought of themselves as pioneers of the "modern" or "progressive" church and celebrated what George Kramer called "a new era of religious architecture." Viewing the history of church architecture in evolutionary terms, they believed that over the centuries, different faith groups and denominations had developed various types of church buildings to suit their special needs and the conditions imposed by the times in which they lived. Now, in the late nineteenth and early twentieth century, it seemed only natural that the evangelical denominations should develop a distinctive style of church architecture. Over the course of half a century, the work of the church had been "revolutionized," asserted Kramer in 1897. It was "altogether different from what it was even a generation ago, . . . and the evolution of the modern church edifice from the primitive meeting-house has been so great, to keep pace with the growing demands, that the structures of even a decade past will not serve the needs of the present day." In 1920, Burroughs summarized evangelical thinking, declaring, "modern church life calls for modern buildings which can adequately express and house the worship and activities of the churches of our day."[14]

In presenting their vision of the modern church the commentators rejected the temporary, utilitarian, plain structures of the past. The Convention of Ministers and Delegates of the Congregational Churches in the United States, meeting in 1852, declared that "the white, staring, tremulous edifices which meet and offend the eye so often in our towns and villages, are at best only tabernacles, and the day for the ark of God to abide in tabernacles should be past." Most commentators recommended building in brick or, preferably, stone, which was thought to be even more elegant and more enduring. They also disdained the plain, secular look of the meetinghouse. They thought a church should have "a churchly appearance." It should not look like an "overgrown barn," as Dexter described the Puritan meetinghouse, or a library, post office, bank, or school. To ensure that the church edifice would be recognized as a religious structure, commentators recommended adding a spire, tower, or steeple, perhaps crowned by "a simple cross, the everywhere recognized symbol of the Christian faith." Such thinking prompted Robert Roeschlaub's design of the spire for Trinity Methodist Episcopal Church (1888) in Denver (Fig. 27). The "needle-thin soaring structure," with its "lofty copper cross," eloquently testified to the building's ecclesiastical function. Stanford White, the architect of the Lovely Lane Methodist Church (1887) in Baltimore (Fig. 28), used the "tall, soaring bell tower" of the Romanesque structure to "give full expression to the religious feeling and mark the building from all points as a church."[15]

Besides giving a building "a church look," spires, towers, steeples, and crosses added the ornamentation evangelical church builders missed in meetinghouses and revival structures. They desired "beauty and impressiveness" in their houses of worship. They joined the "beautification campaign" waged by genteel Americans during the nineteenth century—an effort, described by Richard Bushman, to bring "refinement to dwellings at nearly every level" by building according to the requirements of "taste" rather than "fashion." The Congregationalists became involved as early as 1852; in a work entitled *A Book of Plans for Churches and Parsonages*, officials of the denomination recommended employing an architect who knew how to design a church building "in a tasteful and proper manner." In 1855, the *National Magazine* published an article on Methodist church architecture in which the writer lamented the number of "uncouth and inconvenient" edifices that had been erected and urged more attention to

Fig. 27. Trinity Methodist Episcopal Church, Denver (1888). Photograph by W. H. Jackson, negative number WHJ-2062, courtesy of the Colorado Historical Society, Denver.

building structures "at once convenient, chaste, and tasteful." As late as 1884, the Methodist Board of Church Extension fulminated against "awkward, ill-proportioned, inconvenient" structures that were "not likely to awaken devotional feelings in those who look at [them] or who may enter [them] for worship."[16]

While auditorium church builders rejected the meetinghouses and revival structures of earlier generations, they also dissented from the reigning architectural orthodoxy of the late nineteenth century, whose spokesmen insisted that the Gothic style of the medieval cathedrals was the only truly Christian style of architecture and therefore the only one appropriate for a church building. Evangelicals built auditorium churches in the Classical and Romanesque styles as well as the Gothic, and they often used an eclectic mix of styles, as in First Baptist Church of Dallas (Fig. 29), which Jay C. Henry has described as "Victorian Gothic with selective Romanesque details." They did not slavishly copy the earlier styles but adapted them to current needs. What Henry says of First Baptist applied to most other auditorium churches: "First Baptist is not modelled on any obvious single sources from the Middle Ages. Its plan and spatial configuration are purely modern, nineteenth century solutions to adapt medieval precedent *eclectically* to contemporary Protestant worship. And the details of construction betray the typical nineteenth century love of ornament." Taste and functionalism overruled architectural orthodoxy and purity of style. At a convention of the American Institute of Architects, C. A. Cummings stated the posi-

Fig. 28. Lovely Lane Methodist Church (First Methodist Episcopal Church), Baltimore (1887). Photograph by Dan O'Toole, courtesy of the National Register of Historic Places, Washington, D.C., and the Maryland Historical Trust, Division of Historical and Cultural Programs, Maryland Department of Housing and Community Development, Crownsville.

tion of most evangelical churchmen and architects regarding the style and decoration of the modern church building. "We should be as broad as the diversity of tastes will prompt," he declared. "We should not wish all our churches to be cast in one mould."[17] Evangelicals chose whatever style happened to appeal to the pastor, the church building committee, and the congregation; the architectural boards and departments of the evangelical denominations followed a laissez-faire policy regarding the matter.

In planning their church buildings, evangelicals made size a priority. Their large, urban churches were at least twice as large as the seventeenth- and eighteenth-century meetinghouses and seated a thousand or more persons. Two-story church buildings became increasingly popular during the nineteenth century as evangelicals looked for ways of accommodating increasing worship attendance and expanding church programs. A two-story building cost less to build than a one-story church of the same capacity, and it required a smaller lot, an important consideration in urban areas, where land was expensive. And, as Kidder observed, "a two-story church makes a more imposing and conspicuous edifice than a one-story building, and is preferred by many on that account."[18]

Although evangelicals paid considerable attention to the design of the exterior of the auditorium church building, they regarded the worship space—referred to as the audience room or auditorium—as the most important part of the edifice. They adapted classical and medieval styles in designing the exterior, but in planning the interior, they discovered "no adequate precedent or example." The Boston architect C. A. Cummings had nothing but contempt for "the blind and unintelligent following of medieval traditions" in designing the audience room. Another architect, writing for the *American Architect and Building News,* agreed in condemning the medieval (or "cathedral") style of church architecture. It "has no more affiliation with modern Protestant worship than . . . a Hindoo temple, a Turkish mosque, or a Roman basilica," he declared.

> Almost every distinguishing feature of medieval church design is specially unsuited to present use. The cruciform plan; the division into nave and aisles by obstructing columns; the open timbered or vaulted roofs; the extreme height and length; the traceried windows and stained glass; the paved floors and interior stone or brick faced walls; all that we have been taught to admire in song and story and pictorial art is as foreign to Protestant worship as the barefooted friars, the sackcloth and penance, the processions, the incense, the relics, and the confessional. . . . Our daily life cannot be properly lived in a donjon [*sic*] tower, or even in a baronial hall; nor can we with comfort or propriety wear plate armor or wield the ponderous broadsword. Why then should the religious observances of the day be trammeled by the dress or lodgings of the past?[19]

Condemning "servile copyism," evangelical churchmen and architects championed "fitness to use," which is to say the functionalist aesthetic. They believed the design of the audience room should facilitate the evangelical mode of worship, with its emphasis on the preaching and hearing of the Word.

Fig. 29. First Baptist Church, Dallas (1890).

The shape of the auditorium should be such as to put the preacher and the congregation in the closest proximity. Kidder regarded the "egg oval" used in the Lovely Lane Methodist Church (Figs. 30, 31) as ideal, but he noted that "for various practical reasons, particularly that of expense, it is seldom attempted."[20] During the late nineteenth and early twentieth century, most commentators, including Kidder, favored a rectangular shape for the auditorium, although square and octagonal auditoriums were not uncommon. Commentators differed somewhat over the precise ratio of width to depth, but they generally agreed that the rectangle should be wider than that used for the liturgical churches.

As for the overall size of the auditorium, some commentators, such as Kidder, thought it needed only to be big enough to seat on the main floor the largest congregation expected at an ordinary service. Burroughs recommended a somewhat more commodious auditorium, with seating sufficient to accommodate the church membership. Euster urged evangelicals to build the largest auditorium they could afford. He quoted the Methodist Bishop Charles H. Fowler as saying that the auditorium should be "large enough for all possible occasions. If a magnificent auditorium is all you can secure, get that and leave the rest to coming time." Elaborating on the Bishop's advice, Euster insisted that great size was conducive to evangelism and membership growth. "A large audience room is ever calling for a big congregation," he observed.[21]

Most evangelical churchmen and architects advocated curved seating in the auditorium because it facilitated evangelical worship—as Dexter pointed out, by arranging "the audience socially and sympathetically together while giving them the best position toward the speaker."[22] Curved pews were quite expensive; straight pews built on the chords of their arcs, instead of upon the arcs themselves, offered a less costly alternative.

Instead of a level floor, the audience rooms in some of the larger auditorium churches had curved seating on an inclined floor—the amphitheater plan. It was more expensive than a level floor but was thought to improve acoustics and sight lines. In 1857, architect Edward Burling installed amphitheater seating in the First Methodist Church of Chicago, which accommodated a thousand persons. When other architects began using the amphitheater plan in the 1860s, it was still considered quite innovative. Henry L. Gay's design for the auditorium of the First Congregational Church of Chicago, built in 1869, with a capacity of twenty-two hundred, provoked laughter and ridicule, despite his contention that it had been built on "scientific principles." However, in the 1870s, attitudes began to change. Architect Gurdon P. Randall used the plan in the auditorium of the Union Park Congregational Church (Fig. 32) in Chicago, which seated fifteen hundred persons, and won "an exceedingly favorable" response from the congregation that attended the dedication of the building in 1871. Reporting on the occasion, a writer for the *Chicago Tribune* pointed out "the novel and almost theatrical appearance of this church," but insisted that "this innovation on the established forms of ecclesiastical architecture, so far as the

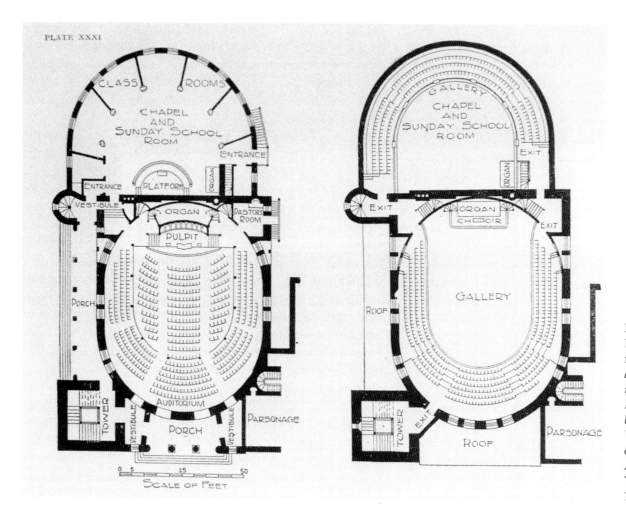

PLATE XXXI

CLASS ROOMS
CHAPEL AND SUNDAY SCHOOL ROOM
ENTRANCE
ENTRANCE PLATFORM ORGAN
VESTIBULE ORGAN PASTORS ROOM
PULPIT
PORCH
AUDITORIUM
TOWER VESTIBULE PORCH VESTIBULE PARSONAGE

0 5   25   50
SCALE OF FEET

GALLERY
CHAPEL AND SUNDAY SCHOOL ROOM
EXIT
EXIT ORGAN
ORGAN CHOIR
EXIT
ROOF
GALLERY
TOWER EXIT ROOF PARSONAGE

Fig. 30. Plans of the Lovely Lane Methodist Church, from F. E. Kidder, *Churches and Chapels: Their Arrangement, Construction and Equipment Supplemented by Plans, Interior and Exterior Views of Numerous Churches of Different Denominations, Arrangement and Cost* (New York: William T. Comstock, 1906), Plate XXXI.

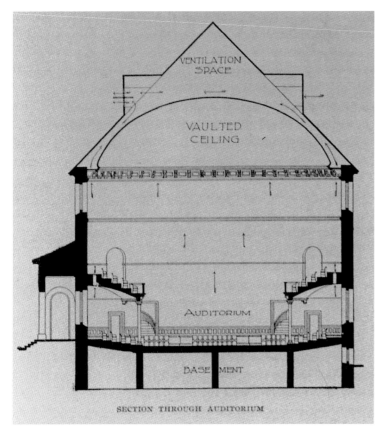

Fig. 31. Section through auditorium, Lovely Lane Methodist Church, from Kidder, *Churches and Chapels,* Plate XXXII.

arrangement of the seats is concerned, gives better seeing and hearing, and a far pleasanter appearance than the old-fashioned system." Rev. C. D. Helmer made the same point in the dedicatory sermon. After declaring his opposition to "Protestant churches imitating the forms of Catholic cathedrals," he went on to contend that "a Protestant service was a social worship, and the amphitheatre was the best form for them, and not long-drawn aisles, dim shadows, and resounding echoes. If the builders of theatres had adopted an amphitheatrical form, was it any reason why the children of light should not do so? They wanted an auditorium in which to hear and see. . . . The congregation of his church had decided to adopt the amphitheatre, and thought a semi-circle could be consecrated as well as a rectangle."[23]

In the 1870s, the theater no longer provoked as much criticism as it had in earlier decades. Still, advocates of the modern church remained somewhat defensive about the use of any form associated with that worldly amusement. In justifying the amphitheater plan, they struck the same pragmatic note sounded by the promoters of the early revival structures. Thus J.A.F., in an article entitled "Modern Church Building" in the *American Architect and Building News,* written in 1879, argued that if church builders wanted the greatest possible number of persons to see and hear a single speaker, they were "almost obliged to adopt . . . the general shape of the old Greek theatre, or of a half amphitheatre." It was, he observed, "an arrangement eminently well suited for the uses of the preacher, lecturer, singer, or actor." If one accepted the new

Fig. 32. Union Park Congregational Church, Chicago (1869). From stereograph by Copelin and Son, ICHi-22322, courtesy of the Chicago Historical Society.

plan, it did not "by any means follow that the church should closely resemble the theatre." In 1897, George Kramer reiterated essentially the same argument. Just because concert halls or opera houses used the amphitheater plan was no reason "the modern type of Church" should not, he declared. "Does preemption give the enemy prior or exclusive right to all features or forms of advantage or comfort? Is not everything devoted to sacred uses sacred? Should not our church be as comfortable and attractive as buildings devoted to secular uses?"[24]

By the late 1890s, curved seating on a level or sloping floor had become fairly commonplace in urban auditorium churches. In the new Methodist Episcopal Church built in 1887 in Fort Worth, the architectural firm Bullard and Bullard featured an auditorium sixty by ninety feet, with curved seating on a sloping floor. Both the Lovely Lane Methodist Church (1887) and Trinity Methodist Episcopal Church (1888) used the amphitheater plan. Affluent African American congregations in large urban centers also adopted it. The Metropolitan African Methodist Episcopal Church of Washington, D.C. (Fig. 33), one of the largest black churches in the United States when it was dedicated in 1886, had curved pews in its auditorium, which accommodated three thousand persons. The fourth house of worship occupied by the congregation of Mother Bethel A.M.E. Church in Philadelphia, built in 1889, used the amphitheater plan. Two early-twentieth-century auditorium churches built by African American congregations in the South featured curved pews: Antioch Baptist Church in

Fig. 33. Metropolitan African Methodist Episcopal Church, Washington, D.C. (1886), courtesy of Library of Congress, Washington, D.C., Prints and Photographs Division, Historic American Buildings Survey, Reproduction number HABS DC, WASH, 489-1.

Shreveport, Louisiana (Figs. 34, 35), designed by N. S. Allen and completed in 1903, and the Sixteenth Street Baptist Church in Birmingham, Alabama (Figs. 36, 37), designed by a black architect, Wallace A. Rayfield, and completed in 1911.[25]

Another innovative feature of the auditorium church besides the shape of the audience room, curved seating, and the amphitheater plan was the large platform. It, too, was designed to facilitate the preaching and hearing of the Word, which evangelicals regarded as the main element of the worship service. The new design used initially by Finney and Beecher caught on quickly. In his 1871 dedicatory sermon in the Union Park Congregational Church, Rev. Helmer praised the fact that "the preacher was no longer raised up and cut off from the audience, but stood on a low and accessible platform." In most auditorium churches, the platform accommodated a preaching desk used to hold a Bible, hymnal, and perhaps sermon notes; chairs for visiting clergy or other guests; and, at the back, choir seating and an organ console. Some commentators recommended a lower secondary platform "to which the evangelist may descend after he has delivered his message, for exhortation and reception of members," and for the administration of the Lord's Supper and similar services (Fig. 38).[26]

Just as evangelicals chose the shape of the auditorium and a seating arrangement that put the preacher and his congregation in the closest proximity, they made the platform project into "the very midst of his audience." They built it high enough to ensure that the preacher could be seen by everyone,

Fig. 34. Antioch Baptist Church, Shreveport, Louisiana (1901–1903).

but not so high as to make him seem remote. Seeing the preacher was vitally important. As a writer in the *National Magazine* noted, "Ideas are conveyed by the *gestures* and *countenance,* as well as by the voice; hence the preacher should not only distinctly see every person to whom he preaches, but the house should be constructed so that every hearer can see him." The architect George Kramer, writing several decades later, agreed. "There is a magnetism in the eye, and an effect in pertinent gestures, combined with the mobility of the facial muscles, of which no speaker should be deprived and no congregation should lose," he observed. Members of the congregation should also be able to hear the preacher. Summarizing evangelical thinking on the subject, Burroughs declared, *"Good acoustic properties are of prime importance.* If the speaker experiences difficulty in speaking, or the singer in singing, or if the hearer finds difficulty in hearing, a chief end of the building is defeated."[27]

The emphasis on good acoustics reflected evangelicals' growing interest in music as an element of the worship service. Most white evangelical denominations had accepted hymn singing by 1800, and during the nineteenth century all but the most conservative relaxed their opposition to organ and other instrumental music in the church. As a result, by the middle of the century their churches, especially the more prosperous ones in large cities, commonly provided space at the back of the pulpit platform for a choir, an organ, and sometimes even an orchestra. In the black churches, acceptance of choral singing and instrumental music occurred somewhat

Fig. 35. Auditorium, Antioch Baptist Church, Shreveport.

Fig. 36. Sixteenth Street Baptist Church, Birmingham, Alabama (1911), Catalog No. OVH 77, courtesy of the Birmingham Public Library Archives.

Fig. 37. Auditorium, Sixteenth Street Baptist Church, Birmingham, Catalog No. 36.60, courtesy of the Birmingham Public Library Archives.

later and after a good deal of controversy. The A.M.E. churches, for example, did not introduce the organ until the 1860s. In the late nineteenth century, urban churches, both black and white, introduced sacred and secular concert music, performed by professional musicians.[28]

In both white and African American auditorium churches of the late nineteenth and early twentieth century, the choir usually sat at the back of the pulpit platform in tiers arranged in a semicircle, facing the congregation. The organ console stood at the base of the choir seats, and an array of organ pipes, highly ornamental as well as functional, "towered over all with their gilt glory." No church could be considered "completely equipped" without a good organ, Kidder asserted; Burroughs declared that a "successful and satisfactory" church building required "an organ of good tone and sufficient volume," centrally located behind the pulpit. If a church had to defer such a purchase, he warned, "the new building is used at a decided disadvantage."[29]

Apart from their usefulness in the production of music, organs came to be seen as emblems of the good taste and wealth of a congregation, and churches competed for the distinction of owning the largest, most beautiful, most expensive organ in the United States. Trinity Methodist Church in Denver, for example, boasted of having the largest organ west of the Mississippi and the fourth largest in the United States. Congregations lacking the money to buy an impressive organ must have been sorely tempted to try the expedient Euster suggested: buy a Kimball organ direct from the factory to save money and then dress it up "to look twice as grand" by adding "about 50 dummy pipes," which "should not cost you more than $60.00 additional."[30]

In Baptist churches the baptistery was another prominent feature of the auditorium, usually located at the back of the platform, above the choir, so that the entire congregation could witness the ceremony of baptism by immersion. Plush or velvet draperies sometimes framed the pool and could be drawn across it when it was not in use. To heighten the sig-

Fig. 38. Platform, First Baptist Church, Dallas, from P. E. Burroughs, *Church and Sunday-School Buildings* (Nashville: Sunday School Board, Southern Baptist Convention, 1920), 72.

nificance of the rite, the rear wall of the baptistery often displayed a painted river scene. The First Baptist Church of Houston, built on Lamar Avenue in 1926, had a baptistery with the traditional river scene. The pastor of the church had visited the Holy Land in 1924, and while he was there, had photographed the River Jordan at the place where Jesus was believed to have been baptized, then had the stones shown in the picture dug out of the river and shipped to Houston. When the baptistery was built, a local artist copied the photograph in painting the mural on the rear wall, and the stones were placed where the water in the mural met the water in the baptismal tank.[31]

Besides designing the auditorium to facilitate their worship practices, evangelicals also introduced features to satisfy churchgoers' increasing desire for comfort and convenience. Among the amenities were comfortable seats. By the 1890s, straight-back pews had largely disappeared, replaced by pews whose backs and seats were curved to fit the human body. Some churches added cushions. Many auditorium churches used "opera chairs"—individual, sometimes cushioned, folding seats. Pews were cheaper, provided more seating in a given space, and, some thought, looked more "churchly," but opera chairs were more comfortable, and most commentators seemed to prefer them. Evangelicals also promoted good lighting in the audience room. The ideal, according to Burroughs, was "a soft sufficient light." To admit natural light during the daytime, evangelicals used large windows and sometimes skylights. Chandeliers and other types of artificial lighting (gas or, preferably, electric) provided illumination in the evening. By the 1870s, heating and ventilating systems had become fairly common in public buildings and upper-class residences, and church officials and architects advised installing such systems in the auditorium as a way of promoting good health as well as comfort. "Impure and oppressive air may effectually defeat earnest efforts to win the lost, as also may discomfort as regards heat or cold," Burroughs warned.[32]

Just as auditorium church builders renounced the utilitarian, plain style of their Puritan forebears, trading the unadorned meetinghouse for more ornamented, "churchly" edifices, they also indulged their newfound interest in beauty in furnishing and decorating the auditorium. "There is abundant room for decoration in the house of God," declared the 1852 convention of Congregational ministers and delegates. Kramer, in his 1897 book, advised church builders that "the seating, furniture and furnishing of a church should be so designed and selected as to serve the double purpose of beautifying and adorning, as well as furnishing."[33]

Elaborate decoration constituted a radical departure for evangelicals, as Bishop Daniel A. Payne acknowledged in describing the interior of the Mother Bethel A.M.E. Church. He had not worshiped in the blacksmith's shop that served as the first house of worship for the Mother Bethel congregation. But he remembered that its second building, though a decided improvement over the first, "was as plain as a Quaker's coat, and perfectly free from ornament, as were all Methodist chapels of those days." In sharp contrast, the third, late-nineteenth-century church building (Fig. 39) featured stained-glass windows using a combination of geometric symbols and traditional Christian images such as the cross, the dove, and the lamb—all painted, according to Payne, "in the colors of the rainbow, with all the tints and hues of the precious stones mentioned in the Revelation of St. John, xxi. 11–21" and "so softly and perfectly blended as to make a glorious scene of divine beauty, and so profuse as to resemble the magnificence of the starry heavens."[34]

Late-nineteenth, early-twentieth-century evangelicals approved stained glass, or less expensive colored glass, not just for its beauty but also for its utility—to "subdue" or "strain" the light coming into the auditorium. And, like organs, stained-glass windows soon acquired symbolic value, testifying to the taste and wealth of a congregation. Indeed, just as Euster had suggested using "dummy pipes" to dress up an inexpensive organ, the Methodist Board of Church Extension advised poor congregations to use "paper imitation of stained glass" to enhance plain glass in existing churches or to apply to the windows of new buildings. The board's catalogue of architectural plans for churches, issued in 1884, included an advertisement for the same by Benjamin D. Price and Co. of Philadelphia, which claimed that "450 Churches have used it."[35]

Some evangelicals continued to be skeptical of traditional Christian art, because of its identification with Roman Catholicism, but that did not diminish their enthusiasm for lavish

Fig. 39. Mother Bethel A.M.E. Church,
Philadelphia (1889), courtesy of Library
of Congress, Washington, D.C., Prints and
Photographs Division, Historic American
Buildings Survey, Reproduction number
HABS, PA, 51-PHILA, 288-2.

decoration of the auditorium. Instead of explicitly Christian images, they employed forms drawn from nature. "An abstract assemblage of stem, foliage, and blossom" decorated the proscenium arch in the Trinity Methodist Episcopal Church auditorium, and the images in the church's stained-glass windows were "analogous not only to jewels but also to plants and flowers." The vaulted ceiling of the Lovely Lane Methodist Church featured a representation of the firmament as it appeared over Baltimore at 3 A.M. on the morning of the dedication of the church, November 6, 1887. Covering an area of twenty-five thousand square feet, the fresco was done in the predominant colors of blue and gold and showed, among other things, "Mars, shining with its own peculiar red light" and "the white light of the 'milky way' with its numerous stars."[36]

The lavish use of color—as in the rainbow hues of the Mother Bethel windows and the blue and gold on the Lovely Lane ceiling—became commonplace in auditorium church interiors. "Nothing . . . is more dull, naked, and even repulsive to good taste than a uniform white upon walls and pews, and wherever paint can go," the convention of Congregational ministers and delegates asserted. Instead of "white-plastered and white-painted churches" the convention recommended buildings done in "a combination of the warmer neutral colors." That was in 1852. A few decades later, evangelicals abandoned neutral colors in favor of the more vibrant, richer hues of "cobalt, ultramarine, carmine, gold, and black." A contemporary described the coloring in the Lovely Lane Methodist Church as "rich and warm, without being brilliant." The "Pompeiian reds" of the walls, carpet, and opera chair upholstery were said to complement the "old brass and gold in the frieze with a particularly happy effect."[37]

The upholstered chairs in the Lovely Lane church were typical of the furnishings found in many of the large auditorium churches, which included expensive wallpaper, draperies, and carpeting, and ornately carved furniture. As a number of historians have observed, the interior design of late-nineteenth- and early-twentieth-century auditorium churches incorporated many features of the middle- and upper-class home: naturally stained wood (used for pews, door frames, and altar rails, as well as wainscoting, ceiling beams, and stairway banisters and newel posts); moldings and cornices; frescoes, wallpaper, carpeting, and upholstery; rich color schemes. Besides the home, the so-called first-class or "palace" hotels constructed in the nineteenth century probably served as models for the interiors of large, urban auditorium churches. As described by Russell Lynes, they had many of the features used by auditorium church builders: rich carpeting, elegant chandeliers, hand-carved woodwork, lavish ornamentation, and modern lighting and heating systems.[38]

The opulence of many auditorium church interiors provoked considerable debate. Like the latter-day Puritans who had deplored steeples and the other forms of ornamentation when they were added to the eighteenth-century meetinghouses, some old-fashioned evangelicals decried the "luxury," "extravagance," and "ostentation" of the auditorium churches and the prevailing notion "that every church has a right to build as expensive a church as it can pay for." Perhaps some of them remembered Finney's admonition in *Lectures on Revivals of Religion,* published in 1835. If the people in the church "are not attentive, they cannot be converted," he observed. So that they "can hear with all their souls," without being distracted by bodily discomfort, the place of worship should be made comfortable. But, he added, echoing Rev. Cotton Mather, "I do not mean *showy.* All your glare and glory of rich chandeliers, and rich carpets, and splendid pulpits, is the opposite extreme, and takes off the attention just as badly. . . . You need not expect a revival *there.*"[39]

The promoters of the modern church countered such criticism with various arguments. As early as 1852, the convention of Congregational ministers and delegates proposed "a safe rule" regarding "the finish and adornment of churches":

> the church should correspond in style to the better class of the dwellings possessed by those who are to occupy the church. If the people are generally poor, so as to be able to have only the plainest houses and the most necessary articles of furniture in them, then it is not to be expected that their place of worship will be other than plain. But if the people indulge in carpets and lounges, in furniture made of rare and costly woods, in mirrors and marbles, and ingenious carvings, and hang their walls with pictures, then it is rightly expected that their house of worship will show something besides bare floors and the array of plain rectangular spaces of unadorned walls. The place of worship does not demand a profusion of ornament. But so far as the ability of the worshipers goes, if it is accompanied

with good taste, it may enrich the house of God with architectural decorations with little danger of carrying the thing too far.[40]

Another argument evangelicals used to justify the construction of expensive, elaborate churches appeared in Rev. Helmer's dedication sermon at the Union Park Congregational Church. He insisted that neither he nor his congregation believed in "extravagance and display." But if they had built a plain church, "the world's people would say the Christians cared little for their God for they built Him such poor houses, while their private houses were sumptuous." Helmer and other evangelicals asserted that "nothing was too good for God."[41]

Black evangelicals had a somewhat different perspective on what some people denigrated as extravagance. Matthew Anderson, pastor of Berean Presbyterian Church in Philadelphia, knew of individuals, including a few of his fellow ministers, who insisted that poor congregations should erect "only plain, cheap church buildings." In opposition to that way of thinking, Anderson's church had contracted a sizable debt in order to build a "well appointed," "attractive" building that would be "an inspiration to the people and a credit to themselves." Describing the structure, Anderson pointed out that "there is nothing about it which is in any way to the Negro a reminder of his past degradation, nor any thing to make him feel that he is an inferior, hence despised and circumscribed, and therefore that only so far he can go and no further. It is the one place he can come and breathe and receive renewed strength and inspiration for the future." Similarly, Bishop Payne declared that the "magnificent temple" built by the Mother Bethel A.M.E. congregation in 1889 "lift[ed] us up above our condition" and "summon[ed] us upon a higher plane of thought and action"; Rev. W. F. Allen of the Colored Methodist Episcopal Church declared that blacks needed "comfortable and respectable houses to worship the Lord in" so they could demonstrate that "they are as good as other people."[42]

Besides exhibiting decoration and furnishings resembling those of middle- and upper-class homes and hotels, the audience rooms of some auditorium churches featured decor similar to that of theaters, concert halls, and opera houses. The large platform that replaced the traditional pulpit as early as the 1830s mimicked the stage, and curved or amphitheater seating, introduced a few decades later, also derived from the theater. Evangelicals adopted both innovations to enhance the preaching and hearing of the Word. Then, during the late nineteenth century, they added performances of sacred or secular music to the worship service.

With so much of the worship service devoted to performance—by the preacher, the choir, or professional musicians—the use of theater decor seemed appropriate. Thus, as Jeanne Halgren Kilde has pointed out, framing the platform became popular. It served to focus attention on the platform in much the same way the elevated pulpit and sounding board in the meetinghouse had accentuated the importance of the preacher. It was usually simply done, using wainscoting, but a few churches employed the more elaborate device of a proscenium arch. In the Trinity Methodist Episcopal Church auditorium (Fig. 40) the arch was "sculpted with papiermache, painted red, green and gold, . . . and studded with ninety-six electric lightbulbs, . . . one for each book of the Bible." Other "theatre references" in the Denver church were "a row of electric bulbs [that] encircled the sanctuary at the lower edge of the gallery" and opera boxes overlooking the stage. The Lovely Lane Methodist Church auditorium displayed ornamentation similar to that of Trinity Church: 340 gas fixtures encircled its ceiling dome. And while Trinity had pews, the Lovely Lane church had upholstered opera seats instead.[43]

Auditorium church builders used features of the theater, opera house, and concert hall partly to facilitate their distinctive mode of worship, but also to create an ambience in the audience room that would appeal to people who prided themselves on (or wanted to demonstrate) their refinement, taste, and gentility. The builders did not feel the need to apologize for or rationalize the use of such decoration, because most people no longer regarded the theater, the opera house, and the concert hall as places of iniquity. They had become respectable. As Lawrence Levine, Richard Bushman, and other historians have shown, they had begun to present "legitimate" drama and "serious" music, and to cater to what contemporary commentators called "the better class, the most refined and intelligent of our citizens," the "high minded, the

Fig. 40. Auditorium, Trinity Methodist Episcopal Church, Denver (1888). Photograph by W. H. Jackson, negative number WHJ-3447, courtesy of the Colorado Historical Society, Denver.

pure and virtuous." Once they became places of "refinement," their decor no longer seemed inappropriate in a church auditorium. Thus a reporter for the *Chicago Tribune* praised the auditorium of the First Congregational Church as "a most handsome combination of the theatre and the church," and a writer in the *Rocky Mountain Christian Advocate* asserted that the audience room of Trinity Methodist Episcopal Church made use of "some of the excellent, well studied features of the theatre and concert room . . . and yet it is churchly in every detail."[44]

"A beautiful interior, as well as an attractive exterior, has much to do with a congregation," Euster observed. The preacher who made a good impression on his congregation could be confident of their returning the following Sunday, he noted. But, he warned, "The impression left by the interior of the church itself has nearly as much influence upon the average man in leading him back to that same Church again next Sabbath. We preachers do not care to acknowledge this, but it is true, nevertheless."[45] Some preachers may have demurred, but most auditorium church builders shared Euster's belief. Not just the theater or concert hall ambience but also other aspects of auditorium church architecture—the eclectic, "churchly" exterior, the comfortable physical environment, the sumptuous audience room—were designed to appeal to the educated, affluent, socially prominent evangelicals living in the large cities of the United States, to draw them to the church and to retain them as members. If the revival structures of the late eighteenth and early nineteenth century reflected the ethos of the Age of the Common Man, the auditorium churches of the mid to late nineteenth and early twentieth century mirrored the values of the Gilded Age.

Although the revivalists used strictly utilitarian structures, and the auditorium church builders constructed "exceedingly magnificent" edifices, both groups regarded their structures as instruments of evangelism. Auditorium church pastors and congregations decorated and furnished their buildings to attract the urban elite, but like the revivalists, they were also committed to "winning the lost," as Burroughs liked to say.[46] Consequently, the auditorium church building often comprised more than a "churchly" exterior and an opulent audience room. In many cases, it was a multipurpose facility designed to bring working-class and poor people under the influence of the gospel, as well as to nurture a predominantly middle- and upper-class congregation.

4

The Multipurpose Church

God, in His providence is moving His church onward and moving it upward at the same time, adjusting it to new situations, fitting it to new conditions and to advancing civilization, requiring us to use the new instrumentalities He has placed in our hands for the purpose of saving the greatest number of human souls.—Russell H. Conwell

In 1853, the convention of Congregational ministers and delegates asserted that "the uses of a church, not to say the proper preaching of the word itself, will demand something more than simply a room in which the Scriptures may be expounded on the Sabbath." Beginning in the middle of the nineteenth century and continuing into the early twentieth century, not only Congregationalists but also Methodists, Presbyterians, and Baptists, African American as well as white, expanded their church buildings to include educational, social, recreational, and institutional facilities. Thus was born the multipurpose evangelical church, one of the "new instrumentalities" championed by pioneers of the "modern," "progressive" evangelical church,[1] and the obvious antecedent of the "full service" megachurches built some one hundred years later.

The most important educational component of the multipurpose evangelical church was the Sunday school. Both white and African American evangelicals made it an integral element of church work. It served primarily as "the nursery of the church"—an institution for indoctrinating church members' children to ensure their becoming professing Christians—but it also offered religious education to adult church members. In addition, some evangelical churches used Sunday schools for missionary work in poor neighborhoods.[2]

Sunday school facilities evolved during the course of the nineteenth century. At first, one or two large rooms sufficed to accommodate the participants. Small groups of scholars gathered around their teachers, with all of the classes sharing the same space. As Sunday school enrollments increased, administrators decided to put the classes of different grades in separate rooms and have the Sunday school students join the congregation for the opening and closing exercises of the worship service. The Akron Plan of the late 1860s provided a way to do that. Developed by Lewis Miller, a Methodist Sunday school superintendent living in Akron, Ohio, and a local builder-architect by the name of Jacob Snyder, it was first used in 1867, in a separate Sunday school building of the First Methodist Episcopal Church. The architect George Kramer then popularized it, incorporating the plan in designs for a number of auditorium churches. During the 1880s it gained increasing acceptance and was widely used throughout the late nineteenth century. Pilgrim Congregational Church (1894) in Cleveland, among others, used the plan (Fig. 41).[3]

An Akron-plan church usually featured a diagonally oriented auditorium with curved seating and a pulpit platform in one corner. In the plans drawn by C. W. Bulger and Son, which P. E. Burroughs presented in one of his books as an illustration of an "expanding auditorium," there were three Sunday school rooms (adult department, senior department, small assembly room) adjoining the auditorium and separated from it by sliding or folding doors or rising partitions (Figs. 42, 43). Opening the doors or partitions enabled the people in the three rooms to participate in the service going on in the auditorium.

While the main purpose of the Akron Plan was to accommodate new developments in the Sunday school, it also proved advantageous in another regard. Evangelicals usually designed their audience rooms to seat the number of persons attending regular worship services. The Akron Plan provided a way to expand the seating capacity of the auditorium to accommodate larger crowds for special occasions or evangelistic services. Burroughs pronounced the plan crucial to successful evangelism. "It is a calamity to be compelled to move from the church building to some hall or opera house or tabernacle in order to accommodate a large attendance," he declared.[4]

In the early twentieth century the appeal of the Akron Plan declined, and evangelicals devised other arrangements for the Sunday school. Administrators had developed a new way of organizing the Sunday school—dividing it into "departments" (e.g., beginners, primary, junior, intermediate, senior, and adult), each of which was "graded" or separated into different age groups. The new departmental, graded Sunday school required more and different kinds of space than earlier plans had provided: individual classrooms for each age

Fig. 41. Auditorium, Pilgrim
Congregational Church, Cleveland
(1894). Photograph by David Thum,
courtesy of the Western Reserve
Historical Society, Cleveland.

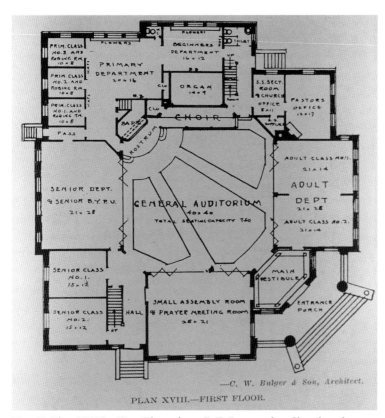

Fig. 42. Plan XVIII—First Floor, from P. E. Burroughs, *Church and Sunday-School Buildings* (Nashville: Sunday School Board, Southern Baptist Convention, 1920), 123.

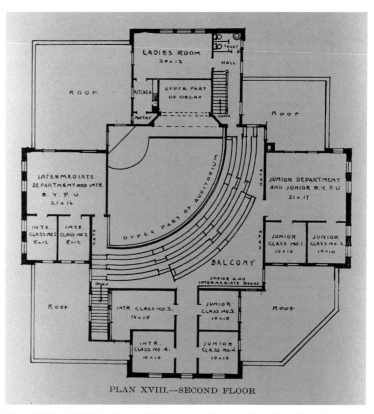

Fig. 43. Plan XVIII—Second Floor, from Burroughs, *Church and Sunday-School Buildings*, 124.

group and a large assembly room for each department, as well as a library and reading room, mission, geography, and teacher-training rooms, and administrative offices.[5] Some congregations met the need by locating the individual Sunday school classrooms and large assembly rooms in the basement of the church, others by adding a wing or wings on the ground floor.

Still others built separate buildings to accommodate the Sunday school. In Philadelphia John Wanamaker oversaw the erection of a four-story structure for the Bethany Presbyterian Church Sabbath School. With a bell tower and spire, the Sunday school building looked very much like a church. Built to accommodate three thousand persons, it had a large hall or "school room" (63 by 58 feet) for the children's classes, which was surrounded by "a series of radiating rooms" used for adult classes. A "huge glass sash" separated the hall from a lecture room with a gallery; it accommodated 350 persons. By the 1920s, many urban churches were constructing separate educational buildings. First Baptist, Dallas, and First Baptist, Jacksonville, Florida, for example, built multistory structures. The one in Dallas had 188 rooms, some large enough to accommodate up to 400 persons. The Jacksonville building, designed by R. H. Hunt Co., featured two elevators and, on the ground floor, a cafeteria the church operated for revenue.[6]

In addition to expanded Sunday school facilities, multipurpose churches featured various kinds of social and recreational facilities. Beginning around the middle of the nineteenth century, evangelical churchmen and architects promoted development of the "social side" of church work. The idea was to make the church attractive to people by "serving the whole man" and "supplying his social as well as spiritual needs," as P. E. Burroughs and Rev. Adam Clayton Powell put it. Some evangelicals focused on particular groups of people: young, single working men and women, for example, who seemed especially vulnerable to temptation; or newcomers to the city, isolated by their lack of family or friends. John Lankford, the Supervising Architect of the A.M.E. Church, observed that social and recreational facilities were "particularly fitted for our churches in the larger towns and cities, for there are many who come from other places, who either join or come under the care of the church, who know few people in the place, except those whom they meet at the church; many have no homes or families in that city, and they use the church and its compartments for both their spiritual and social temple."[7]

The increasing attention evangelicals paid to the "social side" of church work bespoke a general change in their attitudes toward social and recreational activities, which was reflected in such things as the Chautauqua Association and the Young Men's Christian Association. Both of those organizations "eased the way" for Protestant ministers to "make their peace with leisure," according to historian R. Laurence Moore. The Chautauqua Association, founded in 1873 by John Vincent and Lewis Miller (the Methodist who helped devise the Akron Plan), effectively combined religion and social activities in its two-week Sunday School Institutes, which featured "lessons, sermons, devotional meetings *plus* concerts, fireworks, bonfires, humorous lectures, and music in both light and serious forms." The YMCAs promoted "the new gospel 'that physical exercise in all forms can become a mighty factor in the development of the highest type of Christian character.'" Holiness camp meetings and "Christian resorts" established by Methodists, Baptists, and other evangelical denominations during the second half of the nineteenth century also offered summer programs combining piety and leisure.[8]

The Broadway Tabernacle was one of the first evangelical churches to sponsor social events in the church auditorium. Beginning in the 1830s, under the pastorate of Charles Grandison Finney, it rented its audience room to various musical societies for concerts. In later years it also offered a forum for famous speakers such as John B. Gough, Wendell Phillips, William Lloyd Garrison, Ralph Waldo Emerson, and Frederick Douglass. In the 1850s, Tremont Temple in Boston began renting its auditorium for lectures and concerts on weekday evenings. In the post–Civil War period, white and African American evangelicals opened their auditoriums to a broad spectrum of public concerts, cantatas, recitals, lectures, and debates. For example, Concord Baptist Church in Brooklyn, New York, an African American church, presented lectures by prominent black figures such as Ida B. Wells, T. Thomas Fortune, and T. McCants Stewart. Trinity Methodist Episcopal Church in Denver used its audience room, specifically designed for concert performances, to present musical programs, some of them free, featuring classical works as well as popular music.[9]

Other social facilities in African American and white churches included lecture rooms for debates, lectures, elocution contests, and recitations; "social halls" or "social rooms" for musical performances and lectures; one or more "parlors" for smaller gatherings such as teas or the sewing circle, or for meetings of ladies' societies, special committees, or other official bodies; meeting rooms for social clubs (for children and youth as well as adults); and libraries or reading rooms. In the second half of the nineteenth century, some churches added dining or banquet rooms for informal sociables and entertainments as well as more elaborate dinners and banquets. By 1923 the emphasis on such events had grown to the point where Burroughs observed that "the time is quickly coming, if it has not already come, when it will seem . . . incongruous to think of a church building, especially one of large dimensions, without a kitchen. The kitchen, the tea-room and the banquet hall are essential in any well-designed modern church building."[10]

During the latter part of the nineteenth century and continuing into the early part of the twentieth century, evangelical churches expanded their facilities for social and recreational activities. Trinity Methodist Episcopal Church in Denver already had several parlors, a kitchen, and a music room on its "lower level" (the ground floor). In 1926 it completed construction of a three-story annex that housed a gymnasium, lockers, and showers, a kitchen and dining room, several parlors, offices for the church staff, and classrooms for various church activities.[11]

In Philadelphia, the members of Bethany Presbyterian

Church enjoyed social and recreational activities in a clubhouse John Wanamaker built for them in 1890. It featured a swimming pool in the basement; on the ground floor, shuffleboards, billiard and pool tables, a room for games, and a reading room. The second floor had a museum and auditorium, the third a dining room and kitchen as well as a roof garden with comfortable lounge chairs. The Congregational Church of Adams, Massachusetts, built a similar structure. A writer in the *Church Building Quarterly* described its facilities: "On the right of the entrance is the parlor, with a coat room in the rear, and on the left are those indispensable adjuncts of the modern church, the dining room and kitchen." Sixteen Sunday school classrooms opened to a "general assembly room" holding seven hundred persons. The building had a gymnasium and bowling alleys, as well as "rooms for the King's Daughters, the men's Bible class and for social purposes or a library." Like the Bethany clubhouse, the Congregational House also featured two billiard tables, which, the writer pointed out, "seem to belong there as naturally as if they had always been associated with the society of Puritan churches." He could not resist adding that "the lockers and baths, in close proximity, suggest that cleanliness and health are next to, and even a part of, godliness."[12]

Whereas most evangelical churches constructed social and recreational facilities mainly for the enjoyment of their members, the Fourth Presbyterian Church in Chicago also used such facilities to minister to the thousands of unchurched young working-class men and women who lived in the boardinghouses and furnished rooms of a deteriorating neighborhood close to the church—and who were reportedly drawn to a nearby slum notorious for "saloons, dance halls, cheap hotels, houses of prostitution, [and] 'flop-houses.'" In a "club house" built between the manse and the Sunday school building and under the supervision of the Men's Club and the Young Women's Club, young working-class men and women who paid an annual membership fee of one or two dollars found a "home away from home" and wholesome recreation—in separate clubrooms for men and women in which they could relax and read or listen to the player piano, write letters, play cue rogue and shuffleboard (for men only), or sew (for the women). The men and women each had a music room where their orchestras and glee clubs rehearsed, and they shared the use of the gymnasium. There were also classrooms in the clubhouse where they could take evening courses in civics, sewing, salesmanship, business law, shorthand, or typewriting. In parlors sponsored by the Young Women's Club young women could entertain male friends under the watchful eye of a chaperone.[13]

Like the white evangelical churches, many large, urban African American churches added or built facilities for recreational activities. A few provided playgrounds for children. The First Congregational Church, in Atlanta (Fig. 44), was unusual, but not unique, in having a gymnasium; and like some other African American churches it built a separate community center to facilitate its varied social and recreational programs. One of the more unusual recreational facilities provided by an African American church was the Berean Cottage, or Church Home, in Point Pleasant, New Jersey, operated by Berean Presbyterian Church in Philadelphia. It provided accommodations and wholesome recreation for twenty to twenty-five vacationers. The church pastor, Matthew Anderson, said the cottage was "intended to assist in meeting a felt want, not only in the Berean Church, but among the colored people generally, namely, a first-class house where respectable and refined colored people can be accommodated at the sea shore without being subjected to insults and insinuations, and at the same time be protected against those baneful and contaminating influences which are so prevalent at watering places."[14]

Institutional facilities—defined by P. E. Burroughs as those that provided for "community needs" or sought "the betterment of the moral, social and religious life of the community"—constituted an important component of many multipurpose evangelical churches. Among African American churches, Olivet Baptist Church in Chicago (Fig. 45) became well known for such efforts. Under the direction of pastor Lacey Kirk Williams, the congregation bought First Baptist Church on South Park Avenue and Thirty-first Street. Not only did it acquire an impressive neo-Gothic building (described by the *Chicago Defender* as "one of the handsomest and most up-to-date churches on the South side") but it also gained the larger and more varied facilities it needed to expand its community welfare programs. By 1920, the membership had grown to more than eight thousand; Williams and a

Fig. 44. First Congregational Church, Atlanta (1909). Photograph by James R. Lockhart, Georgia Department of Natural Resources, Historic Preservation Division, Atlanta, and courtesy of the National Register of Historic Places, Washington, D.C.

Fig. 45. Olivet Baptist Church, Chicago (1875–1876; originally First Baptist Church).

paid staff of between fifteen and twenty-five persons supervised a day nursery, kindergarten, gymnasium, rooming directory, and employment bureau, in addition to various social and recreational activities.[15]

Like the Olivet church, Trinity Methodist Episcopal Church in Chicago occupied a building previously owned by whites, which it obtained as a result of a transfer in 1917 by the denomination. The *Southwestern Christian Advocate* praised it as "the largest and best equipped plant in all Methodism for Negroes." The complex included "two auditoriums, well furnished, two pipe organs, one costing eighteen thousand dollars, three great pianos, kitchen, dining room, many Sunday school rooms, pastor's study, spacious and well furnished gymnasium, shower baths, [and] hot and cold water." In addition, Trinity had a four-story "community house," which sponsored various institutional programs.[16]

Other African American churches (Baptist and Methodist as well as Congregationalist and Presbyterian) in the North, Midwest, and South maintained facilities for a wide variety of institutional programs. They ranged from savings banks, employment and housing bureaus, medical clinics, and soup kitchens to homes for girls, working women, elderly persons, and unwed mothers, and manual training centers for boys. Some of these programs were for church members, but others provided assistance to people in the surrounding community.

Some white evangelical churches sponsored institutional programs. In the early 1870s Pilgrim Congregational Church in Cleveland provided recreational rooms for young working men in hopes of attracting them away from unsavory places of amusement. When the congregation built its second building, in 1893–1894, it added a large wing dedicated to social and community services (Fig. 46). Bethany Presbyterian Church in Philadelphia also had a number of institutional facilities: a college that offered evening classes in such subjects as book-keeping, stenography, dressmaking, millinery, and mechanical drawing; a parish house that operated a day nursery, kindergarten, and medical dispensary; a "Men's Friendly Inn" that provided meals and lodging for unemployed men; and a penny savings bank.[17]

Perhaps the most famous multipurpose evangelical church, known for a wide range of institutional programs as well as educational, social, and recreational facilities, was another Philadelphia church, the Baptist Temple (also known as Grace Baptist Church), pastored by Russell H. Conwell from 1882 to 1925 (Fig. 47). Dedicated in 1891, the temple was a typical auditorium church, though less "churchly" than most. Edmund K. Alden, writing in the *Christian Union* in 1893, remarked that it presented "the appearance of an institution of some kind"— an art museum or a library, rather than a church. The brownstone structure had no spire or steeple, but the "half rose window" in the facade hinted at its religious function. Situated above the window was a small iron balcony where, on religious holidays, the church orchestra and choir presented programs of sacred music. Inside the temple building were two levels. The Lower Temple, constructed approximately two-thirds below grade, was composed of a lecture room 48 feet

Fig. 46. Pilgrim Congregational Church, Cleveland (1894). Photograph by David Thum, courtesy of the Western Reserve Historical Society, Cleveland.

Fig. 47. The Baptist Temple, Philadelphia (1891), from Agnes Rush Burr, *Russell H. Conwell, Founder of the Institutional Church in America, The Man and the Work* (Philadelphia: John C. Winston Company, 1908), illustration facing p. 154.

by 102 feet, with a 16-foot ceiling, a dining hall and kitchen, an "infant room," four "social rooms," and three "committee rooms." The Upper Temple housed the auditorium and some small offices (Fig. 48).[18]

In the *Christian Union,* Alden wrote that his first thought upon entering the auditorium and seeing its plush-covered opera chairs was that "we are in a music-hall or consecrated theater," but then, he added, "the pulpit and organ reassure us." The ceiling was fifty feet high. Iron trusswork supported the galleries, making posts unnecessary; thus every seat commanded a good view of the platform. The acoustics were said to be perfect. Estimates of the seating capacity of the auditorium varied, from slightly over 3,000 to 3,500; according to one commentator, bringing in 1,000 additional chairs raised the total capacity to more than 4,500. A 250-person choir sat at the back of the platform, and above them were displayed the lavishly ornamented pipes of the great organ. Decorative trusses, stained-glass windows, chandeliers, and beaded board and ceramic tile wainscoting added elegance to the vast auditorium.[19]

The temple baptistery was a long, narrow pool measuring fifteen by sixty feet, situated under and extending the whole length of the platform. For the immersion ceremony, the portion of the platform covering the baptistery was removed, and water flowed through the pool. Made to resemble the site of Jesus' baptism, which Conwell had seen on a visit to Palestine, the pool was banked with flowers, palms, moss, and vines, with a small waterfall at the back. During the ceremony, a wa-

ter pipe under the platform could be opened to create "a beautiful fountain . . . directly in front of the choir." Sometimes the fountain was displayed when the choir performed an oratorio. Then, according to Alden, "the cascade, springing from amidst palms and electric lights, gives a marvelous scenic effect to the volume of the music."[20]

The "Young People's Church" met in the Lower Temple's lecture room (seating capacity, two thousand), which was also used for Sunday school and lectures. Suppers and banquets were held in the five-hundred-person dining room, which had a large kitchen equipped with two ranges, "hot-water cylinders," sinks, and "drainage tanks." The Business Men's Union had a meeting room, and the Young Men's Association and the Young Women's Association their own parlors and reading rooms, also in the Lower Temple. Alden noted "the coziness of these church parlors, with their pictures, easels, vases, libraries, organs, tiled fireplaces, bronzes, and tables covered with the periodicals of the day."[21]

On weekday evenings the church presented a wide range of "entertainments" in both the Upper Temple and the Lower Temple. Those sponsored by the church had a spiritual orientation—concerts and oratorios by the temple choir, recitations, readings and debates by members of various temple societies, lectures by noted churchmen, including Conwell. Other entertainments were more secular—an illustrated lecture on Yellowstone Park, a reading from *David Copperfield,* a "Greek Festival" tableau by Temple College students, concerts by the Germania Orchestra, the Mendelssohn Quintette

Fig. 48. Auditorium, the Baptist Temple, from a weekly bulletin of the Baptist Temple, dated December 6, 1936, courtesy of the Baptist Temple, Blue Bell, Pennsylvania.

Club of Boston, the Ringgold Band of Reading, Pennsylvania, and the New York Philharmonic Club.[22]

The temple also sponsored educational and social welfare programs. In addition to its large Sunday school, it administered Temple College, founded in 1888 to provide tuition-free collegiate education for young working men and women. The college boasted one of the best-equipped gymnasiums in Philadelphia, which could be used by members of the church as well as students. The Temple College Athletic Association (which church members were eligible to join) also enjoyed access to a baseball diamond, a "crease for cricket," lawn-tennis courts, and croquet lawns. A short distance away from the temple, Conwell and his congregation bought a house on the corner of Broad and Ontario Streets and renovated it to serve as the Samaritan Hospital, dedicated in 1892. Like the college, it focused on the needs of working-class and poor people. The founders advertised it as a "Non-Sectarian Corporation for the free relief of needy men, women and children in suffering."[23]

The Baptist Temple provides a good illustration of the way nineteenth- and early-twentieth-century evangelicals combined the auditorium church form and multipurpose facilities, enabling them to appeal to the urban elite while at the same time fulfilling a commitment, inherited from the revivalists, to promote moral reform and to evangelize the masses. Some of the programs of the multipurpose church catered to the predominantly middle- and upper-class church membership. The Sunday schools, the concerts and other musical events, the dining rooms, social halls and parlors, the recreational facilities, all were built for the enjoyment of the church members. Evangelical churchmen and architects believed that such facilities encouraged fellowship and what Burroughs called "solidarity of spirit" among the congregation, which were becoming crucial factors in attracting and holding church members.[24]

However, the evangelical multipurpose church also extended its influence beyond the membership into the surrounding community. In effect, it opened its doors to the inhabitants of the city. Evangelicals regarded public concerts, lectures, gatherings, and similar events as a means of drawing nonmembers to the church, hopefully inducing them to consider attending a worship service or to become members. They turned the church into a kind of cultural center that competed with secular places of entertainment and sought to win people away from their often dubious influence. Conwell justified the temple's sponsorship of "entertainments" on the ground that the church should use "any reasonable means to influence men for good." He believed that by offering wholesome social and recreational programs, the church could win people away from "low and vulgar amusement" and eventually "control the entertainments of the world."[25] Conwell and his congregation were not alone in adopting this moralistic approach to church-sponsored entertainment and leisure activities.

The multipurpose church also functioned as a kind of community center, ministering to the needs of the surrounding neighborhood as well as its own members. Evangelicals used its varied facilities to ameliorate the lives of working-class men and women as well as the unemployed and the poor. Sunday schools, parlors, clubhouses, and other social and recreational facilities, as well as employment and housing centers, savings banks, and medical dispensaries, all constituted an outreach to those classes of people. They represented an extension and elaboration of traditional church-sponsored charitable and benevolent activities. They also served an evangelistic purpose. Offering recreation, employment counseling, medical care, and the like was a way of drawing people to the church and exhibiting the beneficent power of the gospel.[26]

Together, the revivalists and the multipurpose auditorium church builders bequeathed a threefold legacy to later generations of evangelical church builders. One element of the legacy was inventiveness, reflected in the innovative structures devised by the revivalists and the new architectural forms and "instrumentalities" adopted by the builders of multipurpose auditorium churches. A second element was acceptance of "the world." Just as the revivalists and the auditorium church builders drew inspiration from secular architecture (the theater, the concert hall, and the opera house, as well as the home and the first-class hotel), the multipurpose church administrators adapted worldly amusements (social, recreational, and athletic activities) and secular institutions (such as hospitals, savings banks, and employment centers) to religious ends. To those who worried that the church was in danger of "going over to the world," Conwell had an emphatic response. Too many churches, "in coldness and forgetfulness of Christ's purpose, of Christ's sacrifice, and the purpose for which the church was instituted," had withdrawn "so far from the world" that they could not reach the unchurched masses. As Conwell saw it, the danger was "not . . . so much in going over to the world as in going away from it—away from the world which Jesus died to save—the world which the church should lead to Him."[27]

Conwell articulated a third element of the legacy—the commitment to evangelism and to the idea of the church (or the campground, tent, or tabernacle) as an instrument of evangelism. The revivalists and the multipurpose auditorium church builders agreed with Conwell that "the church of Christ should be so conducted always as to save the largest number of souls," and that it should use "anything that helps to save souls."[28] Like the other elements of the legacy, it was a prescription that later generations of evangelicals embraced wholeheartedly.

5

Building for 🍂 Mass Evangelism

Instead of cloud-reaching spires, and churches patterned after ancient cathedrals, we believe that the church building should be a modern lighthouse, a work shop for the Lord. We believe it ought to be practical and simple.—G. B. Vick

In the late nineteenth century, tents and tabernacles reappeared in American cities, the work of a new generation of evangelicals—fundamentalists, pentecostals, and holiness people. They were the religiously disinherited, unwelcome in the mainline evangelical churches, or they were dissident "come-outers" who had separated from those churches because they opposed their modernist heresies.[1] Turning their backs on the mainline denominations, they lured away many of their members in the process of establishing hundreds of independent nondenominational churches and a host of new denominations such as the Church of God (Anderson, Indiana), the Church of the Nazarene, the Church of God in Christ (COGIC) and the Assemblies of God. Because these dissenting evangelicals constituted the immediate ancestors of the late-twentieth-century evangelical generation, their perspective on religious architecture was a particularly significant factor in the evolution of the megachurches. Their emphasis on mass evangelism and on the use of secular building design and modern construction technology exerted a decisive influence.

In their manifold controversy with the mainline evangelicals, the dissenters disparaged not just their religious beliefs and worship practices but also their architecture, railing against "one hundred thousand dollar churches" where "wealth and fashion gather, and the poor have not the gospel preached to them." Such criticism reflected their socioeconomic status. Late-nineteenth, early-twentieth-century fundamentalists, pentecostals, and holiness people were generally less wealthy and less educated than the mainline evangelicals; in the large cities of the United States, they were mostly working-class or poor people. They disapproved of middle- and upper-class congregations who lavished money on themselves and their church buildings yet neglected the poor. They also resented being made to feel unwelcome by architecture and furnishings that advertised churches as worship places for the elite. G. B. Vick, the superintendent of Temple Baptist Church, explained that "one reason why many poor people do not go to church today is that they feel ill at ease and not at home in a church with stained glass windows, a fine carpet on the floor and mahogany pews."[2]

Opposition to "worldliness" also inspired the dissenters' criticism of mainline architecture. As Edith Blumhofer and Joel Carpenter have pointed out, fundamentalists, pentecostals, and holiness people sought to separate themselves from "worldly comforts and pleasures." Thus they scorned mainline evangelicals' preoccupation with refinement and gentility. Instead of pretentious church buildings featuring tall towers, stained-glass windows, and opulently furnished audience rooms, the dissenters advocated structures notable for their economy, simplicity, and utility. They wanted their buildings to be, in Vick's words, "a work shop for the Lord," "simple but comfortable, attractive but not extravagant, inviting to people of all classes and conditions; not too shoddy for the wealthiest and not too fine for the humblest and poorest."[3]

As evangelists of a burgeoning religious movement, fundamentalists, pentecostals, and holiness people devoted considerable energy to recruitment. Their socioeconomic position, along with their antipathy to mainline evangelical church buildings, dictated a reliance, at least in the early years of their movement, on simple, utilitarian structures designed specifically for the purpose of accommodating large numbers of people. Tents and tabernacles, rather than churches, became the main instruments of early dissenting evangelism, especially in urban areas.

The dissenters' tents were much larger than those of the early-nineteenth-century revivalists. During an evangelistic campaign launched to compete with the World's Fair of 1893, held in Chicago, Dwight Moody rented the exhibition tent of Forepaugh's Circus for two Sunday afternoons and filled it with ten thousand persons. J. Frank Norris led a ninety-day revival in Fort Worth, in 1911, in a circus tent Sarah Bernhardt had once used during her national tours. Twenty-four years later, during another evangelistic campaign, in Detroit, he used an even larger, five-pole tent that covered forty-five thousand square feet and seated eight thousand. And in 1922, Aimee Semple McPherson packed some seven thousand persons into a tent provided by the First Baptist Church of San Jose, California.[4]

The dissenters' tabernacles were also large. One of Moody's tabernacles, in Chicago, had eight thousand chairs. Even in smaller cities, Billy Sunday's tabernacles seated five to six thousand. Most of his tabernacles accommodated at least ten thousand, and the Pittsburg Tabernacle seated fifteen thousand. In general, the tabernacles were devoid of "churchly" ornamentation. Some were in fact secular buildings. Moody held revival meetings in theaters and halls, even a saloon, as well as the Brooklyn Rink and the Hippodrome, and Sunday preached in renovated tobacco or cotton warehouses, large halls, and municipal auditoriums.[5]

Perhaps the largest secular building converted into a tabernacle was the Pennsylvania Railroad Freight Depot, donated by John Wanamaker for a series of revival meetings Moody held in Philadelphia during the winter of 1875–1876. It was a long, rectangular building with clerestory windows above shed structures on each side (Fig. 49). Refurbished, the "Depot Tabernacle" housed an auditorium seating ten thousand persons, three large inquiry rooms, and a thirty-foot-wide vestibule around three sides of the building. Inside, the roof trusses were exposed, and a number of bell-shaped light fixtures hung from the ridge (Fig. 50). There were rows of chairs arranged in straight lines, a preaching platform with graded seating for the choir behind it, and biblical inscriptions decorating the walls. According to Herbert Adams Gibbons, the floor of the auditorium "rose gradually so that all could see the speaker and choir," and "the acoustics were so good that even those who were unable to get seats could hear from the

corridor." Although the furnishings were strictly utilitarian, the auditorium was well heated, and the clerestory windows provided both light and ventilation. In the evening, according to Gibbons, "a thousand gas burners, with reflectors in front of the platform, established a new era in lighting."[6]

Tabernacles built specifically for revival meetings reflected secular styles of architecture. A brick tabernacle constructed in Chicago for Moody in the mid 1870s, and financed by a group of businessmen who planned to convert it after the revival into "a row of first class stores," looked like a large warehouse. Several of Sunday's tabernacles resembled a shed-roof crib barn with a "turtle-back" roof, which had a broken gable with clerestory windows that provided ventilation as well as natural light (Fig. 51). Another barnlike tabernacle was the Chicago Gospel Tabernacle, directed by Paul Rader from 1922 to 1933. The "Big Steel Tent," as Rader called it, originated as a temporary revival tent constructed of steel girders, with the sides draped with large sheets of canvas for protection from the rain and the floor covered with gravel. Eventually, Rader enclosed the structure with wooden walls covered with cheap tile, and made it a permanent meeting place.[7] Like the warehouse design used for Moody's Chicago tabernacle, the barnlike design of Sunday's and Rader's structures provided a very economical way of enclosing and roofing a large space, given the state of building technology in the late nineteenth century.

The Union Gospel Tabernacle (Fig. 52) in Nashville, Tennessee, was architecturally more elaborate than most taber-

Fig. 49. Moody's Depot Tabernacle (Old Pennsylvania Railroad Depot), Philadelphia (1875–1876), from William R. Moody, *The Life of Dwight L. Moody* (New York: Fleming B. Revell Company, 1900), 266.

Fig. 50. Auditorium, Moody's Depot Tabernacle, from Rev. W. F. P. Noble, *A Century of Gospel-Work: A History of the Growth of Evangelical Religion in the United States* (Philadelphia: H. C. Watts and Co., 1876), frontispiece. The caption reads: "Messrs. Moody and Sankey in the 'Depot Church,' Philadelphia, Jan. 1876."

nacles, probably because it was intended to serve as a permanent religious and civic meeting place. Built in the early 1890s, it was a Gothic Revival structure featuring a hand-cut limestone foundation and red brick walls, a high pitched gable roof, lancet windows, and buttresses at the corners and on the facade. Other decoration, which was later removed, included crest-tiles (a row of stylized flowers) along the main roof line and crockets on the gables. Despite its Gothic ornamentation, the Union Gospel structure resembled other tabernacles in its barnlike form and great size.[8]

Although the dissenters disparaged the mainline evangeli-

cal churches and probably designed the exteriors of the tabernacles to advertise their differences from them, in planning the interiors they did not hesitate to borrow certain features of the auditorium church. Like the late-eighteenth, early-nineteenth-century revivalists and even the auditorium church builders, the tabernacle builders were pragmatists. They selected architectural forms without regard to their source or association, making use of whatever seemed appropriate to their religious beliefs, their emphasis on mass evangelism, and their worship practices.

So, for example, tabernacles incorporated one or more elements of the auditorium church seating arrangement. The Depot Tabernacle had a sloping floor. In Sunday's Scranton tabernacle, wooden chairs and slat-back benches were arranged around the platform. The Union Gospel Tabernacle followed the amphitheater plan, featuring curved wooden pews on a sloping floor. Moody's Chicago tabernacle had a forty-foot-deep, horseshoe-shaped gallery with banked seats that accommodated twenty-nine hundred persons.[9]

Tabernacles also had platforms like those in the auditorium churches, but they were considerably larger. In Moody's Chicago tabernacle the platform occupied the entire west end of the building, and it was broad and deep enough to accommodate the preacher, an organ, and "five or six hundred singers, ministers, and other distinguished people." The platform in the Chicago Gospel Tabernacle accommodated a three-hundred-voice choir, a full brass band, and two concert pianos. Some of Sunday's platforms were much larger, pro-

Fig. 51. Billy Sunday Tabernacle, Pittsburg (Pittsburgh?; n.d.), from Elijah P. Brown, *The Real Billy Sunday: The Life and Work of Rev. William Ashley Sunday, D.D., The Baseball Evangelist* (New York: Fleming H. Revell Company, 1914), facing p. 189.

Fig. 52. Union Gospel Tabernacle (later Ryman Auditorium), Nashville (1892). Photograph from the Library Picture Collection, courtesy of the Tennessee State Library and Archives, Nashville.

viding space for as many as two to three thousand singers and for his theatrical preaching performance. His contemporaries observed that he used every inch of a large platform while delivering his sermon. Indeed, he employed vigorous gestures and bodily movement more often—and to greater effect—than any of the "sensational" evangelists who preceded him. Two of his associates said that because he knew that "50 per cent of all impressions are received through the eye" and that "people understand with their eyes as well as their ears," he was in "constant movement" while on the platform. It seemed "impossible for him to stand up behind the pulpit and talk only with his mouth." The *Louisville Herald* described him as "a whirling dervish that pranced and cavorted and strode and bounded and pounded all over the platform."[10]

Because of their great size and the huge crowds they attracted, the tabernacles required certain features not found in the auditorium churches. To ensure good acoustics, some tabernacle builders reintroduced the eighteenth-century meeting-house sounding board or its equivalent. Moody preached under a circular sounding board that hung from one of the trusses in the Depot Tabernacle, and there was a large sounding board above the platform in Rader's gospel tabernacle. In some of Sunday's larger tabernacles a device called an "augiphone," fashioned by his building contractor Joseph Spiece, hung above the evangelist's head and amplified his voice (Fig. 53). Spiece also promoted the use of the "turtle-back" roof as a means of enhancing acoustics.[11]

The decor of the tabernacle interior differed significantly

Fig. 53. Interior, Billy Sunday Tabernacle, Syracuse, New York (n.d.). Photograph courtesy of the Archives of the Billy Graham Center, Wheaton, Illinois.

from that found in the mainline evangelical churches. The auditorium church builders favored lavish art work, carving, stained glass, and the like. Whether because of financial constraints, dislike of "one hundred thousand dollar churches," or a neo-Puritan antipathy to "gaudy, pompous, theatrical fineries," the dissenters preferred austerity. They used a minimal amount of decoration in the auditorium—usually religious mottos or Bible verses emblazoned on the interior walls and balcony facings. In a typical Sunday tabernacle, the only ornamentation was a long white banner stretched above the platform, with a message painted on it in three-foot-high letters, such as "GET RIGHT WITH GOD!" Moody used Bible verses rather sparingly in the Depot Tabernacle, but in his Chicago Tabernacle they were more numerous and painted in large red and black letters on the white walls and gallery fronts: on the east, "I am the resurrection and the life"; on the north, "The blood of Jesus Christ, His Son, cleanseth us from all sin"; on the south, "He that believeth on the Son hath everlasting life." On the wall behind the pulpit platform, the painted message read, "NOW is the day of salvation." There was also "an illuminated cross with the words, 'God Is Love,' shining along the crossbeam, and a star positioned at the head."[12] Of course, such displays of religious messages were not mere decoration. They reinforced the word of God worshipers heard in the preacher's sermons and during congregational singing.

The religious inscriptions were one aspect of a larger effort on the part of tabernacle builders to suit their structures to the worship practices of dissenting evangelicals, which contrasted sharply with those of their mainline brethren. As William McLoughlin has pointed out, by the late nineteenth century, many mainline churches had become stolidly middle-class. Their ministers and congregations "wanted no emotionalism in church services, no holiness or perfectionist enthusiasm, no mention of hell-fire, Satan, or the Second Coming of Christ. They had made peace with the world." A similar middle-class ethos dominated the mainline African American denominations, whose spokesmen advocated "intelligent sermonizing" and "music of a refined order" in place of "corn-field ditties," "shouting, jumping, and dancing," and other emblems of a "heathenish mode of worship."[13]

By contrast, holiness people and pentecostals engaged in ecstatic, intensely emotional worship behavior. Holiness churches allowed, even encouraged, individual expression during the worship service in the form of shouting, clapping hands, or dancing; pentecostals demonstrated their encounters with the Holy Spirit by such actions as speaking in tongues, prophesying, or healing. Although fundamentalists eschewed such emotionalism, their worship was also more informal, expressive, and participatory than that of the mainline evangelical congregations. Fundamentalists were not given to shouting, but outbursts of "Amen" or "Hallelujah" were not uncommon. The preacher frequently sought prayer requests, articulated orally or by an upraised hand. As in the holiness and pentecostal churches, congregational singing also provided opportunities for "self-expression" and "emotional release."[14]

Instead of the formal worship environment typical of the auditorium church, which encouraged restraint and decorum on the part of the congregation, the tabernacle builders created a more informal environment appropriate to an expressive mode of worship. The austerity of the tabernacle interior contributed to this effort by concentrating the individual's attention on the worship experience—on the preaching and the music and on his or her own spiritual state—rather than on the decor.

The musical component of the tabernacle service also encouraged informality and participation. Typically, the huge tabernacle choirs performed a few selections, but mostly they assisted congregational singing. In Sunday's tabernacles, musical director Homer Rodeheaver made a point of interspersing performances of the choir with music in which the congregation took part. He would begin the musical program with "some of the old familiar hymns everybody could sing"; then he and the choir would teach the congregation some new gospel songs. Sometimes he encouraged audience participation by what he frankly termed a "stunt"—having the music sung in an "antiphonal" manner. One favorite of the tabernacle audiences, "Brighten the Corner Where You Are," was sung this way: "When the tabernacle was filled we would have one section on one side sing the first phrase of the chorus, then, jumping across the tabernacle, the section on the opposite side sing the second phrase, the chorus choir would sing the third phrase, and then we would pick out the ten back rows of the tabernacle, often nearly a short city block away, to sing the last 'Brighten the Corner.'" Rodeheaver also allowed individuals or groups to choose the songs they wanted the congregation or choir to sing, and he permitted visiting delegations (Boy Scouts, old soldiers, labor unions, women's club or Bible class members, etc.) to sing hymns of their own choice. Sometimes the choir listened while the congregation, or a part of it, performed.[15]

To facilitate evangelism—the main purpose of tabernacle services—tabernacle builders made sure the aisles on the ground floor were wide enough to allow large numbers of people to respond to the altar call or invitation; in tabernacles that had galleries, they constructed stairs or ramps leading down to the platform for the same purpose. By the late nineteenth century, many mainline evangelical preachers had given up the invitation in favor of the "inquiry meeting," which was held after the worship service and provided an opportunity for the "anxious" to pray and talk with the preacher and his assistants. The dissenting evangelicals revived the invitation. At the end of a tabernacle service, the preacher would exhort individuals to "come forward" down the aisles to the platform to profess Christ as their savior and testify to their born-again experience.[16]

The tabernacles functioned as highly effective instruments of evangelism, bringing thousands of converts and new members into the fundamentalist, holiness, and pentecostal churches. Then, in the early twentieth century, as their numbers and financial resources increased, the dissenting evangelicals began building large churches in urban areas of the United

States. They were basically hybrid structures, part tabernacle, part auditorium church, part newly invented. In designing the exteriors, the dissenters broke with traditional religious architecture and experimented with a variety of new styles and construction methods, some of which were inspired by the tabernacles. The interiors of the churches were less innovative. Some were as austere as the tabernacles, while others exhibited the elaborate decoration and opulent furnishings found in the auditorium churches. But whatever their exterior or interior design, all of these churches were planned with the evangelization of the urban masses in mind.

The Baptist Tabernacle (Fig. 54) in Atlanta, pastored by Leonard G. Broughton, actually began as a tabernacle. Its original building was a wooden structure that was eventually bricked over. It was a very simple, utilitarian building, albeit less rough and makeshift than some of Sunday's tabernacles.[17]

Shortly after moving into the structure, Broughton and his congregation became involved in a never-ending effort to expand the seating capacity of the auditorium, partly to accommodate the increasing church membership but also to provide sufficient space for the huge Bible conferences Broughton sponsored each year. When expansion proved unfeasible, the pastor and congregation built a much larger and very different-looking structure a few blocks away from the former building, which opened in March 1911. Designed by Reuben Harrison Hunt, a well-known Chattanooga architect, it featured a neoclassical exterior. Hunt placed the features of a Roman temple (pediment, columns, Corinthian capitols) above an arcade formed by five Roman arches. The exterior walls were red-faced brick trimmed with granite; the roof beams were made of iron and steel. Overall, the building measured 147 by 130 feet, with a vestibule 65 by 22 feet, and 22 feet high. The auditorium was 90 by 90 feet, and 55 feet high; besides the main floor, there were a "gallery" and two balconies. During the dedication week services, September 10–17, an estimated eight thousand persons packed the auditorium, many of them standing, and hundreds more were turned away.[18]

In some ways, the Baptist Tabernacle resembled the mainline evangelical auditorium churches. Its neoclassical exterior was similar to exteriors recommended by P. E. Burroughs and F. E. Kidder, and its auditorium boasted a "gigantic organ," with the pipes and choir loft framed by a proscenium arch (Fig. 55). Still, the overall impression the tabernacle conveyed was that of a dissenting evangelical structure. Consider the reaction of a first-time visitor, Fuzzy Woodruff, the sportswriter for the *Atlanta Constitution.* "It is a structure that will appeal to any man who derives pleasures and benefits from things sportive," he wrote. The first thing that caught his eye was the "big electric sign" on top of the huge building. "It is the same sort of sign as invites the populace in to pay a pair of hard-earned iron dollars to witness Miss Tottie Tiptoes in her justly celebrated musical comedy, 'The Jay Birds.' It's not scary. . . . it's inviting."[19]

Woodruff liked the design of the auditorium, which was arranged "like a modern theater." Only the "stage boxes"

Fig. 54. Atlanta Baptist Tabernacle (1911), from "Sixty-Fifth Anniversary: The Baptist Tabernacle, Atlanta, Georgia, 1898–1963," church brochure in Church Vertical File Collection, Special Collections (Baptist and University Archives), courtesy of Jack Tarver Library, Mercer University, Macon, Georgia.

Fig. 55. Platform, Atlanta Baptist Tabernacle, from P. E. Burroughs, *Church and Sunday-School Buildings* (Nashville: Sunday School Board, Southern Baptist Convention, 1920), 73.

were missing. He liked the feelings the auditorium provoked. It had "good red blood in it." The architect had designed it to make people feel "comfortable and capable of enjoying" the program. During the worship service, "the oppressiveness of the usual church service [was] absolutely absent." The choir members sang "as if they meant it, just as Arlie Latham yells from the coaching lines." So did the congregation. "In most churches," Woodruff noted, "there are three people who hold hymn books and warble softly while the choir is doing the harmony business. In the Tabernacle everybody sings." He described "the well-sustained, harmonious music" as "something like the organized rooting that marks a seventh inning rally. . . . It is pulsating, impressive, but not oppressive. There is not one jot of the funeral dirge in its entire make-up."

And, "wonder of wonders," Woodruff continued, "the congregation can express its feelings," and with as much freedom as sports fans at a baseball game. "If the organist cuts the plate with a tune that appeals, they applaud. If the preacher slips over a Joe Miller, they laugh. If he indulges in a William Jennings Bryan they are as enthusiastic as a political convention. . . . Such is the spirit of the Tabernacle. Any good baseball fan can go there and get his money's worth."[20]

In contrast to the Baptist Tabernacle, the First Baptist Church of Fort Worth, Texas, pastored by J. Frank Norris, was a very utilitarian building. Its main function was to accommodate a huge number of people and facilitate Norris's sensational preaching and dynamic evangelism. The gesturing and bodily movements of the "Texas Cyclone," as he was called, were almost as frenetic as Billy Sunday's. At the climax of the sermon he would "frequently . . . leap from the pulpit platform to the level of the congregation, there concluding his discourse by inviting members of his audience to join him in an act of dedication."[21] His antics were controversial, but they made him one of the most famous preacher-evangelists of the twentieth century.

When Norris became pastor of First Baptist in 1909, the congregation was worshiping in a neo-Gothic auditorium church erected in 1888. After it burned down, in 1912, Norris and his congregation built another neo-Gothic structure, larger (to accommodate the huge crowds Norris was attracting) and less pretentious than the first. It, too, burned, in 1929. Meeting in one "sheet iron tabernacle" after another, Norris and his congregation worked four years to scrape together the money needed to construct a third edifice, which they built on the corner of Fourth and Taylor Streets in the downtown, business section of Fort Worth. A photo taken by W. D. Smith in the early 1940s showed the structure on the far left (Fig. 56). The facade bore no religious decoration, not even a cross, and the structure lacked a tower or steeple. A marquee over the entrance to the auditorium, with large letters proclaiming "Dr. J. Frank Norris, Pastor," made the building look more like a downtown movie theater than a church. Next to the church stood an educational building, which took up much of the corner of Fourth and Throckmorton Streets. It might have been mistaken for a dry-goods or department store were it not for the sign jutting out from the corner of the building, displaying the name of the church and its pastor. In the mid 1940s, two stories were added to the educational building to provide faculty office space for the Bible Baptist Seminary, founded by Norris. (Smith's photograph showed the entrance to the seminary in the four-story building next to the educational building.) The seminary obtained a 199-year lease on the property, which allowed the church to use it on Sunday and the seminary to use it the remainder of the week.[22]

The church auditorium featured a large, sloping cement floor that covered twenty thousand square feet and provided a ten-foot elevation from front to back. Exposed roof trusses recalled the tabernacle mode of construction. A "low sprawling platform" with a "choir loft" and baptistery occupied the north end. Bible verses decorated the platform area and the walls of the auditorium. The day the building was dedicated, fourteen thousand persons attended the services, even though they had to sit on "hard slat benches" and the floor lacked tiles. Ultimately, straight rows of pews replaced the benches.[23]

In 1934 Norris acquired another pastorate, Temple Baptist Church in Detroit. The membership increase he stimulated at the church quickly rendered the existing facility inadequate, so in the late 1930s, he and the congregation embarked on a building campaign. On either side of the existing church building (which was to be used for Sunday school classrooms), they built two three-story Sunday school buildings very similar to the educational building next to Norris's Fort Worth church—simple, boxlike, and unadorned. Across the street, they constructed a new church building measuring 130 by 150 feet. Steel trusses supported the roof, eliminating the need for columns inside the auditorium. A reporter for the *Detroit News* described it as a "4000-seat preaching auditorium . . . designed to be the largest preaching place in Detroit."[24]

Like Norris's Fort Worth church, the Temple Baptist structure had its main entrance at street level. Superintendent G. B.

Fig. 56. First Baptist Church, Fort Worth, Texas (1933). Photograph courtesy of W. D. Smith, Inc., Commercial Photography Collection, Special Collections Division, University of Texas at Arlington Libraries, Arlington.

Vick explained why: "stores, business houses and places of amusement" had found that arrangement to be the best way of "getting the greatest number of people on the inside." After all, he continued, "people are what we are after. Some preachers and churches say there is nothing in numbers. But we believe that to get people saved we must get them under the sound of the Gospel."[25]

The Detroit church also resembled the Fort Worth church in its lack of ornamentation. "No spires or cupolas" graced the exterior, the *Detroit News* reporter pointed out. The walls were of "white glazed material with a black border." The tall narrow windows of the church echoed the neo-Gothic style, but the structure was essentially a rectangular box, with the Bauhaus plainness relieved by Art Deco touches. E. Ray Tatum denigrated it as "a vast, sprawling, empty and hungry looking cavity, resembling as much a poorly planned factory as a huge church auditorium." Perhaps to offset the severity of the building, Norris added a Hollywood touch (possibly borrowed from the Angelus Temple in Los Angeles) in the form of a spotlight atop the old church tower that played over the auditorium an hour before and throughout the evening worship service.[26]

Both of Norris's churches imitated secular styles of architecture. So did two other large, urban churches built by dissenting evangelicals. Tremont Temple Baptist Church in Boston and Calvary Baptist Church in New York City were skyscraper churches—edifices in the form of the new structure developed in the 1880s for high-rise apartment houses and commercial buildings.[27] Both churches were also combination business and church buildings.

Tremont Temple in Boston (Fig. 57) was already well known for its evangelistic emphasis when J. C. Massee assumed the pastorate in 1922. Like Norris, he was a militant fundamentalist with a talent for "selling religion." During his seven years at Tremont, 2,489 individuals joined the church, increasing its membership to nearly four thousand. His Sunday morning and evening worship services averaged between two and three thousand persons. The structure in which he preached was the congregation's third building, constructed in 1894–1896, the previous one having burned in 1893. Designed by Clarence H. Blackall and George F. Newton, prominent Boston architects, the 1896 building was taller than the earlier buildings, but kept the same interior arrangement. Like the earlier buildings, the new structure also included two small stores on the ground floor, whose rental helped support the church.[28]

For the exterior ornamentation of the Tremont Temple the architects chose a combination of Christian and Florentine motifs. The first two stories were done in Indiana limestone and decorated with Christian symbols; the upper portion of the building, constructed of brick and terra-cotta, was decorated in the Florentine manner. Its traditional detailing notwithstanding, Tremont Temple was a thoroughly modern structure—constructed of steel, lighted by electricity, with high-speed Graves' elevators to provide access to the upper stories. The Tremont's three-thousand-seat auditorium (Fig.

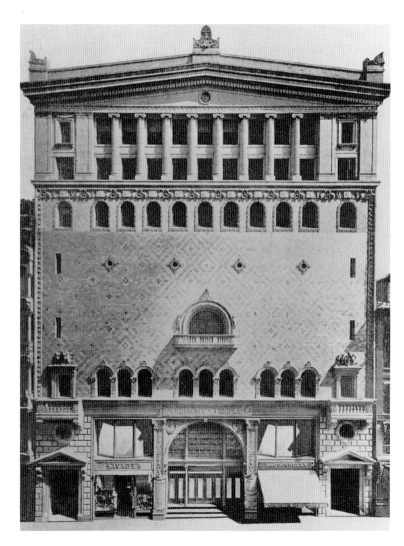

Fig. 57. Tremont Temple, Boston (1896), from
George W. Engelhardt, *Boston, Massachusetts*
(Boston: [Boston Chamber of Commerce?], 1897),
courtesy of the Boston Athenaeum.

Fig. 58. Auditorium, Tremont Temple, Boston (1896), from Charles L. Jeffrey, *Historical Sketch of Tremont Temple Boston* (church pamphlet, [1906]), back cover. Photograph courtesy of the American Baptist Historical Society, American Baptist–Samuel Colgate Library, Rochester, New York.

58), also decorated in the Florentine style, featured carved wood paneling, marble pilasters, bronze gallery and balcony railings, and twelve large stained-glass windows. An elaborate marble arch at the back of the pulpit platform contained the organ pipes. The year after Massee became pastor, the church installed a new Casavant organ with six thousand pipes, which made it larger than any other in the United States at that time.[29] The architecture and furnishings of Tremont Temple presented quite a contrast to the austerity that characterized Norris's churches. Apparently the fundamentalist Baptists who worshiped at Tremont saw no contradiction between their preachments against worldliness and their opulent church building.

The same may be said of Calvary Baptist Church (Fig. 59) on West Fifty-seventh Street in New York City, another highrise, combination church and business building that became a prominent center of fundamentalism in the early twentieth century. Dedicated in January 1931, it occupied a sixteen-story steel and concrete skyscraper that cost two million dollars to build. The church used the first five floors of the building, which housed a lower and a main auditorium as well as Sunday school rooms and various offices. The main auditorium seated more than one thousand persons and featured a five-thousand-pipe organ. The facade was much plainer than that of Tremont Temple, except for the French Gothic tower on top of the building and the embellishment of the entrance and first four stories. The Gothic arch in the center of the structure contained the three main doors to the church. To the right was a

Calvary Baptist Church

DEDICATED
1931

Fig. 59. Calvary Baptist Church, New York (1931), from "Dedication Program of the Calvary Baptist Church, 123 West 57th Street, New York" (New York: privately published for the church, [1931]). Photograph courtesy of the American Baptist Historical Society, American Baptist–Samuel Colgate Library, Rochester, New York, and used by permission of Calvary Baptist Church, New York.

Fig. 60. Moody Memorial Church, Chicago (1925), from postcard by Cameo Greeting Cards, Inc., Chicago, courtesy of the Archives of the Billy Graham Center, Wheaton, Illinois.

separate entrance for the 320-room Hotel Salisbury, operated by the church, which used the eleven uppermost floors of the building.[30]

Three other large, urban churches built by dissenting evangelicals illustrate their receptiveness to modern building designs and construction techniques: Angelus Temple (1923) in Los Angeles, Moody Memorial Church (1925) in Chicago, and Mason Temple (1940–1945) in Memphis. In contrast to the vertical thrust of the skyscraper churches (and many of the mainline evangelical churches), these three structures exhibited a definite horizontal emphasis, reflecting the amphitheater seating arrangement in the auditorium.

Moody Memorial Church (Fig. 60), constructed of brick with terra-cotta trim, took the form of a rectangle with a semicircular end in which the entry doors were located, whereas the Angelus Temple (Fig. 61), built of steel-reinforced concrete, exhibited a true amphitheater form. The Angelus Temple was the plainer of the two, with only a gesture of classical detailing in the pilasters encircling the building. A simple white cross, illuminated at night, stood atop the dome. The Moody Church had no cross but used slightly more ornamentation than the Angelus Temple: Romanesque Revival windows and arches, a corbel table encircling the roof, and intricate brickwork around the entrance and windows. Both buildings featured very large auditoriums, and the free-span dome of the Angelus Temple and the vaulted ceiling of the Moody Church allowed each congregation an unobstructed view of the platform. Moody Memorial provided seating for seventeen hundred in the cantilevered balcony and twenty-three hundred on the main floor. The Angelus Temple, with two balconies, was built to seat a total of fifty-three hundred, but often accommodated up to seventy-five hundred. The Angelus Temple was the cheaper of the two structures, costing approximately $250,000, as opposed to about $1 million for the Moody Church.[31]

The founder of the Angelus Temple, Aimee Semple McPherson, had originally intended to build a wooden tabernacle, but as attendance increased at her evangelistic meetings, she realized such a structure would be inadequate. So she hired a construction company to start work on a church, and the builder-architect, Brook Hawkins, visited one of her meetings so as to be able to tailor the plans to her ministry. With its large seating capacity and excellent acoustics, the temple auditorium (Fig. 62) was perfectly adapted to her style of evangelism. McPherson preached from a platform large enough to hold a one-hundred-voice, white-robed choir, an orchestra that in-

cluded a gold harp and a Steinway grand concert piano, and visiting dignitaries. She incorporated a large measure of theatrics into the temple services, so the platform was also designed to accommodate the elaborate stage sets she used for her "illustrated sermons." It even had an apron that could be raised or lowered by hydraulic pistons—an apparatus she copied from P. T. Barnum's Hippodrome in New York City.[32]

With its soft carpeting, ornate chandeliers, and large Kimball pipe organ, the auditorium of the Angelus Temple closely resembled the audience rooms of the mainline evangelical churches. At the same time, it incorporated two features from the tabernacles. Across the proscenium, an inscription rendered in hand-carved wooden letters proclaimed the message of Hebrews 13:8: "Jesus Christ the same yesterday, today, and forever." And two long ramps descending from the balconies to the platform facilitated the altar calls McPherson issued at the close of services.[33]

The lavish display of the visual arts in the temple revealed McPherson's independent streak. She challenged the dissenting evangelicals' neo-Puritan aversion to decoration in the church by filling the temple with art work: stained-glass windows depicting scenes from the Bible; a baptistery with a painting of the River Jordan behind a real stream and waterfall that flowed into the baptismal tank; and, on the ceiling of the auditorium dome, white clouds painted on an azure background to evoke the promise of the Second Coming of Jesus. The entrance door to the Watch Tower, a room on the third

Fig. 61. Angelus Temple,
Los Angeles (1923). Photograph dated 1939, courtesy
of and used by permission
of the Heritage Department
of the International Church
of the Foursquare Gospel,
Los Angeles.

Fig. 62. Auditorium, Angelus Temple. Photograph dated December 1926, courtesy of and used by permission of the Heritage Department of the International Church of the Foursquare Gospel, Los Angeles.

Fig. 63. Auditorium, Moody Memorial Church. Photograph by Ernest E. Schart, courtesy of the Archives of the Billy Graham Center, Wheaton, Illinois.

floor of the temple where volunteers prayed around the clock in response to requests sent to the church, featured a painting of Jesus kneeling in the Garden of Gethsemane. Inside the room were painted scenes of Jerusalem, the Mount of Olives, and Bethany, and a life-size reproduction of the painting of Jesus on the entrance door.[34]

Like the Angelus Temple, Moody Memorial Church was a

hybrid structure, combining elements of the tabernacle and the auditorium church. Its origins went back to 1915, when Moody's Chicago Street Church (built in 1873) proved too small for the crowds who came to worship. As a solution, Paul Rader, then pastor of the church, arranged for the construction of a wooden tabernacle built on a steel frame. The five-thousand-seat structure, located on a lot at the corner of North and Clark, became the new home of what people had begun to call the Moody Church. After Rader left the pastorate and founded the Chicago Gospel Tabernacle, the Moody congregation built a new church in 1925 to replace the tabernacle and named it the Moody Memorial Church. For many years it was the largest and most influential independent fundamentalist church in Chicago.[35]

The interior of the new church contrasted sharply with the inelegant, uncomfortable tabernacle. The audience room resembled that of an auditorium church (Fig. 63). A four-manual Reuter organ, with approximately forty-four hundred pipes, dominated the platform area, which was framed by a proscenium arch. Stained-glass windows (installed in the mid 1940s) memorialized various pastors and laymen. Seven huge chandeliers, each seven feet in diameter and sixteen feet high, provided lighting. But the Moody Church did have one of the features characteristic of the tabernacles: stairways leading down to the platform that enabled persons seated in the balconies to respond to the altar call.[36]

Compared to the Angelus Temple and Moody Memorial Church, Mason Temple (Fig. 64) was a more utilitarian build-

Fig. 64. Mason Temple, Memphis (1940–1945). Photograph by Gerald Smith, courtesy of the National Register of Historic Places, Washington, D.C., and the Tennessee Historical Commission, Department of Environment and Conservation, Nashville.

ing, especially on the inside. It was built under the direction of its pastor, Charles H. Mason, the founder of the Church of God in Christ (COGIC). Architect W. H. Taylor, one of the elders of the church, and Bishop Riley F. Williams, whom Mason appointed to lead the construction project, decided at the outset "to build a modern building for the church with an outlook to the future." Thus Mason Temple was constructed primarily of steel and reinforced concrete, and the two-story, main entrance bay featured simplified Art Moderne styling

and detail. A tripartite stained-glass window on the second floor featured a portrait of Bishop Mason teaching from the Bible.[37]

The auditorium, measuring 134 by 125 feet, had a seating capacity of five thousand persons on the ground floor and twenty-five hundred in the horseshoe-shaped balcony (Fig. 65). Both areas contained theater-type seats. One of the reasons for the great size of the auditorium was that Mason Temple, as part of the COGIC headquarters, was used not only for regular worship services but also for annual convocations of the denomination's General Assembly. Six steel trusses supported the auditorium ceiling, allowing a clear span of 134 feet. In the middle of the auditorium was an elevated platform, part of which extended into the seating area to provide space for a preaching desk and seating for the senior bishops. In front of the platform was a baptistery with a removable cover; behind it was a graded seating area for a choir of approximately 750 persons. The rostrum, choir stand, and baptistery were all constructed of reinforced concrete. The temple complex also included two buildings that served as dormitories for persons attending the General Assembly convocation, both of which were constructed of reinforced concrete, with exterior walls covered with brick veneer and in the Art Moderne style.[38]

A combination of financial constraints, antipathy to mainline evangelicalism, and a commitment to mass revivalism prompted the dissenting evangelicals to declare their independence from the architectural philosophy of their mainline

Fig. 65. Auditorium, Mason Temple. Photograph by Gerald Smith, courtesy of the National Register of Historic Places, Washington, D.C., and the Tennessee Historical Commission, Department of Environment and Conservation, Nashville.

brethren. Having done so, they constructed a wide range of structures, from barnlike wooden tabernacles to steel and concrete skyscrapers, with auditoriums as austere as the Puritan meetinghouses or as opulent as those of the mainline evangelical churches.

The dissenting evangelicals dispensed with the requirement that a religious building look "churchly." That action, along with their experience using secular (or secular-looking) buildings for religious meetings, freed them from reliance on traditional ecclesiastical models and enabled them to draw inspiration from secular architecture. They developed new and distinctive types of religious structures that combined an auditorium arrangement with design elements characteristic of commercial or civic structures, or even barns, as in the case of Sunday's tabernacles. J. Frank Norris's two churches and Mason Temple could have been mistaken, as some commentators noted, for commercial or educational buildings. Its neoclassical detailing notwithstanding, the Baptist Tabernacle bore a strong resemblance to many banks and civic buildings. Moody Memorial Church and the Angelus Temple (absent the cross) suggested municipal auditoriums rather than places of worship. Tremont Temple and Calvary Baptist Church were skyscraper buildings similar to those built in commercial centers throughout the United States. In some cases, such as Norris's Fort Worth church, financial necessity dictated the decision to build a nontraditional structure. But the modern idiom also proved attractive because of its emphasis on simplicity and functionalism.

The dissenting evangelicals also abandoned the traditional way of identifying or symbolizing the religious purpose of their structures. Instead of a tower, steeple, or cross, they relied, just as secular enterprises did, on some kind of signage to advertise the nature of their business. The Baptist Tabernacle had a big electric sign on its roof; Mason Temple, a sign on a post in front of the church building. Norris used a marquee for his Fort Worth church, along with a sign on the corner of the educational building next to it. Aimee Semple Mc-Pherson put the name of her church on the twin radio antennae surmounting the dome; the modern-day "steeples" advertised both the name of the church and its radio station call letters, KFSG (Kall Four-Square Gospel).

Like the early-nineteenth-century revivalists and the mainline evangelicals, the dissenting evangelicals designed their religious buildings to be instruments of evangelism. In planning their tabernacles, they made them "practical and simple" in order to attract poor and unchurched people who felt ill at ease in a church, and they imitated barns and warehouses in order to obtain meeting spaces capable of accommodating huge crowds. When they began building churches, they continued the emphasis on great size, constructing audience rooms much larger than those in most auditorium churches, so as to be able to use them for revival meetings and worship. That was their solution to the problem they shared with the auditorium church builders: how to accommodate large crowds for special evangelistic services. Instead of incorpo-rating the Akron Plan into their church buildings, the dissenters simply built the largest auditoriums possible. Using modern building materials such as steel and concrete enabled them to construct free-span or vaulted ceilings that covered a more spacious audience room than the auditorium church builders had been able to achieve in wood, stone, or brick. Thus the Baptist Tabernacle, Norris's two churches, the Angelus Temple, and the Moody Church were quite unusual, not just because of their considerable size but also because of their dual purpose. At a time when revivals were generally held outside of churches, in tents and tabernacles, as well as in civic auditoriums and other secular buildings, the dissenters' churches were designed to function as meeting places for revivalism as well as worship.

The dissenters' emphasis on mass evangelism dictated their emphasis on large buildings—what E. Ray Tatum called "bigness."[39] Along with the use of secular building styles and modern construction methods and materials, the stress on great size constituted their most important architectural legacy.

6

The Gathered Church

Religious architecture ought to be a commitment to the real and the true. . . . Imitations of historical styles, the use of imitation materials, the falsifying of structure, the incrustation of buildings with archaic and meaningless symbols, all these common devices are really profanities rather than religious forms.
—Edward A. Sövik, "What Is Religious Architecture?" (1967)

In the aftermath of World War II, the United States experienced a church building boom. At the same time, a revolution in church architecture occurred, as leaders of the liberal, mainline Protestant denominations, as well as other professionals, seized the opportunity to improve church design. The theologian Paul Tillich was perhaps the most eminent of these spokesmen for architectural reform. Others included architects Edward A. Sövik and Harold E. Wagoner, church building consultants John R. Scotford and C. Harry Atkinson, and architectural critics such as James F. White, Paul Thiry, Richard M. Bennett, Henry L. Kamphoefner, Victor Fiddes, Donald J. Bruggink, and Carl H. Droppers. Organizations that promoted the cause of architectural reform included the Department of Worship and the Arts and the Department of Church Building and Architecture, both operating under the auspices of the National Council of Churches, and the Church Architectural Guild of America, founded in 1940 by a small group of architects to promote "excellence in church architecture and allied arts." The *Architectural Record* also voiced support for improvements in church architecture.[1]

The midcentury architectural reformers shared Harold Wagoner's judgment as to the "general mediocrity" of the previous one hundred years of American religious architecture. He blamed it on "a naive 'grass roots' approach" that prevailed until the 1920s and produced, among other structures, the auditorium church, with its "huge sliding doors, sloping floors, polychromed trusses and horrendous arrays of gold-painted organ pipes." Then in the 1920s the trend toward "liturgical formality" started, as Methodists and other mainline, nonliturgical Protestant denominations began building churches in the Gothic style—"puerile American copies of Gothic Cathedrals" he called them.[2]

The architectural reformers also agreed with Edward Sövik that religious architecture should be committed to "the real and the true." In place of an "imitative-traditional" architecture, they urged the development of a modern, recognizably Protestant architecture "suited aesthetically and functionally to the needs of our times." Quoting Louis Sullivan's dictum, "form follows function," they insisted that the form and design of the church building, not just certain features or ornamentation, "should express the beliefs and reflect the practices of the people who worship therein." The ideal of the reformers was the "gathered church," a structure that facilitated the intimate spiritual fellowship and full congregational participation that they believed had characterized the worship services of the early Christians and, centuries later, of the Protestant Reformers in Europe and the Nonconformists in England.[3]

As Sövik once pointed out, "There are any number of ideas which are a part of the Christian vision which cannot be expressed in the material and spaces with which an architect works." But, he added, some ideas, particularly those regarding worship, *could* be expressed in "architectural form." He and other reformers argued, for example, that one way of creating a gathered church was by eliminating the traditional separation between the chancel and the nave. The reformers regarded the chancel-nave arrangement, associated with Roman Catholic and liturgical Protestant churches, as "religiously inadequate for a Protestant architecture." Equally unsuitable was the theater-like arrangement of the auditorium church. Both arrangements separated the clergy and choir from the worshipers, encouraging the former to become performers and the latter to adopt what White called "a spectator role" in the worship service.[4] The reformers interpreted the Protestant doctrine of the priesthood of all believers to mean that the people of God constituted a single, unified body of believers. When they met for worship, they should not play the role of an audience watching a performance, but of a family gathering for a service in which all participated. Members of the congregation should be seated so as to be able to see one another, and the minister should preach and lead the worship service standing among them.

The reformers also recommended a different shape and smaller worship space for the gathered church, as compared to the long, narrow nave of Gothic buildings and the large audience rooms of the auditorium churches. For a "gathered community," the worship space should be nearly circular or square in shape. And it should be much smaller than that of the auditorium churches, whose great seating capacity prevented worshipers from achieving any sense of intimacy or participation. Bruggink and Droppers declared a church capable of seating almost 1,000 on the ground floor and another 200 or so in the balcony too large. A structure whose 420 worshipers were all within a distance of seven pews from the center of worship seemed ideal to them. Scotford believed that members of a congregation seated more than fifteen pews away from the liturgical center (about fifty feet) tended to become mere onlookers rather than participants. In his view the optimum congregational size for participatory worship was about 250.[5]

Another defect of the auditorium church, according to the midcentury reformers, was the placement and role of the choir. Bruggink and Droppers were quite outspoken in their criticism of "choirolatry." The choir not only distracted worshipers' attention from the preacher but also, more significantly, competed with and distracted attention from "the means of God's grace—Word and sacraments." The placement of the choir also prevented it from playing its proper role, which was to assist the congregation in their singing, not to sing for them or entertain them. Therefore, Bruggink and Droppers insisted that "architecturally the choir must be placed with the rest of the congregation." If located in the front of the nave, it should be either to one side of the preacher or seated on the floor level with the congregation; if located in the back of the nave, it should be in a special gallery. The two commentators favored the third arrangement on the ground that it adhered most closely to Reformed ideas about worship.[6]

Although the reformers generally preferred unadorned interior walls, many of them urged greater appreciation for the way art forms could be used to make people "aware of the presence of the holy, making visible that which is invisible." However, they opposed employing them as "mere decoration" or "pious bric-a-brac." Their purpose was to convey meaning, which entailed the use of "abstract or expressive symbols . . . rather than resort[ing] to popular realism."[7]

The midcentury reformers agreed in declaring modern architecture the best option available to Protestants who sought "an honest expression of their faith." Certain characteristics suited it to the theological and practical requirements of the Protestant faith: its honest use of materials and construction techniques, its adaptability to new shapes and forms, its freedom from ornamentation and symbolic content, its simplicity and unpretentiousness. The economy of building in the modern style (as compared with the exorbitant cost of constructing traditional, especially neo-Gothic, edifices) also recommended it. Another compelling reason advanced in its favor was its expressive value. Insofar as the church building functioned as a "witness to those outside the Church," the modern idiom proclaimed the relevance and significance of the church's message in men's and women's lives and for the modern world.[8]

During the postwar building boom, an estimated one quarter to one half of the new churches were in the modern idiom, most of them affiliated with the liberal, mainline Protestant denominations, especially Lutherans, Anglicans, and the Christian Church (Disciples of Christ).[9] Many resembled the "gathered church" advocated by the architectural reformers.

These new, modern Protestant churches rarely accommodated more than three hundred worshipers in the sanctuary. Even the largest urban congregations provided seating for only five hundred to six hundred persons. Architects experimented with a broad range of floor plans for the sanctuary—circular, elliptical, square—in order to bring about a closer union of the minister, choir, and congregation. The shape of the churches also exhibited great variety, since the modernist aesthetic allowed space to be enclosed in many different forms: box, cube, prism, sphere, pyramid, or cylinder, or a combination of those basic solids. The midcentury churches made use of all of the building materials associated with modern architecture: structural iron and steel, reinforced concrete, plate glass, glass brick. Many of the larger churches embodied a basic building type often used for commercial or corporate structures—a steel frame with a lightweight curtain wall of brick, wood, or glass. The framing was often left exposed, instead of being concealed by masonry walls or applied moldings and cornices, and traditional building materials such as wood, brick, or stone were commonly used in their natural finish. The modern churches were generally free of religious symbolism, except that which was integral with the structure itself. In many of the churches the only ornamentation was a large cross made of brushed aluminum or unfinished oak. Clear or tinted glass commonly replaced traditional stained glass. Architects frequently used natural light as an element of design: a shaft of sunlight entering the church through a skylight or window and highlighting the pulpit or baptismal font, for example.[10]

Among the designers of the modern midcentury Protestant churches were several well-known architects: Pietro Belluschi, Ludwig Mies van der Rohe, Richard Neutra, Philip Johnson, Frank Lloyd Wright, Skidmore, Owings and Merrill, Architects, and Eliel and Eero Saarinen. Two churches designed by the Saarinens and built in Columbus, Indiana, illustrate many of the architectural principles advocated by the midcentury architectural reformers. The Tabernacle Church of Christ, designed for a Christian Church (Disciples of Christ) congregation, was completed in 1942 (Fig. 66). Its simple, unadorned exterior reflected both the Disciples theology and the modern aesthetic. Structurally, the church balanced vertical masses (the sanctuary and freestanding tower) with horizontal ones (two Bible school wings not shown in the photograph). The main buildings were constructed of brick curtain walls on a frame of steel beams or reinforced concrete girders. The only applied decoration appeared on the 166-foot tower,

Fig. 66. Tabernacle Church of Christ, Columbus, Indiana (1942).

which featured sections of perforated brickwork that harmonized with the windows of the church, and on the facade of the sanctuary, where panels of pale buff–colored Indiana limestone contrasted with the darker buff color of the brick. The one symbolic ornament was a large wooden cross superimposed upon the limestone panels.[11]

Inside the asymmetrical nave of the church was another large cross, positioned to the right of the pulpit. No other decorated areas distracted attention from the chancel. The colors were muted: the buff-colored exposed brick walls harmonized with the light wood of the pews, screening, and altar furnishings, and with the spun aluminum pulpit and spoon lighting fixtures. Natural illumination entered through a series of tall, thin windows on the western wall of the chancel and a single window on the eastern wall, a feature the Saarinens thought would "add a spiritual quality to the service."[12] The choir sat on the west side of the chancel, partially hidden from view by a wooden partition. On the east side stood the large, prominently placed pulpit, which extended over the chancel steps almost into the congregation.

Like the Tabernacle Church of Christ, the North Christian Church (Fig. 67), designed by Eero Saarinen and completed in 1964, was quite simple and unadorned. It was a single building in the shape of an elongated hexagon, 210 by 106 feet. Dominating the exterior was a slate roof with copper-sheathed ribs that met at the base of a 192-foot spire and cross. The spire rose from the center of the church building. Inside, directly under it, was the Lord's table, an architectural arrangement that re-

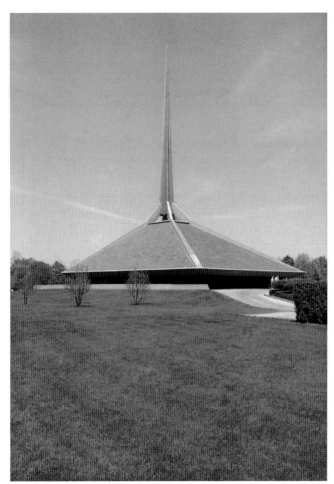

Fig. 67. North Christian Church, Columbus, Indiana (1964).

inforced the Disciples' emphasis on the weekly celebration of the Lord's Supper. The hexagonal auditorium was designed to facilitate the worship practices of the "gathered community": the congregation sat around the Lord's table, the pulpit stood in the midst of the congregation, and the choir occupied pews on the same level as the rest of the congregation.[13]

The mid–twentieth-century reformers presented a new perspective on church architecture, repudiating imitation of historic styles and embracing the modern idiom. In effect, they declared that a church building did not have to "look like a church."[14] Championing creativity, they set the stage for the megachurch building boom that began a few decades later. By that time their perspective had become quite familiar and acceptable to most Americans, and megachurch builders adopted many of the modern forms, construction techniques, and materials used in the "gathered churches." The tentlike form and central spire of Saarinen's North Christian Church became especially popular. Along with the ideas of earlier generations of evangelicals, the mid–twentieth-century perspective became part of the inheritance megachurch builders tapped in designing churches for their growing congregations.

7

Building for ❦
Church Growth

The typical traditional church is no place for the unchurched. —Bill Hybels, *Rediscovering Church* (1995)

Evangelical megachurches emerged as a popular type of church organization and architecture in the 1970s. The pastors and congregations who built them constituted a varied group. Descendants of the nineteenth-century and early-twentieth-century evangelicals, mainline as well as dissenting, made up one component. Recently formed nondenominational congregations constituted a second component. A third component consisted of congregations affiliated with quasi-denominations such as the Willow Creek Association, the Vineyard Christian Fellowship, Calvary Chapels, the Full Gospel Baptist Fellowship, and the Fellowship of Inner City Word of Faith Ministries. The late-twentieth-century evangelicals spurred what amounted to a megachurch building boom. Among the factors contributing to its development were a dramatic increase in the size of evangelical congregations and their willingness to provide financial support for construction projects costing millions of dollars. Both of these factors were in turn related to the general increase in the number of evangelicals in the United States and their rising socioeconomic status.[1]

Another key factor in the development of the megachurch was the campaign Elmer Towns and Jerry Falwell waged in the 1970s to promote what they called, simply, "the large church." Citing the soul-winning records of churches such as First Baptist in Hammond, Indiana, Highland Park Baptist in

Chattanooga, Tennessee, and their own Thomas Road Baptist Church in Lynchburg, Virginia, the two independent Baptist ministers argued that the large church offered the best strategy for reaching the multitudes living in the large metropolitan areas of the United States. Most small churches were unwilling or unable to engage in mass evangelism, they insisted. Big churches were more likely to be faithful to the Great Commission, and, even more important, they also had the necessary resources to prosecute it on a large scale. Using the outreach of radio, television, church newspapers, and Sunday school busing, they could reach families living thirty or fifty miles away. They had auditoriums big enough to hold more people in an evangelistic meeting than all the churches of most cities could engage in a city-wide cooperative program. And only large churches could offer the wide range of services necessary to meet the needs of various segments of the metropolitan population, such as counseling, Christian schools, and recreational and social activities, as well as homes or treatment facilities for unwed mothers, alcoholics, and drug addicts.[2]

Towns's and Falwell's point about the seating capacity of large-church auditoriums is significant. Traditionally, evangelicals had sponsored large evangelistic meetings in nonchurch facilities—camp meetings, revival tents, secular halls, and civic auditoriums—because they were the only spaces large enough to hold crowds of people. In the post–World War II period, parachurch groups such as Youth for Christ, Word of Life, and the Christian Businessmen's Committees began promoting a "new revivalism" in arenas such as Soldier Field in Chicago and Mechanics Hall in Boston. In the late 1950s and early 1960s, Billy Graham galvanized huge congregations in the San Francisco Cow Palace and New York's Madison Square Garden (Fig. 68). Towns and Falwell were no doubt inspired by these examples of mass evangelism. Of course, they did not anticipate building churches that would equal the Garden's capacity of 18,500, but constructing church auditoriums as large as the halls and civic auditoriums Graham and the parachurch groups used was within the realm of possibility. Mechanics Hall in Boston, for example, held six thousand persons.[3] That would enable the churches to open their doors to the unchurched and unsaved, as well as to church members, and to make an evangelistic appeal part of the regular Sunday worship service. As it turned out, large auditoriums became the sine qua non of late-twentieth-century megachurches, with accommodations ranging as high as eight to ten thousand persons.

The so-called church growth strategy promoted during the 1970s, 1980s, and 1990s also played a very important role in promoting the building of megachurches. The leading experts associated with the strategy were three Fuller Theological Seminary professors: C. Peter Wagner, founding president of the North American Society for Church Growth; John Wimber, founding pastor of the Vineyard Christian Fellowship, Anaheim, California, and president of Vineyard Ministries, International; and Carl F. George, director of the Fuller Institute of Evangelism and Church Growth in Pasadena, Califor-

Fig. 68. Billy Graham Crusade, Madison Square Garden, New York (1957), courtesy of Photo Department, Billy Graham Evangelistic Association, Burbank, California.

nia. Other experts included Elmer Towns, dean of Liberty Baptist Theological Seminary and the Liberty University School of Religion; sociologist Wade Clark Roof; church consultants Lyle Schaller, John Vaughan, and George Barna; and a number of pastors including Robert H. Schuller (Garden Grove Community Church, Garden Grove, California), Leith Anderson (Wooddale Church, Eden Prairie, Minnesota), Bill Hybels (Willow Creek Community Church, South Barrington, Illinois), Rick Warren (Saddleback Church, Lake Forest, California), and Walt Kallestad (A Community of Joy, Glendale, Arizona).[4]

In numerous books and articles, as well as seminars, workshops, and pastors' conferences, the church growth experts argued that American society in the late twentieth century was vastly different from what it had been in the 1950s. Therefore the "traditional church," as they termed it, was outdated. They called for a new type of church organization that would be relevant to contemporary American society and culture. Just as late-nineteenth- and early-twentieth-century commentators had promoted the "modern" or "progressive" church, late-twentieth-century church growth experts touted the "innovative" church—what Robert Schuller and Leith Anderson called "a church for the 21st century."[5]

The church growth experts made converting the unchurched and unsaved, thereby increasing church membership, the raison d'etre of the innovative church. They mainly targeted the new generation of Baby Boomers, whose numbers they estimated at some 76 million. Most of the Boomers had been raised in churchgoing families but had dropped out of organized religion. Wade Clark Roof called them "a generation of seekers" and insisted that because they were engaged in a "spiritual journey," they could be reached and brought back into the church.[6]

Other church growth experts shared Roof's optimism. In explaining how to attract the Boomers to church, they emphasized the very different attitudes and lifestyle of the Boomers that distinguished them from their parents. They had grown up in large institutions: "high schools with thousands of students, universities with tens of thousands, companies with large payrolls and employee anonymity, urban apartment buildings, and suburban neighborhoods." They had also imbibed the consumerism that pervaded late-twentieth-century American culture, and that carried over into the religious sphere. Church growth experts often used a shopping mall analogy to explain how many late-twentieth-century Americans decided what church to attend. "People will drive past all kinds of little shopping centers to go to a major mall, where there are lots of services and where they meet their needs. The same is true in churches today in that people drive past dozens of little churches to go to a larger church which offers more services and special programs," Rick Warren observed. In effect, consumerism rather than denominational loyalty motivated the choice of a church. The Boomers, especially, lacked denominational loyalty. "They shop around," Lyle Schaller declared. If and when they chose a church, it was because they believed it would meet their needs or reflect their personal values or lifestyle. They made the decision based on the product rather than on the label or brand name.[7]

Given their distinctive lifestyle and attitudes, Boomers probably would not choose to attend what church growth experts called the "traditional church." In declaring it to be "no place for the unchurched," Bill Hybels offered a terse summary of its deficiencies: "To anybody but the already convinced, the average church service seems grossly abnormal. . . . The music we sing, the titles we choose, the way we dress, the language we use, the subjects we discuss, the poor quality of what we do—all of these lead the average unchurched person to say, 'This is definitely not for me.'"[8]

Adopting the jargon and concepts of the business world, the church growth experts proposed a remedy. To attract the unchurched and unsaved and persuade them to become church members, as well as to nurture the current church membership, the innovative church must adopt a "marketing orientation." That meant, first of all, defining a "target audience"—the individuals the church wanted to attract and serve—and determining, through demographic and market research, its lifestyle, needs, and desires. Then, having done that, the innovative church should be "market-driven." It should focus on what the target audience wanted in a church, which is to say, view potential church members as consumers. "If we recognize church worshipers as consumers," Elmer Towns wrote, "we will recognize church programs as menus, and types of worship as the main entrees in the restaurant."

Just as diners went where the menu suited their taste, so would potential churchgoers.[9] In describing the "menus" and "entrees" appropriate to the innovative church, the church growth experts listed everything from Christmas pageants and athletic teams to efficient traffic control and parking, well-performed music and drama, and an informal atmosphere.

Surprisingly, most church growth experts had very little to say about the architecture of the innovative church. Lyle Schaller was exceptional in this regard. In *The New Reformation*, he speculated about the impact the marketing orientation might have on church architecture. Unlike congregational leaders of the "traditional church," who "affirm[ed] the value of perpetuating the design, the values, the traditions, the heritage, and the symbols" of "church buildings constructed in England and Europe between 1200 and 1800," he declared that leaders of the innovative church would "seek first a functional, attractive, and inspiring structure that is user friendly."[10]

Robert H. Schuller spelled out the implications of the church growth strategy for church architecture in much greater detail than Schaller. The thrust of his thinking appeared in a statement he made in his church growth guide, *Your Church Has Real Possibilities!* Too many church builders, he contended, were *"unconsciously seeking to impress those who were raised in a church—instead of trying to design a structure that would make an impression on non-churched, secular Americans."*[11]

During the late 1950s, 1960s, and 1970s, Schuller implemented the strategy he and other church growth experts recommended. In 1955, as a minister in the Reformed Church in America, he went to Orange County, California, to plant a new church. He decided to call it the Garden Grove Community Church. "I didn't think the name 'Reformed' would bring the *unchurched* people rushing in!" he explained in *Your Church Has Real Possibilities!* Unable to rent a suitable meeting place, he began conducting worship services at the Orange Drive-In Theater, standing on the roof of the snack bar, with his wife playing the two-manual electronic organ they pulled by trailer from their home every Sunday. Schuller later recalled that the ministers of some of the thriving, downtown churches of Orange County professed sympathy for him because of the circumstances in which he was preaching. He replied, "Don't feel sorry for me. After all, I have three things going for me in the drive-in theater that none of you have." They were: "superb accessibility," "virtually unlimited parking space" and seating capacity, and "a much larger market . . . of unchurched people." (Instead of being in one town, the theater was located on the Santa Ana Freeway, which connected three large cities.)[12]

To attract people to his services, Schuller placed advertisements in the newspapers: "Come as you are in the family car. Starting Sunday, March 27, 1955, an exciting new church will begin to operate in the Orange Drive-In Theater!" He also canvassed the Garden Grove area, ringing doorbells and asking people questions: Were they members of a local church? If not, why not? What would they like to see in a church that would attract them to it? He used the information he acquired to develop the various programs his church offered "to meet and fill human needs."[13]

Soon Schuller and his congregation were able to build and move into a small chapel, while continuing the drive-in theater services, and then, in 1961, to erect a much larger building. Schuller knew exactly what he desired in the new building and why. As he explained several years later in *Your Church Has Real Possibilities!* he wanted a structure that would "impress non-Christians and non-churched people," that would "make a big, beautiful impression upon the affluent non-religious American . . . riding by on [the] busy freeway." To do that the building would have to be "pace-setting," beautiful, honest, and modern. Beauty was important, because Schuller believed that people would be "magnetically drawn" to a beautiful church. He also insisted that "honesty impresses!" He had nothing but contempt for churches that used "phony props," "artificial lighting," "carefully contrived staging," "the sentimental-solemn effect" to "manipulate a person's emotions into an unreal religious mood." Why? "Nonchurched people see the phoniness of this," he declared. A modern design was crucial. Too many churches were hampered by "dated architecture," he argued. Their pastors were "trying to impress modern, unchurched people" in buildings designed according to "an out-of-style, out-of-this-world architecture." Such churches announced to everyone who saw them, "This church is old-fashioned, out of date, from bygone generations without any exciting plans for the future."[14]

Thus it was no accident that Schuller hired Richard Neutra,

an architect well known as a modernist. The two men worked together in designing the new Garden Grove Community Church (Fig. 69), which was completed in 1962. Its architecture was modern, but it had some traditional Christian detailing inside and outside, including a bell tower one hundred feet high and a ninety-foot cross atop the fourteen-story "Tower of Hope," which was added in 1968. As Schuller anticipated, the most talked-about feature was the sliding glass wall that could be opened during the worship service, enabling Schuller to preach to and be seen by members of the congregation seated in their automobiles (Fig. 70). Most tuned into the service using their car radios; others heard Schuller via amplifiers in the huge parking lot. In addition, some seventeen hundred worshipers could be accommodated inside the church.[15]

Schuller's innovative approach to building and marketing his church paid off. By 1971, the Garden Grove membership had grown to more than six thousand; ten years later, its membership was estimated at eight thousand. His influence as a church growth expert also expanded, especially after he founded the Robert H. Schuller Institute for Successful Church Leadership. In the 1970s it provided four-day seminars four times a year where some three hundred clergymen and other church people could hear lectures on building a large congregation.[16]

One of those who attended the institute was Bill Hybels. He later met with Schuller to seek advice on buying land for a church building. Schuller told him, "If you give God a thim-

Fig. 69. Garden Grove Community Church (1962) and Tower of Hope (1968), Garden Grove, California. Photograph by Ake Lundberg, courtesy of Billy Graham Evangelistic Association, Charlotte, North Carolina.

ble, perhaps He will choose to fill it. If you give God a five-gallon bucket, perhaps He will choose to fill that. If you give Him a fifty-gallon drum, perhaps He will choose to do something extraordinary and fill even that. If God chooses to do a miracle, you'd better be ready for it. Don't buy a thimbleful of land. Buy a fifty-gallon drum."[17]

Hybels soon became well known as the founding pastor of the Willow Creek Community Church in South Barrington,

Fig. 70. Interior, Garden Grove Community Church. Photograph by Ake Lundberg, courtesy of Billy Graham Evangelistic Association, Charlotte, North Carolina.

Illinois. Nestled among rolling hills, meadows, and woodlands on East Algonquin Road, but easily accessible from two major highways, it was a regional church that advertised itself as "non-denominational." During the 1980s and 1990s, many church growth experts, journalists, and evangelicals pointed to it as the prototypical suburban megachurch built on church growth principles. Indeed, Hybels followed all of the recommendations of the church growth experts. Journalists noted a poster hanging outside his office, displaying questions reflecting his marketing orientation: "What is our business? Who is our customer? What does the customer consider value?" He had a well-defined target audience in mind, composed of suburban, well-educated, professional adult males, age twenty-five to forty-five, married, with children—Baby Boomers whom the "Creeker" staff referred to as "unchurched Harrys." He created a "seeker service" aimed solely at them and scheduled it during the weekend, because, he explained, "if nonbelievers finally decide to attend church, that's when they expect to go." The seeker service was an evangelistic meeting, not a worship service, that combined music, dramatic skits, several brief prayers, and a "message" (not a sermon) by Hybels, all carefully scripted and produced, with considerable attention paid to high-quality performance. The skits presented "life situations" the audience could identify with; the "message" targeted the distinctive social and personal needs of "unchurched Harrys," as did the church's more than one hundred ministries and support groups. The Willow Creek way of "doing church" constituted a wholesale rejection of the "traditional church." Church growth expert Elmer Towns lauded Willow Creek as "one of the most innovative churches in America because of . . . its well-thought-out strategy for reaching the unchurched."[18]

The architecture of the Willow Creek Community Church also signaled a dramatic departure from that of the "traditional church." The church complex, located on a 155-acre site, was constructed in two phases. During the first phase, completed in 1981, the ground-level auditorium and the lower level (made up of offices and activity rooms) were built. In 1989, the church launched a $23 million building campaign to add other facilities: a gymnasium for its youth ministries and sports outreach activities; classrooms, conference rooms, and "small-group" rooms; an atrium with tables, chairs, and a "food court"; and a small chapel with a "sunlight dome," an organ and a piano, and pews for seating.[19]

Viewed from East Algonquin Road and across the pond, the Willow Creek complex appeared as a course of one- and two-story boxlike structures made of brown brick, glass, and steel, attached at various angles and exhibiting varying roof treatments (Plate 1). In the center stood the auditorium, easily recognized by its broad metal roof. Commentators of the 1990s agreed that Willow Creek did not look like a church. Towns thought the structure looked "more like a civic center than a church" and the grounds "more like a landscaped park than a church campus." Other commentators compared the Willow Creek complex to a "well-kept corporate headquarters or a suburban business park" or to a "modern community college."[20]

Hybels seems to have extrapolated a rudimentary architectural philosophy partly from church growth theory and partly from the market research he did in the South Barrington suburbs when he founded the Willow Creek church. On more than one occasion he claimed to have discovered that many young adults were intimidated by imposing church buildings, especially the Gothic cathedrals of Europe, which they also criticized for being uncomfortable and having poor lighting and acoustics.[21] In his view, the unchurched were as alienated by the architecture of the "traditional church" as by its worship services. He insisted that the physical facilities of Willow Creek should be such as to first win the respect of "unchurched Harry," and then make him feel comfortable and relaxed and therefore receptive to the "seeker service." As a tour guide at Willow Creek explained, Hybels believed that a church should fit people's "life experience" and that "you shouldn't go through cultural shock when you go to church."

In developing his architectural philosophy, Hybels noted the kind of secular buildings "unchurched Harry" found attractive—hotels, amusement parks, corporate headquarters—and tried to make Willow Creek look and operate like them. He asserted that the Willow Creek buildings were purposely designed to look like a corporate headquarters. "What we want him ['unchurched Harry'] to do is just say, 'I was just at corporate headquarters for IBM in Atlanta Wednesday, and now I come to church here and it's basically the same.' Neutrality, comfort, contemporary, clean: Those are the kinds of values that we want to communicate." The grounds, archi-

tecture, and technology of Willow Creek, like its services and other programs, were supposed to communicate its emphasis on excellence and high quality, because these were "values" "unchurched Harry" found at Disney World and first-class hotels and in the business world.[22]

The Willow Creek auditorium (Plate 2) communicated the same values Hybels invoked in describing the exterior of the church: neutrality, comfort, contemporaneousness, cleanliness, excellence. Except for the clear glass side walls that provided a view of the grounds and pond outside, it looked like a civic auditorium or a theater, which reflected not only Hybels's preference for secular architecture but also the early history of the Willow Creek church, when it rented the Willow Creek Theater for meetings. On either side of the platform were video screens on which the words of songs, biblical passages, or other messages could be displayed. The auditorium provided seating for 4,550 persons, most of whom could be accommodated in well-cushioned theater seats on the ground floor and in the balcony. Other seating was available on chairs attached to risers, which could be folded flat against the wall when not in use. There were no stairs leading down from the balcony to the platform, since Hybels did not offer the invitation at the conclusion of the message in the "seeker service."[23] Except for the view of the landscape outside and a few potted plants on the stage, the auditorium was completely unadorned. It displayed no Christian symbols or images. Indeed, there were none anywhere in the entire church complex.

Journalists who described the interior of the Willow Creek

church never failed to point out the atrium added during the second building phase (Plate 3). It, too, marked a departure from the "traditional church." It served the purposes of the conventional parlor, fellowship hall, and dining room, but unlike those facilities, it was usable all the time, not just for special events, and its contemporary decor and "food court" gave it a comfortable, shopping mall ambience.[24] Like the Willow Creek auditorium, it was an entirely neutral space, albeit a very comfortable and functional one.

In the 1980s and 1990s some African American evangelicals developed their own version of the church growth strategy, which exerted considerable influence on the building of black megachurches. Like their white counterparts, the African American church growth experts advised targeting the Baby Boom generation, especially the growing number of middle-class and professional blacks, many of whom had moved away from metropolitan areas to the suburbs. The experts noted that many African American Boomers were unchurched and skeptical of organized religion, either because they felt uncomfortable in predominantly white churches or because they were alienated from the black church.

Attracting these disaffected young adults involved a two-pronged effort. Many megachurches made changes and developed programs similar to those implemented by white megachurches. To fulfill Boomers' expectations of cultural relevance and high quality, they featured professional-caliber contemporary music and drama. To address Boomers' personal desires and needs, they offered a plethora of programs and ministries, such as marriage counseling, single parenting and divorce recovery seminars, financial planning workshops, and children's religious, educational, and recreational programs. However, their church growth strategy also prescribed a component not found in the white version. It derived from the assumption that black Boomers were not only searching for spiritual nourishment and practical guidance, like their white counterparts, but also for a way to reconnect with the black community and to identify with the African American heritage. Young black suburbanites, especially, were said to feel increasingly distant from the black culture and community and dissatisfied with the white culture of suburbia. Black megachurches offered them the opportunity to associate with other African Americans, to learn about and appreciate their culture and heritage, and, by becoming involved in the church's community outreach programs, to help revitalize the deteriorating urban neighborhoods they had left behind.[25]

Ebenezer African Methodist Episcopal Church, in Fort Washington, Maryland, offers a good example of a suburban black megachurch that used the church growth strategy to attract black Boomers. The church had been founded in the mid–nineteenth century when thirteen black members, inspired by the belief "that God would have them 'establish a church by colored folks and with colored pastors,'" withdrew from the predominantly white Mt. Zion Methodist Episcopal Church to protest discrimination and segregation. At first they met in members' homes, then in 1856 they built a church in the

Georgetown section of Washington, D.C. In 1983, the black population in Georgetown having declined considerably, the church moved to Fort Washington, Maryland, and Rev. Grainger Browning became the new pastor. Under his leadership the membership increased markedly, and in September 1994 he and his congregation dedicated a new church building located on a thirty-three-acre site near the former church (Plate 4).[26]

According to architect Stan Britt, Browning wanted the shape of the church building to be "reminiscent of an African hut." Designing a hut that could accommodate three thousand persons posed something of a problem. Britt's solution was an octagonal building that would approximate a round structure but would satisfy certain functional requirements (for example, entrances to the sanctuary and the positioning of the pulpit platform) better than a round building. Inside the church, above the entrance to the narthex, was a mural painted by Maurice Jenkins showing a dark-skinned Jesus wearing an African blanket over his shoulder and shepherding a group of people representing every ethnic culture in the world (Plate 5). In the front row on the far left were Pastor Browning, his wife and Co-Pastor Jo Ann Browning, and their son and daughter. In the middle of the group were Bishop Richard Allen and his wife. Allen, the founder of the A.M.E. church, had a special significance for the Ebenezer church: the thirteen African Americans who withdrew from Mt. Zion Church in the 1850s were following his earlier example of walking out of St. George's Methodist Episcopal Church in Philadelphia in 1787 to protest the segregation of its black members. Both the

form of Ebenezer Church and the mural reflected the Afro-centric emphasis that pervaded all of the church's work. An article on the church in the *Christian Century* quoted a member as saying, "There's not a Sunday when something about African-American history or African-American pride is not mentioned. It's always tied into the pastor's sermon."[27]

Located in Prince Georges County, Ebenezer Church attracted a goodly number of affluent blacks, but it encouraged its members to participate in a wide range of ministries and programs serving the African American community as a whole.[28] Through its Manhood and Womanhood Rites of Passage ministries it provided adult mentoring for youths from ten to sixteen years of age. Volunteers in the Cheltenham Ministry worked with adolescents at a youth detention center. The Law Ministry made use of the professional expertise of licensed attorneys whose practices focused on family issues. Other social services were administered by the Family Outreach and Resource Center, and by prison, employment, home shelter, food pantry, drug abuse/HIV/AIDS, and clothing ministries.

Trinity United Church of Christ, on West Ninety-fifth Street in Chicago, provides another example of an African American megachurch that adopted church growth ideas. Its worship center (Plate 6), completed in 1994, was a brick, glass, and steel structure composed of two buildings connected by a glass-covered entry. Above the roof, four steel members outlined the form of a church spire, which was surmounted by a cross.[29]

According to the pastor, Dr. Jeremiah A. Wright, Jr., Trinity was originally part of the "urban strategy" developed by the United Church of Christ, a predominantly white, liberal, mainline denomination. Planted in a middle-income, predominantly black community, Trinity was supposed to attract African American professionals who were presumed to desire what Wright termed "an educated (meaning white) style of worship with a socially conscious focus on ministry." Ten years after the founding of the church, Wright observed, "the congregation made a conscious decision to become a black church in the black community." Recasting the church's cultural and religious orientation from "white" to African American necessitated changes "not only . . . in worship style, but also . . . in focus, in mission, in ministry, in theology, in psychology, and in philosophy." Moreover, instead of targeting a single segment of the black population, black Boomers, Trinity followed the example of other urban black churches in seeking "new members from every walk of life, from every possible level of socioeconomic and educational status, and from every part of the city of Chicago and its surrounding suburbs." By the early 1990s, its new Afrocentric orientation had attracted forty-five hundred active members.[30]

Garden Grove Community Church, Willow Creek Community Church, Ebenezer African Methodist Episcopal Church, and Trinity United Church of Christ testify to the influence church growth experts exerted on both black and white megachurches, and not just on their programs, but on their architecture, in spite of the fact that all but a few of the experts paid little attention to it. Pursuing the ideal of the innovative church, megachurch pastors, building committees, and congregations extrapolated ideas about church design and construction from two components of the church growth strategy: the animus toward the "traditional church" and the emphasis on a marketing orientation. The result was great variety in megachurch architecture.

8

The Megachurch

Every church should be a big church. —Frederick Price

Although journalists, church growth experts, and evangelicals hailed Willow Creek Community Church as a prototype, our sample of sixty-three megachurches reveals that their architecture varied more than the prototype suggested. Some of the megachurches we visited were plain, utilitarian structures that recalled the seventeenth-century meetinghouses and the nineteenth-century tabernacles. Others exhibited a more elaborate architecture comparable to that of the auditorium and "gathered" churches. Megachurches also differed in the size and number of their buildings, as well as their shape and visual emphasis, and their decor ranged from very austere to highly ornamental. Unlike Willow Creek, many megachurches featured "churchlike" details such as crosses, towers, spires, even stained-glass windows.

The variety reflected the fact that not all megachurches were "seeker churches" like Willow Creek. Some incorporated elements of the seeker orientation, describing themselves as "seeker-friendly" or "seeker-sensitive" or "seeker-oriented," while others advertised themselves as "family churches" and sought to attract a wider range of people than just the Boomer generation.

Differences among evangelicals regarding their basic conception of the church building also produced architectural variety. Virtually all evangelicals agreed that the church building was not a sacred place. Nor was it an end in itself. Some regarded it as simply a "tool for ministry." Such thinking attached little importance to the building's architecture and provided a rationale for economical, unpretentious, strictly utilitarian facilities. Other evangelicals, however, viewed the church building not just, or only, as a tool for ministry, but as a facility designed and built to honor God. Conceiving the building in that way elevated the importance of its architecture. Few late-twentieth-century pastors or congregations wanted to be considered stingy. Jerry Falwell, for example, disparaged what he called "rinky dinky 'chicken coop churches,'" explaining that "a cheap church makes God look cheap." Lynne Hybels insisted that "'Good enough' is just not good enough when it comes to honoring God through the church," that "our attitude ought to be to pay tribute to Him with the best we can offer." Believing that "God deserves our very best" led many evangelicals to underwrite costly facilities featuring luxurious appointments such as plush carpeting and upholstered theater seats, gleaming tile restrooms, expensive woodwork, and the like.[1]

And finally, the architectural variety reflected the choices megachurch builders made regarding the design/construction process. Some pastors and congregations employed an architect or architectural firm to develop a design appropriate to the church's theology, worship and other programs, budget, and aesthetics, and to supervise the construction of the building. Assuming a high level of creativity and skill on the part of the designer, an architect-designed building promised a degree of individuality, even distinction. However, pastors and congregations that chose a design-build firm or a package builder were likely to get a more conventional building, less tailored to their needs, since such firms used "standard materials, finishes, and structural systems."[2]

The variety of megachurch architecture notwithstanding, megachurch builders agreed on one thing—that the church building was an instrument of evangelism and that architecture could and should be used to make an impression on the unchurched and unsaved that would lead them to attend a worship service or become involved in some other church-sponsored program or activity. Of course, this was not a new idea among evangelical church builders. But megachurch builders gave it a new twist. In accord with the "marketing orientation" recommended by church growth experts, they regarded the megachurch structure and its architecture as an advertisement for the "product" and "services" offered by the church.

In adopting the merchandising strategies of the business world, megachurch builders seized the opportunities created by recent and ongoing changes in American society: the population shift from the center city to the suburbs and, later, to the "edge cities" mushrooming within or adjacent to major metropolitan areas or along tollways and interstates; the expansion of millions of miles of highways, expressways, and freeways throughout the United States; the preeminence of the automobile as a mode of transportation; and the advent of what Kenneth T. Jackson has called the "drive-in culture."[3]

For example, when First Baptist Church of Jacksonville, Florida (Plate 7) decided to remain downtown rather than move to the suburbs, as many other center city churches were doing, it took advantage of the metropolitan expressway system and reinvented itself as a regional church, drawing congregants not just from the surrounding neighborhood or the downtown, but from all of Jacksonville and even from as far away as St. Augustine and St. Mary's, Georgia. Signs painted on several of the church buildings declared, "Welcome / First Baptist Church / Minutes Away by Expressway." An elevated rapid transit system under construction in the mid 1990s, with a stop at First Baptist, promised to provide another convenient mode of transportation to the church. The church also made it easy for congregants to park their cars and find their way around the church complex and into the auditorium. By the mid 1990s it had built three large parking garages featuring elevated walkways that linked them to the various buildings in the church complex. It also maintained several ground-level parking lots and was considering building yet another parking garage.[4]

Another downtown church, Dauphin Way Baptist Church, responded to demographic shifts in Mobile, Alabama, by moving to a more advantageous location within the metropolitan area. Though small by megachurch standards, the new nineteen-acre site was adjacent to the city's main traffic arteries. A church booklet published to promote the building campaign pointed out that the new location would put the church "in the very heart of Mobile" and noted that "almost every church member and potential member will be within 15 minutes drive of our church. Each day more than 60,000 ve-hicles will pass our church on Dauphin Street and on I-65. What a witness for Mobile!"[5]

While some downtown churches remained in the center city, others moved to the outskirts, seeking more land as well as improved accessibility. Second Baptist Church of Houston had relocated as early as 1957, settling on a twenty-five-acre campus in a developing area of southwest Houston. In the mid 1970s First Baptist, Houston, also left the center city, choosing a strategic site on Katy Freeway at Loop 610 West.

These and other downtown megachurches that moved away from the center city saw the same advantages in the suburbs that newly formed congregations envisioned. Because of the increase in individual mobility facilitated by widespread use of the automobile, worshipers were willing and able to commute to a church located a considerable distance from home. The expansion of the highway system made suburban sites easily accessible. Like First Baptist, Jacksonville, suburban megachurches could function as regional churches. Thus in the mid 1990s, Willow Creek Community Church drew congregants not only from the northwest suburbs of "Chicagoland" but also from the North Shore and as far away as Milwaukee. When Saddleback Church occupied its new campus in Lake Forest, California, located just off the 241 Toll Road and convenient to five other major highways, it fully expected to become a regional church, drawing worshipers from as far away as San Juan Capistrano.[6]

Undeveloped or newly developing areas in the suburbs proved especially attractive to megachurch builders. Since the cost per acre was less than in already developed areas (and much less than in metropolitan areas), megachurch builders could "think big"—planning huge campuses of one hundred acres or more and an entire complex of buildings rather than just a large auditorium and Sunday school building. (In our sample, Bellevue Baptist Church in Cordova, Tennessee, boasted the largest campus, 376 acres.) Locating in an undeveloped or newly developing area was also a way of avoiding the zoning and related controversies in which many megachurches became embroiled in the late twentieth century.[7]

Besides accessibility and relatively low-cost acreage, suburban locations, especially in undeveloped or newly developing areas, offered the promise of increased worship attendance and church membership once new residential areas opened up near the church. In 1999, Prestonwood Baptist Church vacated its North Dallas complex, which it had occupied for only ten years, and dedicated a new one in a rapidly developing area on the outskirts of Plano, Texas. Since the new location was easily accessible from the Tollway, Prestonwood anticipated retaining a large number of the members who resided near the former church building, about seven miles away. In addition, the pastor and congregation saw the Plano area as a very promising mission field and thus an opportunity for further growth. In messages to his congregation during the building campaign, Pastor Jack Graham declared that 74 percent of the people of Plano were unchurched and urged his congregation to join him in "conquer[ing] this land and this community for the glory of God."[8]

Like First Baptist, Jacksonville, suburban megachurches made ample parking space a priority. "You want people to perceive that you have room for them," explained church growth expert George Hunter. Another reason was that megachurches located on major highways were inaccessible to pedestrians, and public transportation was usually unavailable. Most members and visitors came to church in automobiles. One of the reasons Prestonwood church had moved from its former location was the lack of sufficient parking space, which church officials blamed for a decline in membership growth. When the church relocated to its new 138-acre campus in Plano, church officials ensured that there would be ample parking. Three thousand spaces were developed in the initial building phase, to be expanded later to a total of five thousand.[9]

As the foregoing discussion suggests, the church growth experts' invocation of the shopping mall analogy was not mere rhetoric. Many suburban megachurch builders followed the merchandising path charted by the shopping malls of the mid to late twentieth century. Megachurch builders imitated the shopping malls in moving away from the center cities to the suburbs in order to capture a growing retail market—a "mission field" in evangelical terminology. Like mall builders, megachurch builders erected very large buildings and located them on extensive campuses that were easily accessible to highways. Megachurch builders also followed the shopping mall model in eschewing the traditional sidewalk or street orientation and opting instead for a large building or buildings situated in the middle of a vast parking lot.[10]

Two "seeker sensitive" megachurches in our sample even appropriated the shopping mall style of architecture: Faith Community Church in West Covina, California, and A Community of Joy in Glendale, Arizona. Indeed, the origins of Faith Community Church (Plate 8) linked it with the shopping mall. The previous church building had been a remodeled Dollar Saver supermarket. In the mid 1990s, the congregation bought a building where Hughes Aircraft had once manufactured torpedoes and flight simulators for Stealth bombers. Besides the low price, ample space (165,000 square feet), and parking for eleven hundred cars, another attractive feature of the building was its location, accessible from not one or two, but four freeways. "Within twenty minutes of the facility there are millions of people," associate pastor Jim Hayford noted. Architects David Miller and David Gilmore planned the adaptation of the flat-roofed, boxlike industrial facility to its new purpose.[11]

The shopping mall look of Faith Community Church was intentional. A *Los Angeles Times* story published in 1996, when the adaptation was under way, quoted the pastor as saying, "We did not want a traditional church atmosphere. What we were aiming for was the feeling of a mall. A place that's familiar, a real gregarious place." In talking with another *Times* reporter the following year, he observed, "Malls are a neutral place and people feel comfortable in malls. So when people come into our church, they will say, 'Here's a familiar place. I feel safe and secure here like in a mall.'" Architect Gilmore said that his "mission" was "to create an environment free of religious symbols." Instead of traditional church furnishings, he envisioned "calming pools of cascading water" and "movable kiosks" vending cappuccino, hot dogs, and popcorn. Lack of space ruled out the "full-blown food court" the pastors and some members of the congregation wanted, so they settled on the kiosks instead.

What one of the *Times* reporters called "a mall-like ambience" began in the huge concrete expanse of the parking lot. One entered the church through a postmodern portico (with a glass-paneled roof forming the arch) that relieved the blank wall of the building. The revamped interior featured new windows and new spaces defined by freestanding walls pitched at striking angles.[12] Color-coding made the building user-friendly: to help persons find their way around it, the walls in different areas were painted green, yellow, and purple and coded accordingly; for example, "G-auditorium," the multipurpose auditorium used for young people's and children's activities, could be found in the area with green walls. A twenty-five-hundred-seat auditorium, a "courtyard" used as a fellowship area, and office space occupied the remainder of the interior.

The influence of the shopping mall style was even more conspicuous in A Community of Joy (formerly Community Church of Joy) in Glendale, Arizona. In 2000, Kid Kountry—the name spelled out in bright primary colors that contrasted with the adobe-pink and sand colors of the exterior walls—dominated the campus. It looked like a toy or children's clothing store, but in fact it was the church's preschool and day care facility (Plate 9). Along with a multipurpose conference/banquet center that resembled a ten-screen mall movie theater (Plate 10), Kid Kountry was part of the initial phase of an extensive building program begun in the late 1990s, when the church moved to its 175-acre campus in a newly developing area called Arrowhead Ranch. The first building phase was completed in 1998. Until a proposed worship center was built, the church was holding worship services in the conference/banquet center, which seated between seventeen and eighteen hundred.[13]

Just as the pastor of Faith Community Church justified the mall ambience by saying that it made people feel comfortable, the Community of Joy church administrator explained that "we asked the architect to design buildings that would meet people's everyday thinking." The church had been criticized for looking like a shopping mall, but, he observed, "that's where people go."

A Community of Joy provides a good example of what Mark Gottdiener called a "themed environment." Just as amusement parks and restaurants used architecture and decor to create a "themed space" (think of Disneyland and the Hard Rock Cafe), the Joy church not only looked like a shopping mall but also offered its "customers" the experiences they enjoyed in the mall: consumption, entertainment, and community. Its shopping mall ambience advertised the fact that Joy was a "full service" church. Just as mall-goers could choose from a wide array of consumption opportunities, visitors to Joy could select from myriad facilities and programs.

The architecture and decor of the shopping mall also advertised the church's emphasis on excitement, energy, enthusiasm—in a word, joy—not only in its recreational and social programs but also in its worship services. Joy was a "seeker-oriented" church, and Pastor Walther P. Kallestad used what he called "entertainment evangelism" to appeal to the unchurched. He based his approach on two assumptions: that many unchurched people found Christianity "boring," and that entertainment could be used (and redeemed) for the proclamation of the gospel. In 2000, each of church's four worship services targeted a slightly different audience, but all of them accentuated entertainment in the form of contemporary music, drama, and multimedia presentations. And, finally, just as the shopping mall offered visitors a sense of community, Kallestad envisioned his church as "a strong and caring community" that would "attract people of all ages and walks of life with programs that provide a positive influence in their lives." By the spring of 2000, besides the banquet/conference center, four other components of the proposed "intergenerational" community were already in operation or about to open: Kid Kountry; the Joy Community School for grades K–8; Joy Celebration Village, a "retirement resort" for seniors; and Arrowhead Memorial Gardens at Joy, offering mortuary services as well as a cemetery and mausoleum. Later phases of the Joy Community building program were to include a worship center that would also serve as a "performing arts" facility (with four thousand seats and a retractable roof to permit scheduling "concerts under the stars"), a chapel, a hotel,

Plate 1. Willow Creek Community Church, South Barrington, Illinois (1981, 1992).

Plate 2. Auditorium, Willow Creek Community Church.

Plate 3. Atrium, Willow Creek Community Church.

Plate 4. Ebenezer A.M.E. Church, Fort Washington, Maryland (1994).

Plate 5. Mural, Ebenezer A.M.E. Church.

Plate 6. Trinity United Church of Christ, Chicago (1994).

Plate 7. First Baptist Church, Jacksonville, Florida (1994).

Plate 8. Faith Community Church, West Covina, California (1998).

Plate 9. Kid Kountry, A Community of Joy, Glendale, Arizona (1998).

Plate 10. Conference/banquet center, A Community of Joy.

Plate 11. Midwest Christian Center, Tinley Park, Illinois (1989).

Plate 12. Oak Cliff Bible Fellowship, Dallas (1995).

Plate 13. Calvary Church, Naperville, Illinois (1993).

Plate 14. Vineyard Christian Fellowship, Anaheim, California (1991).

Plate 15. Mariners Church, Irvine, California (1996). The auditorium is on
the left; on the right can be seen part of the Life Development Building.

Plate 16. Fellowship Church, Grapevine, Texas (1998).

Plate 17. First Baptist Church, Houston (1977). The structure with the peaked roofs seen above the roofline of the church is a high-rise apartment building some distance from the First Baptist campus.

a youth and recreation center, a "state-of-the-art aquatics center," and "50+ acres of parks, lakes, and recreational areas."[14]

Like the two shopping mall megachurches just described, many other megachurches exhibited the influence of secular building design, especially that used for commercial or corporate buildings. In style and mode of construction, several megachurches resembled the utilitarian buildings used for warehouses or in strip shopping centers: Midwest Christian Center in Tinley Park, Illinois (Plate 11), Oak Cliff Bible Fellowship in Dallas (Plate 12), and Calvary Church in Naperville, Illinois (Plate 13). Boxlike, with metal roofing, they exhibited minimal detailing except for the facade or entrance.[15] The builders' main concern was to find the most economical way of enclosing a large space for worship and other activities of the church. Whether intentionally or not, these structures advertised the builders' indifference to the church building and its architecture. They reflected many evangelicals' conviction that the people, not the building, constituted the church. The construction administrator of First Baptist, Jacksonville, expressed this utilitarian ethos in describing his own church's new worship center. We wanted "nothing fancy, just a functional building in which we could worship and preach the Lord," he said.

Other megachurches followed the corporate style of architecture used in the design of many large office buildings and civic or educational institutions. As Richard Longstreth has pointed out, this style represented a significant change from that of nineteenth- and early-twentieth-century commercial buildings. The earlier buildings were designed to be seen from the front. Beginning in the mid 1950s, however, architects began to design buildings that were freestanding or grouped in clusters and surrounded by large amounts of open space. The facade was de-emphasized; buildings were conceived of as three-dimensional objects to be read as a solid mass and defined more by the roof than the walls.[16] The late-twentieth-century megachurches that made use of this new design appeared as massive structures or complexes set in a large parking lot. The gross form of the main building or its roof treatment, rather than the facade, defined these churches architecturally.

Several megachurches in our sample exemplify the adaptation of late-twentieth-century corporate design, including Vineyard Christian Fellowship and Mariners Church, both in Orange County, California; Fellowship Church in Grapevine, Texas; First Baptist Church and Second Baptist Church in Houston, Texas; and the First Evangelical Free Church in Rockford, Illinois. All were rather plain, unornamented structures that exhibited little or no evidence of their religious function. Like Willow Creek Community Church, another example of the corporate style, they resembled educational, civic, or corporate office buildings or complexes rather than churches.

The Vineyard Christian Fellowship worship center (Plate 14) was, in fact, the former Rockwell International Testing Laboratory, which the congregation purchased in 1991 and adapted to religious purposes. Like Mariners Church (Plate 15) and Fellowship Church (Plate 16), it was a "seeker-sensitive" church. The minimalist, modern look of the three mega-churches advertised their nontraditional orientation. In particular, the sleek metal crosses on the Fellowship Church facade communicated the "high tech" ambience of a church that offered innovative, "culturally relevant" worship services and other programs. Fellowship marketed its "product"—"Innertainment for the Heart"—in brightly colored brochures and mailers featuring sophisticated graphic design and wordplay. The weekly church bulletin was a 4 ¾"-square booklet designed to look like the informational insert accompanying a compact disc recording.[17]

Three megachurches that had originally been downtown churches but had moved to the suburbs also chose the corporate style for new buildings erected in the late 1970s and 1980s. All of them featured very pronounced horizontal lines and minimal ornamentation. The new First Baptist, Houston, complex, opened in 1977 (Plate 17), was composed of mostly rectangular structures as well as two with curving walls that enclosed pie-shaped spaces, one of which was the auditorium. Steve Seelig, one of First Baptist's pastors, conceded that it "has always looked like an office building to me," but added, "It's very functional." In 1980, the First Evangelical Free Church of Rockford, Illinois (Plate 18) constructed a sprawling, flat-roofed facility in the Bauhaus style, its dominating horizontal lines relieved only by a freestanding bell tower, also in a modern idiom. At Second Baptist, Houston, a dome surmounted by a Celtic cross distinguished the otherwise plain, red-brick worship center, dedicated in 1986 (Plate 19). The combination of the traditional element and the overwhelmingly secular, modern style of architecture reflected Second Baptist's dual mission. It promoted itself as a "family church," but its slogan—"the Fellowship of Excitement"—advertised its "seeker-sensitive" orientation. Pastor Edwin Young once observed that his "aim was to develop a wonderful environment, full of love and fun and light. I wanted to make it so that a secular, unchurched person could go there and not be threatened."[18]

Their distinctive form and detailing distinguished two other corporate-style megachurches from the rather plain structures just discussed. They were Saddleback Church, located on a seventy-four-acre Foothill Ranch site in Lake Forest, California, and Prestonwood Baptist Church in Plano, Texas. Saddleback was a "seeker church." Pastor Rick Warren built his four-thousand-plus congregation using the "Saddleback Strategy" he developed in the early 1980s, which targeted unchurched, well-educated, professional Baby Boomers who felt uncomfortable in the "traditional church." Embarking on a long, multiphase building program in the early 1990s, Warren envisioned a parklike campus. "People always say they feel closer to God in nature," he told a *Los Angeles Times* reporter. "When God made Adam and Eve, he put them in a garden, not a skyscraper." Elaborating on his architectural philosophy, he added, "We see our buildings as tools for ministry, not monuments. We're much more into putting money into landscaping, trees and a park atmosphere than making an architectural statement."[19]

The first permanent structure erected on the Saddleback campus was a multipurpose building used as a temporary worship center, which opened in September 1995 (Plate 20). The plain rectangular building had a modified barrel vault roof instead of the more conventional gable or circular roofs seen on most megachurches. Some members fondly referred to the building as "our airplane hangar." Others thought it looked like a gymnasium.[20] In keeping with Warren's naturalistic emphasis, both the exterior and interior of the glass and steel building incorporated earth-tone slate tiles, adobe, and wood. Large, floor-to-ceiling windows allowed natural light to flood the worship space. Warren wanted the landscape to be visible from inside the church, but he also wanted the worship space to be visible from the outside. That way, in southern California's balmy climate, Saddleback worshipers could sit outside the auditorium where they could watch the worship service through the windows and hear the preaching and music over loudspeakers.

Prestonwood Baptist Church in Plano, Texas, also began an ambitious building campaign in the 1990s. In 1999, it completed a huge, $56 million, 460,000 square-foot structure made up of a Main Building that housed an atrium, a seven-thousand-seat worship center, and various administrative offices and production facilities; and a Children's Building (Plate 21). The structure exhibited many of the elements characteristic of the megachurches discussed so far: circular as well as rectangular shapes, a horizontal as opposed to a vertical emphasis, and a focus on the roof as the defining feature of the building. The roof was circular in some places, barrel vault in others. The rectangular Children's Building was rather plain and utilitarian, whereas the partly circular, partly rectangular Main Building featured an unusual amount of ornamentation compared to most megachurches. David Shanks, the director of design for HH Architects, the firm that planned the church, said that his client wanted the building to reflect a "'cutting edge' image." Writing in *Texas Architect,* Susan Williams observed that "in renderings the curved front of the worship center resembles the concourse side of a baseball stadium more than it does a church." At the same time, however, the facade of the Main Building featured elements reminiscent of traditional church architecture but translated into the modern idiom: flying buttresses, clerestory windows, and a three-hundred-foot band of stained glass under the eaves. The eclectic design was HH Architects' response to its client's request for "a huge, yet warm, contemporary design that incorporated many traditional elements such as arches, balustrades and materials that are pleasing to look at and touch."[21]

All of the megachurches considered thus far were basically boxlike buildings, whether square or rectangular. Other megachurches were circular, hexagonal, octagonal, or twelve-sided. The use of the circular or polygon form was significant for two reasons. First, it recalled the tents evangelicals have used throughout much of their history. Second, unlike square or rectangular buildings, it prefigured the shape of the worship space inside. In effect, the builders of the circular or polygon megachurches followed the advice of the midcentury architectural reformers who had argued that the very form of the church building should express the beliefs and worship practices of its congregation.

The dome offered one way of approximating the tent shape. Both Brentwood Baptist Church in southwest Houston and Crenshaw Christian Center in Los Angeles chose the geodesic dome for this purpose. The Brentwood dome (Plate 22), 120 feet in diameter and 60 feet high, housed an auditorium seating eighteen hundred persons. The Crenshaw Christian Center FaithDome (Plate 23) had an inside diameter of 320 feet; its center was about 75 feet high. It boasted the largest seating capacity of any twentieth-century evangelical megachurch: 10,145 theater seats on a sloping floor surrounded the platform, creating a "church-in-the-round."[22]

Besides Brentwood and Crenshaw, another predominantly African American megachurch, the World Changers Ministries Christian Center, in College Park, Georgia, built a domed worship center (Plate 24), but instead of the geodesic form, it used a domed roof supported by circular walls. Like the FaithDome, the World Changers auditorium was designed as a church-in-the-round, with eight thousand seats encircling the platform.[23]

Instead of a dome, several other megachurches used a segmented roof covering a circular, hexagonal, octagonal, or twelve-sided building. The worship center and chapel of North Phoenix Baptist Church (Plate 25) came the closest to evoking the tent of any of the megachurches in our sample. The massive rectangular buttresses of the octagonal Family Worship Center in Baton Rouge, Louisiana (Plate 26) compromised the tent form somewhat, but gave the structure an impression of solidity not found in some other megachurches.[24]

Another tentlike polygon structure was the worship center of Southeast Christian Church in Louisville (Plate 27). The twelve-sided building was constructed of precast concrete panels, with blue mirror walls covering about a third of the perimeter. Its auditorium provided seating for ninety-one hundred persons on four different levels besides the ground floor. In size and height (297,000 square feet, eight stories), the worship center ranked among the largest of the late-twentieth-century megachurches. Commenting on the building, architect David Miller suggested that its distinctive shape and "simple but profound grandeur" communicated its religious function. Had the center been designed in "a traditional rectangular shape," he noted, "it would have looked like an airport terminal."[25]

Except for its unusual shape, the Crystal Cathedral (Plates 28, 29) belongs in the same class as the corporate-style megachurches discussed earlier. As the architectural critic Paul Goldberger remarked at the time of its dedication, it could easily "be mistaken . . . for a jazzy corporate headquarters." Erected in 1980 by Robert Schuller and the Garden Grove Community Church, it is one of the most distinctive megachurches, architecturally speaking, in our sample. But like the others, it, too, was designed as an advertisement to attract the unchurched and the unsaved to the gospel. Indeed, shortly after the cathedral was constructed, Schuller referred to the building as a "22-acre shopping center for Jesus Christ." Schuller collaborated on the design of the cathedral with the architectural team of Philip Johnson and John Burgee, famous for their "image making skyscrapers." Johnson regarded the commission as "a unique opportunity . . . to create a star of glass." Schuller embraced the building project as a way of continuing the church growth strategy he had helped develop.[26]

Although his congregation had grown spectacularly since the 1960s, Schuller still targeted the unchurched and the unsaved. And, based on church growth theory, he had very definite opinions as to the kind of structure likely to attract people in Orange County. When Johnson and Burgee showed him their first design, a masonry structure in the form of a Greek cross, Schuller rejected it. He said, "I was hoping for a great idea. . . . You've given me a traditional church. I'm not traditional. This is California. People here don't come to church to be closed up in a box. They want to be close to green, [sic] to water and sun."[27]

In an interview published in 1984 in *Christianity Today*, Schuller explained the rationale behind the design of the Crystal Cathedral auditorium. He said he focused his Sunday morning service not on the already saved, but on the unconverted, and he wanted the space in which they met to seem inviting and comfortable. "To convert them, first you need to *relax* them so they will listen to you. That is what Richard Neutra, our church architect, taught me 29 years ago," he said. Although Neutra spoke as a "secularist," Schuller observed, "what he said had the ring of truth to it." Indeed, Neutra's teaching provided the perfect prescription for "a place where secular, cynical, untrusting people would come." It explained why "we have no stained glass windows, but lots of water and natural plantings," Schuller noted. "The human being must be back in his natural habitat, with structures that don't provoke cross-cultural conflicts, but make him receptive to our message."[28]

One hundred twenty-eight feet high, the cathedral took the form of an elongated four-pointed star, which measured 207 feet from point to point in one direction and 415 feet from point to point in the other. Descriptions of the building focused on the effect created by the 10,900 panes of reflective glass that composed the walls and roof. Commentators called it "a vault of shimmering transparency," "a gigantic crystalline form," "a trompe-l'oeil of light."[29]

Like the earlier Garden Grove church, the Crystal Cathedral accommodated drive-in worshipers. It had two doors, each ninety feet high, which opened to reveal the platform inside the auditorium, so that people sitting in their automobiles could watch the service. Johnson called them the "Cape Canaveral" doors, "a technical wonder." Other architects might have demurred at devising such theatrical effects, but Johnson and Burgess were sensitive to the fact that they were designing a building for a television evangelist. "The opening of those doors will look great on TV. Dr. Schuller knows exactly what he's doing," Johnson declared.[30]

Just as the design of the auditorium evidenced the influence of the church growth strategy, its ambience advertised

Schuller's distinctive "possibility" theology. After attending the dedication service, Goldberger described the auditorium as "full of a kind of flowing energy, an energy that is ideally suited to the sort of joyful worship that Dr. Schuller's liturgy entails. And because the sun and the clouds and the sky are all visible through the glass, there is a sense of nature present at all times—this is not a church in which one withdraws from the world, but one in which one embraces it." Schuller himself drew the connection between his optimistic theology and the architecture of his church: "I believe in the Resurrection. That is the capstone of my faith, my philosophy, my knowledge, my theory of the church. So in its emotional tone the structure should breathe in harmony with the gospel of the resurrected Christ. That means joy, not gloom."[31]

Originally, the Crystal Cathedral featured no Christian symbolism or other "churchly" ornamentation on the outside, and only a plain cross in the auditorium, at the edge and to the side of the platform. Several years later, however, Schuller asked Johnson to add a freestanding tower. He may have been responding to criticism of the secular look of the Crystal Cathedral. Schuller conceded that "the cathedral doesn't say from the outside what it is," and said that when it was being planned, he and Johnson had discussed "some kind of statement that . . . would mark it as a gathering place for the people of God," but "we couldn't afford it at the time." The 234-foot Prayer Spire, as the new tower came to be known, was completed in 1990. Johnson described it as "a Gothic tower, a Gothic spire in polished stainless steel."[32]

All of the megachurches considered thus far were emphatically modern in design. Late-twentieth-century megachurch builders' acceptance of modern architecture was nothing new, of course. In the earlier part of the century dissenting evangelicals had drawn inspiration for some of their buildings from modern commercial or civic structures.

There were good practical reasons for building in the modern idiom: it was cheaper than building in the traditional style, and it worked just as well in the design of economical, strictly utilitarian church buildings as in the construction of more expensive, distinguished edifices. In addition, the modern idiom may have appealed to recently organized megachurch congregations made up primarily of the unchurched or converts from other denominations and who lacked a consensus on what a church should look like; or to congregations that had no denominational affiliation and therefore no architectural tradition to draw upon.

It is striking how often and with what obvious pride megachurch builders used the term "contemporary" to describe the design of their modern churches. Megachurch pastors and members presented themselves as "conservatives" in matters of theology—the Willow Creek Web site announced: "Our message is as old as the Bible itself. We embrace historic Christian teaching."[33] But just as they touted "innovative" methods of evangelism and worship practices, many evangelicals embraced modern architecture. It satisfied their desire to appear up-to-date, even "pace-setting," to use Robert Schuller's phrasing. In this regard, late-twentieth-century evangelicals resembled the nineteenth- and early-twentieth-century mainline evangelical church builders who prided themselves on their "progressive" views of church architecture.

As Peter Williams has pointed out, the later generation generally preferred "the less radical modes of the modern styles." With the exception of the Crystal Cathedral and Calvary Assembly of God, in Winter Park, Florida (to be discussed later), megachurch builders typically chose the kind of modern architecture that seemed familiar and comfortable. Some even employed structural or ornamental elements to relieve the austerity of a modern design and, at the same time, make their buildings more expressive of their religious function. As we saw earlier, Robert Schuller recognized the desirability of offsetting the starkly neutral look of the Crystal Cathedral by adding the Prayer Spire. Although the polished stainless steel construction was designed in the modern idiom, its vertical thrust evoked the Gothic to signal religious purpose. (Even so, two commentators demurred that the freestanding structure looked "more like the outline of an expressionist skyscraper than a conventional spire."[34]) Similarly, the architects who designed Prestonwood Baptist Church incorporated "traditional elements" to temper the very contemporary, "cutting-edge" design of the church building. At Brentwood Baptist Church, a gable-roofed entrance with a spire and cross was grafted onto the geodesic dome to give a "churchly" look to the worship center. And at First Baptist, Jacksonville, the architects used lancet windows to relieve the austerity of the nondescript, utilitarian building housing the new auditorium.

The modern idiom facilitated the megachurch builders' "marketing orientation." Commentators on late-twentieth-century business architecture have noted management's predilection for using buildings to express "corporate identity." Looking beyond mere functionalism, management sought to make buildings "impelling symbols of corporate virtues and management intentions," according to Per Olof Berg and Kristian Kreiner. In a discussion of business and office park buildings in the United States and Great Britain, Alan Phillips observed that the high-profile, advanced-technology corporations that built the parks sought to advertise "a prestige product by association with good architecture, good art and a good landscape design."[35] By the same token, megachurch builders used the modern idiom to advertise their break with the "traditional church." Recall Bill Hybels's catalogue of the "values" the Willow Creek Community Church building and landscaping were intended to communicate: "neutrality, comfort, contemporary, clean." (Significantly, these were the very "values" Hybels perceived in corporate headquarters.) Or consider the words of the pastor of Faith Community Church: "We did not want a traditional church atmosphere. What we were aiming for was the feeling of a mall." Megachurch builders used the modern idiom to advertise all of the "virtues" and "intentions" that distinguished their church facilities and programs from those of the "traditional church," such as accessibility, convenience, comfort, innovation, excellence, and relevance (contemporaneousness).

It was not only suburban "seeker churches" that used buildings and architecture in this way to project their "virtues" and "intentions." Statements by Bishop Arthur M. Brazier, an African American megachurch pastor, bespoke a different perspective on the work of the church in the inner city, as compared to the suburbs, but his use of architecture to communicate that perspective was similar. His church was the Apostolic Church of God, a holiness-pentecostal church in the Woodlawn neighborhood of Chicago's South Side. Surrounded by abandoned, disintegrating buildings, its several structures occupied almost an entire city block. The focal point of the complex was a tall tower marking the entrance to a plain but massive red-brick building called the Dorchester sanctuary (Plate 30).[36]

In building their church, Brazier and his congregation demonstrated their determination to stay in a rapidly deteriorating neighborhood that had become notorious for its gangs and drug dealers. "The fact is that the Lord pressed upon the minds of the members of this congregation, many of whom didn't live in this community, to stay and help reach this community, . . . to do something to affect [sic] the redevelopment of this community," he declared.[37] The fortress-like invulnerability of the Dorchester sanctuary conveyed the congregation's intention very well, at the same time that it evoked something of the divine. "I wanted the sanctuary to show the magnificence of God, to show His omnipotence—that He is strong and stable and eternal," Brazier explained. The tower, which was his idea, also communicated symbolic meaning. Formed by two closely spaced slabs of unequal height, it

stood in marked contrast to the horizontal line of the main building. Modern in design, it nevertheless worked as a powerful traditional religious symbol, directing attention away from the church's sordid, earthly surroundings to the heavenly realm of God.

Like Brazier's church, most of the other megachurches in our sample displayed various types of signs and symbols to signal their religious "intentions." Such devices were usually quite large and simple in content, because, like the signs lining commercial strips or expressways, they were designed to be seen from afar by passing motorists and to be comprehended easily and quickly. Thus the cross on the roof of Southeast Christian Church measured one foot in diameter and rose forty feet above the peak of the roof. On a clear day, according to church officials, it could be seen six miles away. At night, illuminated by six floodlights, it signaled the church's commitment to "evangelizing the lost" and "edifying the saved."[38]

The sign in front of Trinity United Church of Christ, displaying a digitized message, and the one used by Midwest Christian Center, positioned so as to be visible from the highway alongside the church, were similar to signs used by commercial enterprises. Even more so was the sign exhibited by Fellowship Church. Indeed, Pastor Ed Young readily admitted to borrowing the idea for it from a commercial enterprise. In 1998, flying over Las Vegas one night and seeing all the neon lights below, he remembered that the previous year Dr Pepper had placed advertisements on the roofs of two Grapevine schools located under a flight path used by the

Dallas–Fort Worth Airport. Soon after Young returned from his trip, airline passengers flying over Fellowship Church could look down and see its name painted on the roof in giant red, white, and blue letters. In a story about the sign, the *Fort Worth Star-Telegram* quoted Young as saying, "We unashamedly try to be as strategic and intentional as possible to get the name of our church out there." He thought the church might learn something from Dr Pepper and Las Vegas: "Our culture doesn't have much to say, but it knows how to say it. The church has everything to say, but we don't know how to say it."[39]

The religious symbols found on most megachurch exteriors were usually traditional in concept, despite the fact that the buildings were generally quite modern in design. Crosses proved to be the most popular, but megachurch builders also used spires, towers, domes, and the like. The crosses varied in design, from the simple, unadorned version found on the Southeast Christian Church, to the Celtic cross used on the dome of Second Baptist, Houston, to the abstract renderings mounted on the worship centers of two Phoenix, Arizona, megachurches, North Phoenix Baptist Church and The Valley Cathedral. The photograph of The Valley Cathedral (Plate 31) illustrates the contrast between the traditional spire and cross on the church's former worship center and the modern rendering on the current worship center. Generally, crosses were displayed on the roof, as seen in Carpenters Home Church, in Lakeland, Florida (Plate 32), Phoenix First Assembly of God, in Arizona (Plate 33), and other tentlike churches. Some churches, such as Calvary Church, presented their crosses as freestanding forms, while others, such as Fellowship Church, affixed them to the worship center. The attached brick and glass tower of the worship center of Oak Cliff Bible Fellowship in Dallas framed a white cross. Elmbrook Church in Brookfield, Wisconsin, enclosed a cross in a "light scoop" formed by the steel trusswork that created the dramatic pitch of the roof (Plate 34). During the day the "scoop" admitted natural light that bathed the auditorium platform below, which created a particularly dramatic effect during morning worship services, when it transmitted eastern light from the rising sun. At night, backlighting in the "scoop" made the cross stand out in bold relief, transforming it into a dark shape visible at a considerable distance from the church.[40]

Whatever their design and no matter how displayed, the crosses constituted a kind of generic religious symbolism, easily recognized emblems that indicated the Christian orientation of the buildings they adorned. Used as a marketing device, such symbolism provided a way of advertising the churches' nonsectarian ethos to the great undifferentiated mass of the unchurched and unsaved, thereby casting as wide a net as possible.

Of course the *absence* of religious symbolism also constituted an advertisement. Some megachurches, especially "seeker churches" such as Willow Creek and Vineyard, purposely omitted religious symbols from their buildings, so as to present the neutral look believed to attract the unchurched Boomer generation.

Eschewing both neutrality and generic Christian symbolism, some megachurches featured displays that communicated their particular theological orientation. The tongues of fire painted on its pediment identified the West Angeles Church of God in Christ in Los Angeles as a pentecostal church (Plate 35).[41] Both Carpenter's Home Church and Phoenix First Assembly of God exhibited large images of Jesus on the exteriors of their worship centers, the one on the Lakeland church showing him working as a carpenter, the even larger one on the Phoenix church presenting him as a white-robed, standing figure. Considering evangelical Protestants' traditional antipathy to representational art on or in the church, the images were unusual, but they graphically conveyed the emphasis both churches placed on Jesus' life and sacrifice.

Equally unusual was the "Christian signage" displayed on the Saddleback Church worship center, which recalled the biblical passages inscribed on the interior walls of some early-twentieth-century fundamentalist tabernacles and churches. It took the form of a reflective-glass "scripture wall" running the length of one side of the building. Etched into the glass were words in capital letters—"OUR PURPOSES: MAGNIFICATION, MEMBERSHIP, MATURITY, MINISTRY, MISSION"—and various biblical verses elaborating on each of the five purposes. The messages on the scripture wall were more or less legible, depending on the time of day and whether it was cloudy or bright. A reporter for the *Orange County Register* thought they looked "more like design than words." However, Tim Stafford, writing in *Christianity Today,* saw the wall in a quite different (and much more positive) light and ap-

preciated the spiritual as well as the architectural message it conveyed. Looking at the glass, he observed, "you see simultaneously three scenes. Through the glass, you look in to the interior of the worship center. Reflected in the glass you see an immense outdoor vista of sky, palms, and patio. And etched into the glass are words, so that a message stretches over the indoor and outdoor scenes. . . . The effect is subtle, since the color is all in the outdoor reflection, while the words are a glass gray. Yet the wall unmistakably communicates that this church is governed by a purpose, inside and out."[42]

Although modern corporate and commercial architecture exerted considerable influence on late-twentieth-century megachurches, not all of them bore its imprint. The church growth experts' denigration of the "traditional church" notwithstanding, several megachurches in our sample imitated the Federal-style churches favored by eighteenth- and early-nineteenth-century Congregationalists, Presbyterians, and Baptists, or, reaching further back in time, the Gothic churches of the Middle Ages. These were first and foremost megachurches, however, and their physical and spatial requirements inevitably forced a compromise of the historic styles.

While the use or evocation of a historic style implied disapproval of the modern idiom favored by most megachurch builders, the builders of the neo-Federal or Gothic megachurches agreed that architecture could and should be used as a marketing device. Like their modernist counterparts, they, too, sought to attract the unchurched and the unsaved, especially those who thought a church should "look like a church" and were put off by neutral, secular-looking church architecture, or who appreciated the "visual linkages" to their historical and theological heritage.[43] In effect, these megachurch builders employed the very strategy the church growth experts recommended—"packaging" their "product" in such a way as to stand out in the religious marketplace and attract individuals shopping for "something different."

The Federal-style church, combining a rectangular red-brick meetinghouse, a neoclassical portico, and a Gibbsian tower and spire, had become an icon of American church architecture by the early twentieth century. During the 1950s, Southern Baptists were particularly attracted to its design. So it is not surprising that when the pastor and congregation of the Roswell Street Baptist Church in Marietta, Georgia, planned the construction of a new auditorium, they chose the historic style rather than a modern one (Plate 36). Dedicated in 1958, the facility was a rectangular building constructed of red brick and decorated with white trim, and featured a neoclassical portico with Doric columns and a steeple rising from the front of the main structure. Educational and office wings were added later, distorting the original form. In 1979, having outgrown the 1958 auditorium, the congregation built a new, much larger worship center accommodating thirty-three hundred persons. Although it exhibited some traditional features—a red-brick entrance, Georgian windows, even an oddly shaped steeple (which served as a prayer tower)—overall it constituted a less faithful replica of the Federal-style model.[44]

Among the largest of the Federal-style structures was the worship center of the Dauphin Way Baptist Church of Mobile, Alabama, dedicated in 1988 (Plate 37). A church booklet described it as a combination of "the classic beauty of the Colonial-Georgian Style with the functionality of modern church design." To be sure, it was a red-brick building with white trim and neoclassical detailing, a temple-like portico, and a stereotypical Gibbsian tower and spire rising from the main body of the structure. But it was huge (126,000 square feet)—built on a much larger scale than any eighteenth-century church or, for that matter, the 1958 Roswell Street Baptist Church auditorium. It had to be huge to accommodate the church's large membership (more than eight thousand) and its many programs and activities. It departed from the Federal-style model not just in size but also in form. An octagonal rather than a rectangular building, it boasted not one but three porticos (the "Great Hall Entrance," with six columns, and the others with four columns each).[45]

Some megachurch builders, rather than trying to imitate the Federal-style church building, presented an allusive rendering of it. The architects who designed First Baptist Church of Raytown, Missouri (Plate 38) used visual references to evoke the eighteenth-century church—the steeple, the red-brick walls and white trim, the modernistic, enclosed portico—although the effect was compromised by the shape of the structure (five-sided as opposed to rectangular), the porte-cochere in front of and the truncated towers on either side of the entrance, and the stained-glass windows (brought from the previous church building) on the portico and between it and the towers.[46]

Notwithstanding its postmodern broken pediment and the fact that it served as a porte-cochere, the portico of Bellevue Baptist Church, in Cordova, Tennessee, signaled another attempt to evoke the traditional Federal-style church (Plate 39). Builder Roe Messner faced the same problem confronted by other designers of mega-versions of the eighteenth-century church: how to give the building a traditional appearance and also accommodate the very large membership and the many and varied programs characteristic of a megachurch. In 1989, at the time of its dedication, the new Bellevue structure was a large, flat-roofed, rectangular building with a sanctuary seating seven thousand persons. Additions to the building made it even larger (470,000 square feet) and turned it into a U-shaped structure enclosing a freestanding building. As in the case of the Dauphin Way Baptist Church, the size and, ultimately, the shape of Bellevue Baptist Church subverted the attempt to evoke the historic model. So did the embellishment of the pediment, which featured a cross with its rays penetrating a stained-glass image of the world, illustrating the Scripture command printed below it: "Send out thy light and thy truth. Psalm 43:3."[47]

Although the Gothic churches of the Middle Ages represented an alien architectural and theological tradition, the pastors of two pentecostal megachurches drew upon the neo-Gothic idiom in designing their structures. Earl Paulk, Jr., the senior pastor of the Cathedral of the Holy Spirit in Decatur, Georgia, chose the historic style to symbolize his spiritual authority (as a bishop in the International Communion of Charismatic Congregations) and what he believed to be the distinctive, providential mission of his church. He claimed to have had "direct experiential contact" with God or the Holy Spirit and also voiced the conviction that his church was "unique," that it had been "Called of God for a Special Purpose" and had been granted "the anointing and power of the Holy Ghost." Early in 1986, he quoted Oral Roberts as saying, "'There is not a Holy Spirit directed cathedral in the world.'" Soon afterward Paulk declared that God had commanded him to build a 7,777-seat "Cathedral to the Holy Spirit."[48]

Construction began on Easter morning in April 1988. Three years later the new structure opened its doors (Plate 40). The $12 million, steel-frame, metal-roofed, brick and concrete structure encompassed approximately 150,000 square feet. A church leaflet described the architecture as a blend of "Gothic design with a contemporary layout." The irregular polygon shape was contemporary (and similar to the tentlike churches discussed earlier in this chapter), but the one-hundred-foot tower, with its crocketed spire, was neo-Gothic. According to the church leaflet, it closely resembled the towers of "small Gothic cathedrals of the 13th century which are found in Germany." Another traditional feature was the "typically Gothic rose window" in the tallest of the three neo-Gothic windows above the entrance. Inside was a seventy-seven-hundred-seat sanctuary replete with neo-Gothic furnishings and ornamentation.[49]

Mike Hayes's purpose in constructing a neo-Gothic building was "to put the romance back into church." Architect Nick

Plate 18. First Evangelical Free Church, Rockford, Illinois (1980).

Plate 19. Second Baptist Church, Houston (1986). The steeple seen on the left, above the roofline of the church, belongs to the Federal-style church building constructed in 1968 and currently used as a chapel.

Plate 20. Saddleback Church, Lake Forest, California (1995).

Plate 21. Prestonwood Baptist Church, Plano, Texas (1999).

Plate 22. Brentwood Baptist Church, Houston (1986).

Plate 23. FaithDome, Crenshaw Christian Center, Los Angeles (1989).

Plate 24. World Changers Ministries Christian Center, College Park, Georgia (1996).

Plate 25. North Phoenix Baptist Church, Phoenix; worship center (1977) on the left, chapel (1985) on the right.

Plate 26. Family Worship Center, World Ministry Center of Jimmy Swaggart Ministries, Baton Rouge, Louisiana (1985).

Plate 27. Southeast Christian Church, Louisville (1998), courtesy of Jimmie Wallace, Photographer, Louisville.

Plate 28. Crystal Cathedral (1980) and Prayer Spire (1990), Garden Grove, California, courtesy of and used by permission of Crystal Cathedral Ministries.

Plate 29. Auditorium, Crystal Cathedral, courtesy of and used by permission of Crystal Cathedral Ministries.

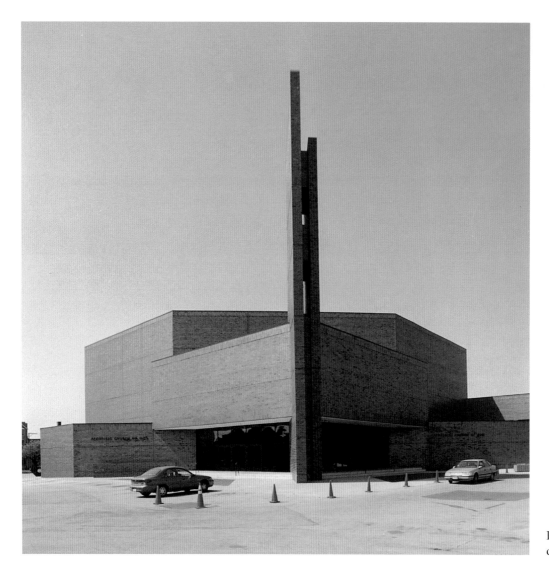

Plate 30. Apostolic Church
of God, Chicago (1992).

Plate 31. The Valley Cathedral, Phoenix (1990–1991).

Plate 32. Carpenter's Home Church, Lakeland, Florida (1985).

Plate 33. Phoenix First Assembly of God, Phoenix (1985).

Plate 34. Elmbrook Church, Brookfield, Wisconsin (1994).

Cade recalled that at their first meeting, the senior pastor of Covenant Church in Carrollton, Texas (Plate 41) requested "something in a Texas Gothic vernacular." Hayes had toured all the great cathedrals of Europe and found them inspiring. He also wanted something different from the typical evangelical megachurches of the 1970s and 1980s. They were too "civic-oriented"—you couldn't tell the difference between them and a convention center. He wanted a building that looked like a church. Executive Pastor Jerry Parsons also emphasized his and Hayes's desire for a "churchly" structure. The previous house of worship had been a metal building that "looked like a Sam's Club," Parsons explained. "We want people to know this is a church. We told the architect, 'We want it to look like a church and sound like a cathedral but [be] constructed with contemporary materials.'"[50]

Dedicated in 1995, Covenant Church was a steel-frame building with rough-textured concrete block walls and a metal roof. A church booklet named the style "Texas Gothic Cathedral." The Texan element was "the white and cream limestone-look"; Gothic detailing gave the building what Parsons called "the cathedral effect." Thus the church exterior featured pointed arches, flying buttresses, and a steeply pitched roof over the front entranceway. The auditorium featured an "open-girder system" in the ceiling (exposed steel trusses supporting a low, flat roof). According to Parsons, it was designed "to get the echoes," meaning reverberation similar to that produced by the vaulting in the nave of a medieval church.[51]

Overall, the architecture of the Cathedral of the Holy Spirit and Covenant Church paled in comparison with that of the medieval Gothic churches. In contrast to the heaven-pointing medieval churches, the two late-twentieth-century imitations seemed uninspired, ill-proportioned and heavy, utterly earthbound. The orientation of the two megachurches was basically horizontal, rather than vertical, a function of the broad roof span of the cathedral and the flat-roofed structure extending behind the front part of the Covenant Church. Both structures suffered from architectural ambiguity. The use of neo-Gothic elements suggested a liturgical church, whereas the size and horizontal emphasis of the structures denoted an evangelical megachurch.

The builders of two other megachurches, instead of grafting neo-Gothic features such as crockets, rose windows, and buttresses onto a boxlike or polygon structure, simply evoked the historic form, using the idiom of modern architecture. In effect, they adopted an approach similar to the one used by the builders of some of the Federal-style megachurches.

The Coral Ridge Presbyterian Church in Fort Lauderdale, Florida (Plate 42) featured an eclectic mix of neo-Gothic and other elements. The tower and the modified cruciform shape of the sanctuary were neo-Gothic, but the simple, geometric lines of the tower and the use of faceted glass in the tower and church windows hinted at Art Deco. And the sanctuary roof outlined a fish, an early Christian symbol used in the design of a few mainline Protestant churches in the 1950s and 1960s. The centerpiece of the Coral Ridge complex was the 303-foot carillon tower (believed to be the tallest in the United States when it was built), with a 90-foot stainless steel spire surmounted by a 22-foot cross. Its great height and brilliantly colored faceted glass windows, which were illuminated at night, made it an effective advertisement for the church, as well as a tool of evangelism, visible day and night from a long distance. At the base of the tower, directly above the entrance to the church, stood a 27-foot figure of Christ, and engraved over the doors were the words "Come Unto Me."[52]

In comparison with the Coral Ridge church, the main building of Calvary Assembly of God in Winter Park, Florida (Plate 43) presented a more coherent interpretation of the Gothic. Composed of cylindrical forms arranged in tiers, it was a strikingly modern structure, but the multiple truncated "towers," especially the two tallest ones at the front entrance, clearly suggested the form of a medieval Gothic church.[53]

When late-twentieth-century evangelicals began building megachurches they confronted a wide range of design choices. The second half of the twentieth century produced no distinctive, dominant style of church architecture; because none of the evangelical denominations mandated a specific building design or style, affiliated pastors and congregations were as free as their independent, nondenominational counterparts to select whatever suited their taste and budget. In effect, each megachurch devised its own architectural philosophy. The reigning idea seemed to be "every man (or pastor or church building committee) his own architect"—a kind of architectural antinomianism.

The variety of megachurch architecture reflected the evolutionary history of the late-twentieth-century structures. For example, the secular look of most megachurches recalled the seventeenth-century meetinghouses and the late-nineteenth-century and early-twentieth-century tabernacles and temples. Even when megachurch builders employed towers, spires, crosses, and other kinds of Christian symbolism, they did so sparingly and more in the spirit of the architects of the mid-twentieth-century "gathered churches" than that of the late-nineteenth-century auditorium church builders. Most megachurches, particularly those designed as circular or polygon structures, exhibited a horizontal rather than a vertical orientation, which was similar to that of the nineteenth-century revival tents and tabernacles as well as the Angelus Temple and Moody Memorial Church. The use of the modern idiom had a precedent in the "gathered churches" as well as the early-twentieth-century fundamentalist, holiness, and pentecostal structures that imitated commercial buildings such as department stores, theaters, warehouses, and municipal auditoriums.

Even the great size of the megachurches reflected their continuity with earlier structures. The megachurches dwarfed the meetinghouses and the "gathered churches," and most of them were much larger than the auditorium churches in terms of campus acreage and square footage of the church complex. The average seating capacity of the megachurch auditoriums—around 4,000—also exceeded that of the auditorium churches, which was about 2,300.[54] The four largest megachurches in our sample were Southeast Christian with a seating capacity of 9,100; First Baptist, Jacksonville, with 9,200; Carpenter's Home Church with 10,000; and the Crenshaw Christian Center FaithDome with 10,145. However, the tabernacles built by the dissenting evangelicals were even larger. Dwight Moody's "Depot Tabernacle" in Philadelphia seated 10,000; other tabernacles built for him in Chicago and Boston seated 8,000 and 6,000, respectively. Most of Billy Sunday's tabernacles accommodated around 10,000. Of course they were temporary structures built to provide space for a revival campaign of limited duration. But the more permanent tabernacles were comparable in size to larger-than-average megachurches. The Union Gospel Tabernacle held between 3,000 and 6,000; the Chicago Gospel Tabernacle, 5,000; and the Atlanta Baptist Tabernacle, 8,000. Even the large churches built by some fundamentalists and pentecostals compared favorably in size with the very large megachurches: Temple Baptist Church and Moody Memorial Church accommodated 4,000; Angelus Temple, 5,300–7,500; Mason Temple, 7,500. And First Baptist Church of Fort Worth, seating 14,000, exceeded all of the late-twentieth-century megachurches.

Megachurch builders agreed with Frederick Price that "every church should be a big church." They considered great size an important marketing device, believing that a very large church building in and of itself drew newcomers. The experience of Second Baptist Church of Houston and Southeast Christian Church seemed to prove them right. During the first year Second Baptist occupied its newly built auditorium, the average worship attendance increased by 2,842 persons, and it became necessary to put chairs in the aisles to provide extra seating. After only fourteen months in the new auditorium, the church had to go to two Sunday morning services to accommodate its growing congregation. In 1998, before Southeast Christian Church moved to its new location, the average worship attendance was 10,865. More than 15,000 persons attended the three Dedication Weekend services for the new complex, in December of that year, and the first five weeks in the new worship center saw about a 40 percent increase in attendance. A record 20,761 persons attended the Easter weekend services. Attendance dropped somewhat later on, but the average worship attendance of 13,565 for 1999 represented a significant increase over that of the previous year. And it rose again during 2000 to 14,151.[55]

Increasing worship attendance at Second Baptist, Southeast Christian, and many other megachurches reinforced evangelicals' commitment to evangelism and to the megachurch as the best instrument for fulfilling it. "Any church in a large, growing community that is practicing the 'Great Commission' cannot keep from growing," declared the author of a pamphlet published by Roswell Street Baptist Church. "To criticize a church for being big is to imply disbelief in Christ's commission." The author's conclusion: "Big is Beautiful."[56]

9

The "Full Service" Church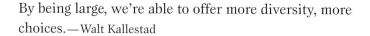

By being large, we're able to offer more diversity, more choices. —Walt Kallestad

One Sunday morning in the mid 1990s, while researching an article on megachurches for *Atlantic Monthly,* Charles Trueheart browsed among the information tables set out on the Mariners Church patio advertising the church's "various 'ministries,' support groups, and fellowship opportunities" (Plate 44). The broad range of offerings included parenting groups, twelve-step recovery meetings, classes on "divorce dynamics" and "life development," a brunch for "women in the workplace," a men's retreat, several "grief support ministries," and numerous sports leagues and recreational activities. The patio scene, complete with a cappuccino cart, soft rock music, and "hundreds of people standing and talking together in the sunshine," exhibited a "full service" megachurch at work, recruiting participants for the vast array of programs and activities it offered in addition to regular weekend worship services.[1]

The full service strategy was exactly what the church growth experts prescribed as the key to increased church membership and congregational vitality. Elmer Towns and others recommended offering "multiple services," just as shopping malls did, to provide "a quality ministry to the total man for the glory of God." Megachurches throughout the United States, in the inner cities and large metropolitan areas as well as in the suburbs, those with predominantly black or multiracial congregations as well as those with predominantly white congregations, all embraced the concept of the full service church. Like Walt Kallestad, pastor of A Community of Joy, other megachurch builders insisted that the great size of their facilities enabled them to offer "more diversity"—a broader range of ministries—than smaller churches could. Adapting to the "mall mentality" of late-twentieth-century American consumers, megachurch builders offered "one-stop" shopping to meet their congregants' myriad needs and wants, not just religious programs but therapeutic, educational, recreational, social, and community service programs. The idea was to provide what church growth experts called "multiple entry points" or "side doors" into the church community.[2]

Given the great number and variety of its ministries, the full service megachurch became what Lyle Schaller and others called the "seven-day-a-week church." Kallestad claimed that the Community of Joy offered "something seven days a week for everyone: support groups, 12-step groups, dance academies, sports enthusiasts." Willow Creek Community Church sponsored ninety-one ministries in the mid 1990s, and the church calendar published for February 1996 showed meetings, classes, or events scheduled for every day of the week, in the morning, afternoon, and evening. Black megachurches offered a similarly varied range of ministries. "We don't see church as just a place to go on Sunday morning," Bishop Arthur Brazier of the Apostolic Church of God observed. "It is a place where we can go if we want to learn a foreign language, or if we're interested in how best to handle our home finances, or if we need marriage counseling. If we're interest-

ed in how singles can work together or if we're interested in helping the teens, we can do that through the church."[3]

While some megachurches targeted the special needs of Baby Boomers, such as day care during church events or classes on single parenting or dieting, most aimed their programs at a broader constituency. Like First Baptist Church in Dallas, they sought to make the church "the center of life for your whole family."[4] In addition, most megachurches instituted "outreach" programs designed to draw people from the larger community to the church or to provide assistance of various kinds to those in need.

The wide range of new or expanded facilities developed by late-twentieth-century megachurches for purposes other than worship included libraries and bookstores (with names like The Garden of Readin' or The Living Word or Our Daily Bread), as well as television, video, and cassette tape production studios. Many megachurches had nursery or day-care facilities featuring fanciful furnishings and decor designed to appeal to the juvenile imagination and religious sensibility (Plates 45, 46). Separate buildings for children, such as Kid Kountry at the Community of Joy and Small World Village at Phoenix First Assembly of God (Plate 47), were not uncommon, especially on the larger megachurch campuses. Prestonwood Baptist Church included in its complex a ninety-three-thousand-square-foot Children's Building that contained three indoor playgrounds as well as numerous classrooms and, on the third floor, an eight-thousand-square-foot room that could accommodate six hundred children playing games at one time. Willow Creek Community Church and Southeast Christian Church built youth centers, and Ebenezer African Methodist Church renovated its former church building, a short distance away, for a youth facility.[5] Amphitheaters used for outdoor dramas and concerts, as well as special religious services, also became increasingly popular features on megachurch campuses.

Most megachurches expanded their educational offerings far beyond those of late-nineteenth- and early-twentieth-century urban churches. Virtually all megachurches had Sunday school classrooms for adults and children. Some housed their classrooms in temporary modular buildings, while others used large multipurpose rooms, such as a fellowship hall or gymnasium (which could be subdivided by means of folding walls or movable partitions), or the chapel (generally reserved for adult classes). Megachurches with Sunday school enrollments in the thousands built educational wings or separate, multistory educational buildings.[6]

Besides Sunday schools, some megachurches operated so-called Christian Academies or Christian Schools, some of which offered only preschool and/or elementary education, others kindergarten through twelfth grade. They enrolled anywhere from 150 to more than 1,000 students, and their facilities varied from a few rooms in a wing of the church's main building to classrooms in a separate building. Bible institutes, Bible colleges, and/or seminaries operated at some of the larger megachurches.

Late-twentieth-century megachurches also expanded their social and recreational programs beyond those of earlier evangelical churches. Concert series opened the sanctuary to the general public for the purpose of entertainment. Since most megachurches charged admission, concerts were a way of raising revenue for the church, but their main purposes were to foster good relations with the larger community and to attract hundreds, even thousands, of persons who would not otherwise come to the church. The Apostolic Church of God presented free concerts featuring talented local singers and musicians as well as nationally known artists and orchestras, while Elmbrook Church hosted concerts by the Milwaukee Symphony Orchestra. The ten-thousand-seat auditorium of Carpenter's Home Church was specifically designed for concerts and dramatic productions, as well as conferences, and the church regularly rented it for "special events" featuring talented artists and gifted speakers. Coral Ridge Presbyterian Church sponsored one of the longest-running concert series, which began in the 1970s and featured a wide range of music, everything from classical to pop and country, and from gospel to contemporary Christian music. In the 1980s it averaged some two thousand persons per concert.[7]

Although comparatively few megachurches offered concert series, pageants celebrating secular or religious holidays became a staple of megachurch entertainment and evangelism in the 1980s and 1990s. Some megachurches charged admission, but most did not. The pageants were considered an investment in evangelism, and megachurch pastors claimed they brought a hefty return—in the scores of people won for the Lord. A Bellevue Baptist Church bulletin credited its annual musical pageants with 77,267 decisions for Christ over a twenty-five-year period.[8]

The themes varied. Fourth of July pageants featuring music and fireworks blended patriotism and religion. Explicitly religious pageants were even more prevalent. Robert Schuller's church began staging "The Glory of Christmas" in 1980. A few years later Tommy Barnett, senior pastor of Phoenix First Assembly of God, became famous for his church's annual Easter and Christmas pageants. Although some people criticized Barnett for his emphasis on the spectacular, he justified it as an evangelistic tool. "It gets their attention," he retorted. "People will come to see a pageant who won't come to church." By the 1990s both the Crystal Cathedral and Phoenix First were presenting multiple performances, drawing thousands of spectators, and inspiring other megachurches, black as well as white, to follow their example. In 1995, Brentwood Baptist Church produced an Afrocentric Christmas pageant, "Black Nativity," a gospel song-play by Langston Hughes. Pastor Joe Samuel Ratliff described it as "reminiscent of one of the most significant events of our faith and also reflective of the rich and vibrant African American Heritage that is ours."[9]

These were technically sophisticated, professional-caliber, multimedia productions that would have been impossible without the financial resources and the numerous staff and volunteers megachurches commanded, and, even more important, their large auditoriums and "high-tech" sound and lighting equipment. Barnett's Easter pageant of 1996 included a theatrical reenactment of Jesus' crucifixion and ascension, flying angels, a laser-light show, and a multicolored "dancing" fountain of water. A cast of five hundred performed in the Southeast Christian Church Easter pageant. The stage set was two hundred feet wide, with towers almost three stories high rising up into the balcony area, as well as a "mountain" from which Jesus delivered the Sermon on the Mount (and which rotated to display the manger scene in Bethlehem and the tomb where Jesus was buried).[10]

Besides using their auditoriums for concerts and pageants, megachurches provided other spaces for socializing and entertainment. These were mainly for members of the church rather than the larger community. "Food and fellowship" facilities—like the atrium and "food court" at Willow Creek Community Church—were especially popular. They were touted as an innovation in church architecture, but in fact, they were not altogether new. During the late nineteenth and early twentieth century, in both white and African American urban churches, luncheons, teas, suppers, and banquets, as well as other kinds of socializing, occupied a prominent place in the church schedule, and "parlors," "social halls," "dining rooms," and kitchens were regarded as indispensable. In early pentecostal, holiness, and fundamentalist churches such facilities were less common, but they were not totally absent; the Chicago Gospel Tabernacle and the Baptist Tabernacle in Atlanta had restaurants, and the Mason Temple complex included a large dining hall and kitchen.

The megachurch dining halls and fellowship centers (also called dining rooms, fellowship halls or banquet centers) often combined the functions of the earlier social halls and dining rooms. Some were simply large, open rooms into which chairs and/or tables could be moved; others were more elaborately furnished and equipped. They were used for a wide range of meetings and gatherings: "family nights," businessmen's and women's luncheons, singles group meetings, even dinner theaters. The fellowship hall at Coral Ridge Presbyterian Church accommodated 1,000 persons; at First Baptist Church, Jacksonville, 1,200; at Roswell Street Baptist Church, up to 1,500. When Southeast Christian Church opened its new facility in December 1998, it boasted what was probably the largest fellowship hall ever built by any megachurch in the United States. The main room, on the second floor of the worship center building, seated 1,000 persons for dinner, or 1,400 in chairs arranged for an audience. Another room, on the first floor, accommodated 1,000 and had partitions that could be used to divide the space into as many as six different areas. Each of the two rooms had a stage. On the second floor were also a large kitchen to provide food service, multiple serving counters and drink stations designed to speed guests through the food lines, and an elevator to deliver food to the floor below for overflow crowds.[11]

In addition to dining and fellowship halls, a few megachurches had restaurants or snack bars. In the early 1980s, First Baptist Church of Houston opened its Garden of Eatin' restaurant, and Second Baptist Church of Houston soon followed suit with a snack bar/restaurant called the Second Helping, offering "a healthy lunch or dinner for all of our church family and their guests in a Christian atmosphere." Adjoining it was the Terrace Room, which provided additional restaurant seating and could also be used for fellowship and meetings. First Baptist Church of Dallas also had a restaurant.[12]

The snack bar at the Cathedral of the Holy Spirit was located in the John Garlington Mall (Plate 48). Originally intended as a "Christian shopping mall," the facility featured an "atrium" decorated with large "landscape murals" painted by members of the church's "Artists Guild" and furnished with a fountain, a piano, plants, street lamps, and tables and chairs. The mall also housed the Cathedral Shoppe (a gift shop), a tape library, and various church offices.[13]

Being a full service megachurch entailed offering varied recreational programs—for adults as well as children and youths—and extensive indoor and outdoor facilities in which to enjoy them. Late-twentieth-century megachurches put much more emphasis on recreation than their predecessors. A growing recognition of the church's responsibility to "the whole person" and the so-called leisure revolution following World War II prompted many evangelicals, especially Southern Baptists, to expand their recreation programs, hiring staff members to supervise them, targeting adults as well as children and youth/teens, and expending millions of dollars on facilities. Fundamentalists and pentecostals lagged behind other evangelicals in this regard.[14] Stephen Strader of Carpenter's

Home Church remembered that in the 1970s, when his church was located in downtown Lakeland, it purchased a Pepsi Cola bottling building and a bowling alley next door to use for a gymnasium and a fellowship hall. Some of the brethren thought having a gym was "extremely carnal," he said. He explained that traditionally, "the Assemblies of God . . . focused on church. The Baptists have been way ahead of us in building fellowship halls, gymnasiums and the like." Strader's church was only the second Assemblies of God church in Florida to have a gymnasium.

Organized sports and a myriad of athletic activities constituted the largest element of most megachurch recreational programs. Megachurches sponsored sports leagues and teams for all ages, and their large campuses made it possible to provide indoor courts and outdoor playing fields (lighted for use in the evening) for team practice and home games. At some megachurches the recreational facilities were fairly rudimentary, and those of black megachurches were generally less extensive than those of white megachurches. But virtually all of the megachurches in our sample had at least a gymnasium with one or two basketball/volleyball courts.

Like North Phoenix Baptist Church (Plate 49), some megachurches built separate structures for their recreational programs, variously known as family life centers, Christian life centers, or, simply, sports and fitness centers. At Second Baptist Church of Houston the Family Life Center was an integral part of the new worship center dedicated in 1986. It housed four racquetball courts and two full-size basketball/

volleyball courts; an eight-lane bowling alley, a walking/jogging/running track, an aerobics room, and an exercise/weight room. Both the men's and women's locker rooms featured a lounge area, wooden lockers, a dry sauna, a steam room, a whirlpool, and showers. A 175-seat theater in the center served as a "movie/video showplace" for screening 16mm and VCR movies and live television events on a regularly scheduled basis. A "game room" offered table tennis, foosball, table shuffleboard, pool, snooker, and bumper pool; a "crafts room" served as a center for ceramics, painting, photography, calligraphy, quilting, woodworking, and stained glass.[15]

The Sports and Fitness Center at Prestonwood Baptist Church was designed as a multipurpose structure. It had six large classrooms and open assembly space for Bible study. In addition there were three basketball courts (two with regulation wood floors, one with a regulation synthetic floor) with dividers to enable six half-court games to be played simultaneously; volleyball and rollerblade hockey facilities; an exercise room with equipment for up to thirty people; and a grill and snack area.[16]

Virtually all megachurches, black as well as white, regarded their recreational programs and facilities as tools of evangelism. The leaders of Prestonwood Baptist Church expressed the prevailing view in an article on the Sports and Fitness Center the church planned to build. They estimated that during its first three years, it would draw a total of 21,005 participants, many of whom would be guests or visitors to the church rather than members. "Through sports and fitness, we will reach out to those around us with the message of salvation in Jesus Christ," they declared. When Southeast Christian Church dedicated its Activities Center, the activities minister reminded those attending the ceremony of the purpose of the facility: "We want to introduce people to the body of Christ."[17]

Unlike educational, social, and recreational programs, the megachurches' "institutional" or community service programs—often called "outreach ministries"—did not require many special or very extensive facilities on the church campus. Megachurches often leased or owned buildings off-campus for such purposes. Of course, whether located on the campus or in the larger community, the community service facilities were as much a part of late-twentieth-century megachurch architecture, broadly interpreted, as were the educational buildings, fellowship halls, family life centers, and other structures or spaces discussed thus far.

In general, the community service programs targeted a constituency very different from those persons who attended the megachurch concert series and pageants or used their social and recreational facilities. In the words of the Vineyard Christian Fellowship mission statement, they mainly served "lost, broken, poor people, who need the resources that God has freely given the church." Most megachurches operated "food pantries" and "clothes closets" for the needy, with designations that reflected the evangelical penchant for religious-sounding names such as "God's Provisions" at The Valley Cathedral and "Joseph's Storehouse" at the Cathedral of the Holy Spirit. West Angeles Church of God in Christ sponsored a Skid Row ministry that served two thousand meals a week. The Family Outreach and Resource Center of Ebenezer African Methodist Episcopal Church, headquartered on the grounds of its former church building, a short distance away from the church campus, distributed food and clothing, in addition to offering substance-abuse counseling and other programs.[18]

The Vineyard church operated an extensive on-site ministry in a former Rockwell Laboratory warehouse renamed the Benevolence Warehouse and Community Room. At noon every Sunday following the worship service, church members served Lamb's Lunch to as many as three hundred to four hundred "guests" in the Community Room. Afterwards there was a "short bilingual service that include[d] worship, teaching with drama, [and] ministry," followed by a distribution of groceries or clothing at the Benevolence Warehouse. The predominantly black New Birth Missionary Baptist Church in Decatur, Georgia, offered similar services to the homeless and the families of prison inmates, and also sponsored a transitional home for battered women and their children. Brentwood Baptist Church built a four-unit cottage that provided temporary housing for individuals suffering from HIV/AIDS. Other megachurch community service ministries included drug and alcohol abuse counseling facilities, pregnancy support centers, and homes for unwed mothers, usually located away from the church campuses in facilities owned or leased by the church.[19]

All of the community service facilities discussed so far exhibited a strong evangelistic orientation. Whatever the service rendered—information, counseling, residential treatment, clothing, groceries, even a single meal—it was accompanied by a religious message transmitted during organized worship or individual witnessing. Soul-winning was the overriding aim. So-called economic development projects, preeminently the work of black megachurches, had a different objective: revitalizing the surrounding community by building nursing homes, senior citizen centers, restaurants, shopping centers, and especially residential housing. Some of the megachurches established their own economic development corporations, while others cooperated with civic agencies or local or national interdenominational organizations.[20]

Bishop Arthur Brazier of the Apostolic Church of God served as chairman of the board of two economic development corporations: the Woodlawn Preservation and Investment Corporation, which was involved in the rehabilitation of 300 apartments and the new construction of 330 homes in the Woodlawn neighborhood; and the Fund for Community Redevelopment and Revitalization, which undertook the rebuilding of both Woodlawn and the North Kenwood/Oakland area. Of the several black megachurches in the New York metropolitan area that sponsored economic development projects, probably the best known was the Allen African Methodist Episcopal Church, in Jamaica, New York, pastored by Rev. Floyd Flake. It built a 300-unit housing complex for senior citizens and more than 100 single-family homes, and also transformed a row of deteriorating stores into a modernized strip mall. Neighborhood renewal plans initiated by two black megachurches in Houston produced community facilities other than housing and shopping centers. The 7,300-member Windsor Village United Methodist Church sponsored a Power Center, which included a school, a bank, and a health clinic, as well as a $1 million chapel donated by former heavyweight champion Evander Holyfield. In 1996, the 10,000-member St. Agnes Baptist Church began building a neighborhood complex on a 131-acre tract in southeast Houston, the site of its former church building. Softball fields, a golf driving range, and picnic grounds were completed by August, and the church was about to begin converting the former sanctuary into a business development center to encourage aspiring entrepreneurs. The objective of the St. Agnes project was not just economic development and empowerment. Pastor Gene Moore, Sr., described it as a way of gaining control over the social environment. "We are building our own city right out here," he declared. "We will develop as much as God will let us develop. That way you can control your environment. Until a community controls its environment, you are not going to keep drugs and crime out."[21]

Significantly, whereas most of the community service programs and facilities sponsored by black megachurches emphasized evangelism, the economic development projects exhibited more of a social gospel orientation. Their goal was community revitalization rather than individual regeneration. Bishop Brazier voiced the rationale that undergirded the community renewal efforts of the Apostolic Church of God, and probably most other black megachurches: "We have to recognize that as Christians we have a civic responsibility. We have to do things for the betterment of our community, but that may not directly relate to converting people to Christ." Citing projects sponsored by the Woodlawn Preservation and Investment Corporation and the Fund for Community Redevelopment and Revitalization, he declared, "Our efforts as a church are made because it is our civic responsibility, not because of any concern as to whether anyone is going to become a member of this church."[22]

Besides evangelism and community service, one other purpose of the megachurch full service programs and facilities merits consideration—fostering a sense of community among the members of the church. This was important because many evangelicals viewed the larger community and culture outside the church as alien, even threatening.

White evangelicals, especially, regarded themselves as a beleaguered minority in the United States. "The church today has become a sub-culture," declared Nelson Price, the pastor of Roswell Street Baptist Church. "We can fulfill our role as salt and light, but it is no longer the dominant influence it once was. The enemy's now on our shores in the form of materialism, secular humanism, new age philosophy and homosexual activism." Like Price, other megachurch pastors regularly inveighed against the "very non-Christian, and of-ten anti-Christian, secularistic culture" that seemed to pervade American society. Social problems such as crime, drugs, racial tension, and school shootings also fed evangelicals' anxieties.[23]

In an ocean of secularism, the full service white megachurch served, in the words of the senior pastor of Second Baptist, Houston, as an "island" to which the entire family could "retreat" for education, fellowship, and recreation. Few white megachurches aspired to the kind of comprehensive, cradle-to-grave community Walt Kallestad envisioned, but most offered programs and facilities sufficient to meet virtually all the educational, social, and recreational needs and desires of their members, filling most of their after-work hours and weekends. Megachurch members could have their children cared for or educated in church-operated nurseries, day-care centers, or schools that promised a "Christ-centered, loving environment." Eschewing purely secular amusements, they could find uplift as well as entertainment at megachurch concerts or enjoy the Bible-based pageantry of the annual Easter or Christmas production. In their workplaces and residential subdivisions, they encountered constant reminders of their minority status, but at lunch in the megachurch restaurant or "food court," or attending "family night" in the fellowship hall, they could socialize with people whose lifestyle and values (not to mention religious faith) matched their own. Not least among the attractions of the full service megachurch was the "Christian environment" it provided "for recreation and relaxation."[24]

To the extent that they facilitated church members' retreat from an outside world they regarded with apprehension, these "island" communities encouraged what one critic called an "inward-turning, country club atmosphere" and another termed a kind of "Christian cocooning." They seemed more like "lifestyle enclaves" than true Christian communities. Even some evangelicals recognized the danger. In a sermon entitled "Enclaves and Community," the pastor of Mariners Church warned his congregation against becoming an isolated, self-centered enclave, "a little private gated community." Jesus, he reminded them, "tears down walls between you and between you and the community."[25] Community outreach services sponsored by white evangelical megachurches did take members out of their enclaves into the larger community, but only temporarily—and the evangelistic motive that inspired such services reflected the same saved/unregenerate dichotomy that influenced their retreat from "the world."

African Americans also experienced a strong sense of community as members of black megachurches, and like white evangelicals, many of them regarded the megachurch as a retreat. Indeed, the black church had long served as "a refuge in a hostile white world." In the late twentieth century, the civil rights revolution notwithstanding, persistent racism, discrimination, and de facto segregation ensured that it would continue to do so. For African Americans living in impoverished neighborhoods like Woodlawn, megachurches such as the Apostolic Church of God offered a haven from poverty, unemployment, prostitution, drugs, and gangs. For middle-

class African Americans who had "made it" and moved to the white suburbs, megachurches such as Ebenezer A.M.E. Church, Oak Cliff Bible Fellowship, and St. Luke "Community" United Methodist Church provided an opportunity to reconnect with the black community, to discover their African American heritage (and introduce it to their children), perhaps even to help revitalize inner-city black neighborhoods.[26]

Even so, black megachurches were much less likely than white megachurches to function as lifestyle enclaves. This was partly because African American congregations tended to be more heterogeneous than white congregations in terms of income, education, and social status. In addition, as Robert M. Franklin has pointed out, rather than encouraging retreat from the larger community, African American congregations empowered members to minister to it. Black megachurch members' sense of racial and community solidarity also tempered the us-them mentality characteristic of late-twentieth-century evangelical religion. Equally important, the legacy of the black church focused attention on the needs and problems of the surrounding community. Historically, the black church had served as "the spiritual, emotional, cultural, political, educational, economic, and intellectual center of the community," and many black megachurches assumed that role.[27] If the white megachurch functioned for many of its members as a kind of oasis, the black megachurch constituted more of a fountainhead, the source of economic, social, and spiritual renewal in the community at large as well as in the congregational community.

As the church growth experts anticipated, the "multiple entry points" or "side doors" of the full service megachurch have brought us to the worship center. Notwithstanding the attention evangelicals devoted to expanding the megachurches' educational, social, recreational, and community service programs, they considered worship paramount. So, too, the space provided for worship constituted the focal point, and perhaps the most revealing component, of megachurch architecture.

10

The Worship Center

Praise ye the Lord. Praise God in his sanctuary. . . .
Praise him with the sound of the trumpet: praise him
with the psaltery and harp. Praise him with the tim-
brel and dance: praise him with stringed instruments
and organs. Praise him upon the loud cymbals: praise
him upon the high sounding cymbals. Let everything
that has breath praise the Lord. Praise the Lord.
—Psalm 150:1, 3–6

In most late-twentieth-century megachurches, one ap-
proached the auditorium—or worship center, as it was generally called—through a lobby or atrium. The main purpose
of this entranceway was to encourage fellowship. On weekdays and evenings, it provided church members an opportunity to meet and converse. Before and after worship services,
it allowed visitors and members to gather for conversation,
exchange greetings with the pastors and staff, or sign up at
one of the ministry tables for church-sponsored activities.
Lobbies and atriums also served as reception areas or welcome centers. Ever mindful of their commitment to evangelism, megachurch builders used them to make a positive impression on visitors. In most cases, the lobby was the first area
visitors encountered upon entering the church structure, and
as Southeast Christian's guest services coordinator observed,
"the first impressions we make on people often determines
[sic] whether they will return a second time."[1]

At some California megachurches, outdoor patios served

the same purpose as the lobbies and atriums found in most other megachurches. Before and after worship services at Saddleback Church, members and visitors gathered on the main patio alongside the front of the worship center. Palm trees and other plantings and a few concrete benches created a pleasant setting, and a "ministry canopy" sheltered tables that provided information about the various ministries sponsored by the church. Mariners Church also held before-and-after-worship activities on its patio. The church auditorium had a large foyer, but members preferred the outdoor area. Indeed, when Mariners first moved to its new location, it reduced the number of Sunday worship services from three to two in order to allow more time for "the patio experience." (The longer interval between services also facilitated parking.) "We promote a lot of just hanging out on the patio," observed Jan Lynn.

The style and decor of megachurch lobbies and atriums varied almost as much as the megachurch exteriors. The Faith Community Church "concourse," as it was called, was a long, wide corridor that led to the auditorium and other areas of the church building (Plate 50). Except for the information table just inside the main entrance and the banners hanging from the roof trusses, it was quite barren. By contrast, the lobbies of Coral Ridge Presbyterian Church and First Baptist Church, Raytown (Plate 51) featured faceted or stained-glass windows and Scripture verses on the walls. The inscription over the main door of the Coral Ridge lobby, "Go ye into all the world," reminded members of their evangelistic duty. At First Baptist, Raytown, the biblical message read, "I was glad when they said unto me, Let us go into the house of the Lord. Psalm 122:1."

Just as some megachurch exteriors drew inspiration from commercial or corporate architecture, some megachurch lobbies resembled those of secular buildings. The plush-carpeted lobby of First Baptist, Houston (Plate 52), with its ultramodern seating arrangements, suited the corporate style of the church exterior. Dauphin Way Baptist Church, Covenant Church, and Oak Cliff Bible Fellowship (Plate 53) imitated the decor of a formal hotel lobby, with a marble floor and chandelier, as well as occasional furniture, framed art on the walls, and a very large artificial flower arrangement on a table in the middle of the floor. The minimalist style of the Apostolic Church of God lobby suggested a movie theater (Plate 54).

The shopping mall inspired the reception area of the Midwest Christian Center (Plate 55). An information booth stood just inside the main entrance to the church at the beginning of a corridor referred to as "the mall." Decorated with lampposts and greenery, the corridor accessed children's rooms on either side and ended in a lobby adjacent to the auditorium, where a bookstore called The Word Shoppe was located. Dominating the lobby was a huge sculpture entitled *The Rapture*. Vineyard Christian Fellowship combined reception facilities and informal seating areas in such a way as to suggest a convention center lobby (Plate 56). A sculpture entitled *The Divine Servant*, depicting Jesus washing Peter's feet, alleviated the rather stark expanse of the lobby and added a religious note to an otherwise neutral space.

Plate 35. West Angeles Church of God in Christ, Los Angeles (1987).

Plate 36. Roswell Street Baptist Church, Marietta, Georgia; former auditorium (1958) on the right, current auditorium (1979) on the left.

Plate 37. Dauphin Way Baptist Church, Mobile, Alabama (1988).

Plate 38. First Baptist Church, Raytown, Missouri (1999).

Plate 39. Bellevue Baptist Church, Cordova, Tennessee (1989).

Plate 40. Cathedral of the Holy Spirit, Decatur, Georgia (1991).

Plate 41. Covenant Church, Carrollton, Texas (1995).

Plate 42. Coral Ridge Presbyterian Church, Fort Lauderdale, Florida (1973, 1990).

Plate 43. Calvary Assembly of God, Winter Park, Florida (1985).

Plate 44. Patio, Mariners Church, Irvine, California (1996).

Plate 45. Promiseland play area, Willow Creek Community Church, South Barrington, Illinois (1992).

Plate 46. Seven Days of Creation, Fellowship Church, Grapevine, Texas (1998).

Plate 47. Small World Village, Phoenix First Assembly of God, Phoenix (2000).

Plate 48. John Garlington Mall, Cathedral of the Holy Spirit, Decatur, Georgia (1991).

Plate 49. Family Life Center, North Phoenix Baptist Church, Phoenix (1986).

Plate 50. Concourse, Faith Community Church, West Covina, California (1998).

Plate 51. Lobby, First Baptist Church,
Raytown, Missouri (1999).

Plate 52. Lobby, First Baptist Church, Houston (1977).

Plate 53. Lobby, Oak Cliff Bible Fellowship, Dallas (1995).

Plate 54. Lobby, Apostolic Church of God, Chicago (1992).

Plate 55. The mall, Midwest Christian Center, Tinley Park, Illinois (1989).

Plate 56. Lobby, Vineyard Christian Fellowship, Anaheim, California (1991).

Plate 57. Atrium, Second Baptist Church, Houston (1986).

Plate 58. Atrium, Prestonwood
Baptist Church, Plano, Texas (1999).

Plate 59. Atrium, Southeast Christian Church, Louisville (1998), by permission of Southeast Christian Church.

Plate 60. Auditorium, Carpenter's Home Church, Lakeland, Florida (1985).

Plate 61. Auditorium, Second Baptist Church, Houston (1986).

Plate 62. Auditorium, Fellowship Church, Grapevine, Texas (1998).

Plate 63. Auditorium, Oak Cliff Bible Fellowship, Dallas (1995).

Plate 64. Auditorium, Southeast Christian Church, Louisville (1998), by permission of Southeast Christian Church.

Plate 65. Auditorium, First Baptist Church, Houston (1977).

Plate 66. Auditorium, Elmbrook Church, Brookfield, Wisconsin (1994).

Their great scale distinguished the multistory atriums of Second Baptist Church, Houston, Prestonwood Baptist Church, and Southeast Christian Church from the lobbies of other megachurches. In addition to a visitor information counter, the Second Baptist atrium offered an informal seating area that included park benches, abundant greenery, lampposts, and a fountain (Plate 57). The Prestonwood atrium, with exposed trusses evoking the groining of a Gothic church, extended across the front of the main building. Besides providing access to the worship center, it also served as a welcome center and a temporary fellowship hall (Plate 58). A circular welcome center (twenty-four feet in diameter) dominated the Southeast Christian atrium (Plate 59). Along the rear wall stretched a forty-eight-foot registration counter where people could sign up for special events or the various ministries offered by the church. At the west end were stairs, escalators, and elevators accessing the upper levels of the worship center; at the east end, to the right of the welcome center, were chairs, end tables, and lamps arranged to form a casual seating area. Various types of greenery and floral arrangements decorated the atrium, including artificial fig and olive trees around the welcome center, specially chosen for their "biblical connections."[2]

In designing the worship centers, megachurch builders borrowed features from both the mainline and dissenting evangelicals. In size the worship centers more closely resembled the tabernacles and temples of the dissenters than the auditorium churches built by mainline evangelicals. As noted in chapter 8, the late-twentieth-century worship centers boasted, on average, about twice the seating capacity of the late-nineteenth-, early-twentieth-century urban auditorium churches. Their larger memberships and worship attendance, as well as their emphasis on evangelism, demanded the greater capacity; and improvements in building technology made it possible. Especially important was the ability to construct large balconies and roofs capable of spanning huge spaces without relying on supporting columns inside the auditorium that would have blocked the view of the platform. Recall that the circular auditorium of Robert Mills's Sansom Street Church in Philadelphia, built in 1812, measured only ninety feet. By contrast, the wall-to-wall roof span of the Southeast Christian Worship Center extended nearly three hundred feet, and the inside measurement of the Carpenter's Home Church auditorium (Plate 60) was 308 feet. The geodesic dome made it possible for the Crenshaw Christian Center to span an even larger space; the FaithDome had an inside diameter of 320 feet.[3]

The shape of the worship centers varied, influenced partly by the taste and theology of the builders and partly by the exterior form of the building and the shape of its roof. Although some megachurch auditoriums were rectangular or square, most were wedge-shaped or semicircular.[4] Their antecedents were Moody Memorial Church and the Angelus Temple, circular or nearly circular structures. Most megachurch worship centers also resembled those two churches in having stairs leading down from the balcony to the platform area (Plate 61) to enable individuals to respond to the invitation or altar call, which was a standard practice in most late-twentieth-century evangelical megachurches.

From the auditorium churches megachurch builders borrowed amphitheater-style or graded seating in pews or theater seats. Such an arrangement ensured that every seat would be "a good one," the Southeast Christian architect maintained. He and other megachurch builders took pride in what they regarded as optimum sight lines in the worship centers. At Southeast Christian, for example, a person sitting in the first balcony in the seat furthest from the pulpit was 128 feet away; in the upper balcony, 145 feet. In the auditorium of First Baptist, Jacksonville, the sight lines were 143 feet on the first floor, slightly more in the balconies. The Cathedral of the Holy Spirit claimed that the sight lines in its auditorium (slightly less than 150 feet) put "most of the congregation within the reach of eye contact of the speaker." Of course these three churches ranked among the largest of the megachurches. Smaller worship centers had better sight lines. In the Elmbrook Church auditorium, no one sat more than 104 feet from the pulpit; in the Roswell Street Baptist Church worship center, no seat was more than 100 feet away.[5] These sight lines were not as good as those in most of the late-nineteenth-, early-twentieth-century auditorium churches, but given the greater size and seating capacity of the megachurches, they were the best the builders could achieve. No doubt they seemed quite acceptable to late-twentieth-century churchgoers accustomed to huge superdomes or stadiums and large civic auditoriums.

Megachurch builders modified some of the components they borrowed from earlier evangelical structures, such as the platform area and the preaching desk, to accommodate changes in evangelical worship practices that occurred during the second half of the twentieth century. The changes were partly an outgrowth of the church growth strategy and partly a result of a worship renewal movement. Much of the criticism the church growth experts aimed at the "traditional church" pertained to its worship service. They contended that it had little appeal for the "'sight-sound-sensation' generations"—young adults born between the late 1960s and early 1980s and "reared in a culture that placed a far greater emphasis on visual communication, on music, on sensations, and on feelings" than did the culture of their parents. To reach them the experts recommended worship forms and practices that were "simple," "up-beat," "user-friendly," "from the heart," "informal," "participatory," multimedia, even "multi-sensory."[6]

As if in response to their urgings came a grassroots worship revitalization movement led by Jesus People and neo-pentecostals. The Jesus People introduced a worship style characterized by expressiveness, spontaneity, and emotionalism. Neo-pentecostals added an emphasis on the work of the Holy Spirit during corporate worship, engaging in such practices as glossolalia (speaking in tongues), raising arms, clapping hands, "dancing in the Spirit," and uttering "sacred expletives" such as "Hallelujah!" "Glory to God!" and "Thank you Jesus!" Both groups regarded "Spirit-filled" worship as a way of facilitating and expressing worshipers' experience of the immediate, felt presence of God. Music, rather than the spoken or printed word, became the principal medium of worship. And the music was different—not traditional hymns and gospel songs, but contemporary Christian music (Christian rock and so-called praise and worship music produced by Maranatha! Music, the Vineyard Music Group, Integrity, Bill and Gloria Gaither, and others). Indeed, the new music became the main conduit for the influence the worship revitalization movement exerted on mainstream evangelical churches.[7]

Most late-twentieth-century megachurches used what came to be known as contemporary Christian worship in one or more of their worship services. Not surprisingly, it became the principal mode of worship in seeker, seeker-sensitive, and seeker-oriented churches. Most other megachurches offered a "blended worship service," which combined traditional elements such as hymns and Scripture reading with contemporary elements such as praise and worship.[8]

The main components of a contemporary or "blended" worship service were preaching and music. Whereas earlier evangelical congregations viewed the preaching of the Word as the focal point of the worship service, most predominantly white megachurches allotted it less time. At the Community of Joy and Second Baptist Church, Houston, the sermon (or "message," as it was called) lasted only fifteen to twenty minutes; at Elmbrook Church and Willow Creek Community Church, thirty to thirty-five minutes. In black megachurches, however, preaching continued to be regarded as the highlight of the worship service. Frederick Price's sermons in the Crenshaw Christian Center FaithDome were about an hour long.[9]

Music dominated the contemporary and "blended" worship services in both white and black megachurches. John D. Witvliet described contemporary Christian music as sounding like "commercial, popular music"—repetitive, "fast-paced," and using "simple harmonic structures." The texts were based on "scriptural hymns of praise" and "narratives of religious experience." The language of the songs was "vernacular, even colloquial, in style, diction, and form."[10]

The praise and worship segment of the contemporary music program lasted twenty to forty minutes. Led by a "praise team" or "praise band," members of the congregation sang choruses. They did not use hymnals; the words were displayed on large video screens on either side of or above the platform. While singing together, many congregants offered individual expressions of praise by clapping hands or swaying to the music, raising one or both arms to heaven, and, in pentecostal churches, shaking tambourines, speaking in tongues, even "praise dancing" in the aisles or in the space in front of the platform.[11] Besides the praise and worship segment, the contemporary Christian worship service in most late-twentieth-century megachurches featured several musical selections by one or more of the following: the choir and/or orchestra, a "praise band," various vocal and instrumental ensembles, and individual artists.

With so much of the worship service space dedicated to performance, and to different kinds of performance, megachurch builders decided that the traditional auditorium church platform had become outmoded. They needed more space. Not so much for preaching, since many of the younger, more urbane megachurch pastors disdained the platform-strutting, Bible-thumping style popularized by some older preachers, but for the large choirs and orchestras that performed during the musical segment of the worship service. They also needed a more flexible, multipurpose space to accommodate everything from preaching to rock bands and "worship teams," dramatic skits, pageants, concerts, and pastors' conferences.

In enlarging the platform, megachurch builders borrowed architectural forms from the theater, just as the builders of the nineteenth- and early-twentieth-century auditorium churches had done. In some cases they modeled the platform area on the proscenium stage, using a curtain or curtains, rather than a proscenium arch, to define the performance space and focus attention on the platform. Willow Creek Community Church, Calvary Church, Fellowship Church, Valley Cathedral, and Phoenix First Assembly of God all based the design of the platform area on the proscenium stage or on a modified form of it that featured steps from the platform to the auditorium floor. If the church had a choir, it was seated in a loft at the back of the stage or stood on movable risers. The curtain could be drawn back or lifted to display the choir and other performing groups or artists, or the setting for a dramatic skit, and then closed to form a backdrop for the preaching event on the forestage. Fellowship Church (Plate 62) added another theatrical element, used by little-theater groups in the United States and in experimental theaters such as the Royal Court Theatre in London, in the form of an exposed catwalk and lighting system above the stage and spotlights on the balcony railing.[12]

Another platform design developed by megachurch builders was an adaptation of the "thrust stage" (also referred to as the "open stage") that revolutionized theater design in Europe and North America. In Canada and the United States, the theaters designed by Tyrone Guthrie at Stratford, Ontario (1953) and Minneapolis, Minnesota (1963) provided the best-known examples.[13] A large number of megachurches appropriated this design, including Oak Cliff Bible Fellowship (Plate 63), Southeast Christian Church (Plate 64), First Baptist Church of Houston (Plate 65), and Elmbrook Church (Plate 66).

Unlike the platform in the auditorium churches and the proscenium stage in some late-twentieth-century megachurches, the thrust stage jutted out into the auditorium, and the seating curved around it in an arc of about 180 degrees. Thus it proved quite adaptable to both the amphitheater seating arrangement and the circular or polygon church buildings popular among megachurch builders. Moreover, it provided much more performance space, and more flexible space, than the traditional platform and even the proscenium stage offered. Elmbrook Church, which had an orchestra of thirty to forty persons, was able to remove part of the stage to create an orchestra pit when it presented large musical productions. At Southeast Christian Church the orchestra pit could be completely or partially covered with modules to make a flat platform area of varying size, or the modules could be removed to accommodate a forty- to fifty-piece orchestra. The church's worship minister observed that the design offered "much more flexibility and creativity in the placement of musicians, singers and drama."[14]

Beyond these advantages, another feature of the thrust stage attracted megachurch builders. In extolling the virtues of the new stage design, Guthrie had declared that "the dominant consideration is the great advance in the intimacy, the fact that by bending the rows and getting them round an open stage you can get so many people close to the actors." Because the audience was "so arranged that spectators can see one another around, and beyond, the more brightly lighted stage," the new design made theater-going "a sociable, a shared experience." Like Guthrie, megachurch builders sought to create a sense of togetherness or community—a sense of "intimacy" they called it—within the congregation and between it and the persons on the platform. In combination with amphitheater seating, a platform modeled on the thrust stage seemed an ideal way to achieve it, especially because megachurches borrowed not only the "thrust" of the open stage but also the steps leading up to it on all sides. The steps were thought to promote intimacy by enabling the preacher to maintain eye contact with the congregation while making his way from the platform to the auditorium floor. They were also said to minimize the "sense of separation" caused by the elevation of the platform, thereby making the preacher seem more accessible. Steps across the front of the platform also facilitated the invi-

tation: the preacher could walk down into the area in front of the platform to issue the call, and respondents could kneel or stand on the steps, or the platform itself, after coming forward.[15]

Guthrie had recommended the open stage theater as a way of combining "intimacy with capacity." The Tyrone Guthrie Theater, for example, held 1,400 persons, but no spectator was more than seventeen meters (about fifty-six feet) from the center of the stage. To preserve intimacy, Guthrie favored limiting seating capacity. Indeed, he criticized the Stratford, Ontario, theater, which seated 2,225 people, for being less intimate than he would have liked. And he heaped scorn on the "giant Concert Halls" with sixty-foot stages and seating for 3,500 persons that had been built in several large Canadian cities following World War II. In such an auditorium "the human being is completely lost," he complained. "An actor on that stage looks like a peanut. You can sit in the front row and the corner people in the same row are half an acre away in one direction and half an acre in the other direction. It is no sort of view."[16]

Megachurch builders, unwilling to sacrifice large seating capacity, sought other means of achieving intimacy. Along with the thrust stage, they adapted the huge video screens—also called Jumbotrons or I-Mag (image-magnification) Screens—commonly used for entertainment in large sports facilities and civic centers or for advertising, as in New York City's Times Square. Carpenter's Home Church (1985) was one of the first churches in the United States to use such technology, and the first to use two such large screens (twenty feet on the diagonal). Pastor Stephen Strader recalled that in the early 1980s, when he and his father were planning their new church, they got the idea for the video screens from a week-long seminar presented by Bill Gothard, an independent Baptist who headed a parachurch ministry that became very popular in the 1970s and 1980s. Attended by ten to fifteen thousand persons, the seminar used a huge video projection screen to present information. Gothard himself did not lead the seminar in person, but appeared on the giant screen—"so impressive and impactful," Strader remembered, "better than if he were live."[17]

By the 1990s video screens were ubiquitous in megachurch worship centers, usually located on one or both sides of the platform. They displayed the words of hymns and choruses, Scripture quotes, sermon outlines, computer-generated graphics, and church-produced videos, as well as images of the preacher or musical performers on the platform. Because of their great size (the two screens at Prestonwood Baptist Church measured 28.5 by 16 feet, for example), the video screens dominated the platform area. Some megachurches devised ways of concealing them when they were not being used. At the First Baptist Church in Raytown, Missouri, a stained-glass window above the baptistery divided in the middle, each portion retracting to reveal the video screen when it was needed. The builders of Southeast Christian Church preferred a more ostentatious display of the "leading-edge technology." Five fourteen-foot screens aimed at various segments of the balconies formed the exterior of the audio-video gondola suspended above the platform; a sixth twenty-foot screen, located behind the choir loft, could be made to descend when needed and disappear when not in use.[18]

Megachurch builders acclaimed the new technology as a way of ensuring that everyone in the congregation could see well what was taking place on the platform. It solved the problem of the peanut-sized preacher—the huge video screens made him or her look larger than life-size (Plate 67). Megachurch builders also contended that the screens created a sense of closeness or intimacy between the preacher and other persons on the platform and the worshipers in the audience. The editor of the *Southeast Outlook* explained that "image magnification enables every member of the congregation— even those in the second balcony—to see facial expressions of speakers. The eye is naturally drawn to the larger image." But while members of the audience might be able to see the facial expressions of the speaker, the speaker could not make eye contact with them—or see *their* facial expressions. Seeing the preacher on the video screen was like watching television. As Anthony Robinson noted, the churchgoer experienced the kind of "pseudo-intimacy" television offers: "though a million people may be watching the same program simultaneously, viewers feel as if they are being personally addressed."[19]

New types of preaching desks (or "pulpits," as megachurch builders called them) constituted another means of achieving an intimate, immediate relationship between the preacher and the congregation. Some megachurches continued to use a stationary preaching desk, which remained on the platform throughout the service. However, the new concept of the platform as a multipurpose space dictated a different sort of pulpit. Just as the platform became a stage for various kinds of performance, the pulpit became a piece of stage furniture, part of the set used during the preaching of the Word. It had to be movable. As a consequence, it became smaller and plainer— a perfect symbol of the diminished role of preaching in the worship service as compared with music.

Among the new-design pulpits were Plexiglas lecterns, which were used at Willow Creek Community Church, Southeast Christian Church, and Fellowship Church. The megachurch pastors who used them consciously exploited their symbolic meaning—not, of course, the diminished significance of preaching, but the different kind of authority assumed by the person standing behind the pulpit. Just as some of the younger megachurch pastors, hoping to appear more "user-friendly," preferred to be called by their first rather than their last name ("Pastor Bob" rather than "Reverend Russell," for example), they also preferred a preaching desk that was "less exalted, removed, or fortresslike." Using a pulpit just large enough to hold notes or a Bible, these megachurch pastors gave the impression of engaging in conversation with the congregation rather than lecturing them. The practice of moving from behind the pulpit and walking down the platform steps to get closer to the congregation conveyed a similar impression. The Southeast Christian worship minister explained his church's decision to use a Plexiglas pulpit as follows: "One reason we wanted a see-through pulpit is sort of symbolic," he observed. "That's the kind of Christian we're supposed to be—transparent. We wanted something simple and small, something that didn't present a barrier between the preacher and the congregation."[20]

To complement the new platform designs as well as the new forms of worship that had inspired them, megachurch builders installed elaborate lighting and sound systems so sophisticated they had to be operated by professional technicians. These systems reinforced the theatrical ambience of the megachurch. Lighting technicians and worship directors could manipulate the light in the worship center, using special effects to create whatever mood or atmosphere was required. The Prestonwood Church visitors' information sheet suggested the wide range of special effects the eight-hundred-plus theatrical lights could produce in its auditorium: "any color, brightness, moving, spot, stationary, or speciality light can be achieved."[21]

In an article on church architecture published in *Christianity Today* in 1998, Tim Stafford noted that "electronics are a fundamental part of new church buildings. . . . Even modest churches have sound systems that would outdo entire recording studios a generation back." Providing a good sound system for a megachurch proved challenging because some of its architectural features created acoustical difficulties. Very large, circular worship centers were especially problematic. While sound waves reflected "evenly and predictably off flat and angular surfaces," they reflected "wildly off curved surfaces," resulting in a "chaotic mix of original sounds and echoes." Moreover, each of the two main components of the worship service, music and speech, required a different acoustical environment. Music demanded hard, reflective surfaces, which were ill suited to the hearing of the spoken word. High-decibel contemporary Christian music, especially, required a certain kind of acoustical environment. Theater-style seating, as opposed to pews, posed yet another problem. When empty, the theater-style seats folded up, exposing their hard undersides, which caused echoes in the worship space. Pews that were cushioned and soft absorbed sound. Like the empty theater seats, windows also reflected sound. However, carpeting absorbed it and consequently diminished the quality of congregational singing. Tile or cement under the seats ensured a livelier room and more enjoyable congregational singing because the sound bounced off it.[22]

Southeast Christian Church boasted a "one-of-a-kind, custom-designed sound system" engineered to enhance both congregational and performed music, as well as preaching. The megachurch hired Michael Garrison Associates, based in Fresno, California (which had previously designed systems for Crenshaw Christian Center) to design and install all of the sound, as well as the lighting and video systems in the worship center. To eliminate the acoustical problems posed by the large, circular, reverberant worship space, the senior consultant with MGA, David Kennedy, persuaded architect David Miller to make two major changes. One was to lower the wor-

ship center ceiling and expand the size of the gondola, which reduced the room's cubic footage from three million to two million (without reducing floor space or seating capacity), thereby eliminating one-third of the reverberation. The other was to modify the cylindrical shape of the worship center by staggering the walls, the balcony face, and the seating sections. That reduced echoes that would have traveled back to the platform. Other structural changes included reducing the number of windows in the worship center, angling those that remained, and installing wall panel material in various places to absorb some reverberation.

MGA housed a major portion of the sound, lighting, and video equipment for the worship center in the gondola suspended from the ceiling over the platform. (Church members dubbed it "The Enterprise," after the *Star Trek* space ship.) In addition to the loudspeakers and amplifiers in the gondola, MGA placed more than three hundred other speakers throughout the worship center and installed two hundred thousand watts of amplifiers in six rooms encircling it. To produce the best acoustics for different types of sound, MGA created a computer-controlled system capable of altering the acoustic environment electronically, using digital processors. In effect, the Electronic Acoustic System, as it was called, could make the worship center sound smaller or larger. A reporter for the *Southeast Outlook* explained that the EAS worked "much like a home stereo system that has settings for stadium, nightclub, concert hall or studio sound. The system operator can choose to make the room sound smaller during a sermon, or 'enlarge' it to sound like a cathedral when the Worship Choir sings. Those settings, and many others in between, are preset in a computer, and can be changed with the push of a button." Worship minister Greg Allen pointed out the implications for congregational singing: "It will sound like you can hear yourself singing." Members of the congregation would be able to hear their own voices because "they will be miked and the sound will be fed back out into the sanctuary."[23]

Using stage designs and sound and lighting systems borrowed from the theater did not preclude retaining some or all of the elements of the traditional platform area. "Choirolatry" reigned in most late-twentieth-century megachurches as it had in the auditorium churches, and the "worship choirs" that performed during the weekend worship services were usually quite large, numbering one hundred persons or more. A number of megachurches had tiered choir lofts centrally located behind the preacher and facing the congregation. However, only a few retained the array of organ pipes once considered the sine qua non of an elegant auditorium church (Plate 68). A significant number of megachurches used electronic organs or synthesizers, which, of course, had no pipes.

The baptistery continued to be a prominent feature in most megachurches, because baptism was one of their most meaningful rituals. Like First Baptist, Jacksonville, some megachurches baptized new converts at almost every worship service. "Everything is focused on the preaching from the pulpit and the baptismal service," declared the construction administrator of the Jacksonville megachurch. Illuminating the bap-

tistery during the worship service (Plate 69) underscored the importance of the baptismal ceremony.

As did First Baptist, Jacksonville, most megachurches located the baptistery in the center of the back wall of the platform. Instead of the idealized River Jordan scenes commonly used in the auditorium churches, megachurch builders and pastors found other ways of ornamenting the baptismal tanks. At First Baptist Church in Houston, the baptistery featured "a representation of what the sky might have looked like when Jesus was baptized." The Resurrection Window over the baptistery at Second Baptist, Houston, exhibited images relating to the death and resurrection of Jesus. Roswell Street Baptist Church (Plate 70) and Dauphin Way Baptist Church framed their baptisteries with woodwork done in the neo-Georgian style. Like Prestonwood Baptist Church (Plate 71), several megachurches placed a stained-glass window above the baptistery. Others, like North Phoenix Baptist Church, presented the baptismal tank in a more naturalistic setting, surrounded by lush greenery and potted plants. However presented, the baptistery served as a symbolic reminder that all of the members of the church had "come into the body of Christ through baptism." And to render the baptismal ceremony meaningful to the congregation as a whole, not just to the new believers and their families, it was displayed on the large video screens. The "enhanced" baptismal ceremony became yet another way to promote a sense of intimacy and community in the megachurch congregation.[24]

The decor of most megachurch worship centers was less

elaborate than that of the auditorium church interiors. This was partly a function of the modernist, commercial aesthetic many megachurch builders adopted, and partly because wall-to-wall, multilevel seating left little space for decoration. On the Calvary Assembly of God worship center ceiling, a corona suggestive of the crown of thorns duplicated the outline of the stage below (Plate 72). In some megachurches, the baptistery and/or organ pipes were lavishly decorated. Other megachurches displayed some kind of religious symbolism, usually a large cross hanging over the platform or affixed to its back wall. Above the Southeast Christian platform, on either side of the video screen, were displayed images of a cross and a dove. In the Apostolic Church of God, doves and the words "Jesus Christ is Lord" were carved into the brick walls above the choir loft (Plate 73).

In 1994, Robert E. Webber, a widely respected authority on worship, observed that "free church people" (which included evangelicals), who had traditionally rejected the visual arts in worship, were "increasingly recognizing that the visual arts help the worshiper see what is otherwise hidden; that the visual arts therefore assist us in praising God; and that the visual arts provide a form of witness." As evidence of the change, Webber cited the greater attention paid to the liturgical furnishings of the worship center, such as the pulpit and the baptistery, and also to "secondary visuals that assist the function of worship such as stained glass windows, sculptures, crosses, paintings, banners, bulletin graphics, and audio visuals." In 1999, Davin Seay, writing in *Worship Leader,*

heralded a "Christian arts renaissance" among Protestants. "Now, on the cusp of the new millennium," he declared, "churches and congregations across the country and around the world are moving to reclaim their artistic birthright, rediscovering the potency of art as a means of proclamation, celebration and kinship with the Creator."[25]

As we saw in chapter 8, some megachurch builders incorporated the visual arts into the exterior design of their structures, using crosses, depictions of Jesus, and etched, stained or faceted glass windows to proclaim the identity and purpose of the church. In megachurch lobbies and worship centers the visual arts registered an even greater impact, in the form of banners, carved wood, paintings, murals, stained glass, and sculpture.

Megachurch builders generally used the visual arts to serve a didactic purpose—to communicate a religious message, not to induce an aesthetic experience or provide interesting architectural detail. Stained-glass windows generally taught a biblical message. Thus the three-hundred-foot band of stained glass installed above the main entrance of Prestonwood Baptist Church presented symbolic images of Christ as he appeared in the sixty-six books of the Bible (Plate 74). The stained-glass window above the baptistery of the Oak Cliff Bible Fellowship also used symbols (a crown, a red cross, and wings, among others) to depict biblical themes. In addition to the Resurrection Window over the baptistery, the worship center of Second Baptist Church, Houston, had a stained-glass window in the ceiling, lighted by the dome, which symbolized the Word of God, with a border of sixty-six "monograms" or "keys" representing each of the books of the Bible. The Revelation Window to the right of the Second Baptist platform (as viewed by the congregation) focused on "the many promises" revealed in the apocalyptic vision described in the book of Revelation (Plate 75).[26]

African American megachurches also employed the visual arts for a didactic purpose—to reinforce an Afrocentric approach to the Bible and black history. In a 2001 National Public Radio commentary, Robert M. Franklin, president of the Interdenominational Theological Center in Atlanta, pointed out that African American Protestant Christians, traditionally "people of the book who regard words as the ultimate vehicles of truth," were "now paying more attention to the evocative power of visual images and symbols." They were "insisting that church art inspire worshippers to remember and respect the sacred sacrifice of the nameless, faceless millions who gave so much to America and the world." As a result, black churches were not only presenting Jesus and other biblical personages as African American, "but the formerly taboo and offensive subject of slavery is finding its way into sacred art. Church artists are portraying the journey from Africa to the New World, the horrors of enslavement, and even organized resistance to slavery."[27]

Franklin observed that African Americans' interest in sacred art seemed particularly strong in black megachurches. The mural in Ebenezer A.M.E. Church, discussed in chapter 7, comes to mind. St. Luke "Community" United Methodist Church in Dallas made even more extensive use of the visual arts. Under the guidance of Rev. Zan Wesley Holmes, Jr., who became pastor in 1974, the church developed a distinct Afrocentric orientation. By 1993, St. Luke's membership having reached about thirty-five hundred, Holmes and his congregation decided to construct a $1.8 million addition to the original church building to house a new auditorium and various offices. Certain features of the auditorium (Plate 76), designed by architect Norcell Haywood of San Antonio, evoked phases of African American history. The triangular shape of the choir loft, for example, was intended to recall the Egyptian pyramids. In addition, fifty-three stained-glass windows designed by Laura Jean Lacy, a member of the congregation, celebrated African American heroes and heroines such as Martin Luther King, Jr., Malcolm X, Sojourner Truth, and Harriet Tubman, as well as ordinary blacks in various historical and geographical settings (Plate 77). "You can't stand in this sanctuary and not get in touch with your African-American heritage," Holmes declared.[28]

Like St. Luke's, Trinity United Church of Christ used visual art both to enhance the worship environment and to reinforce the church's Afrocentric orientation. In the early 1970s, when the Trinity congregation made what pastor Jeremiah Wright described as "a conscious decision to become a black church in the black community," a dramatic change in the worship service occurred. Prior to the 1971 decision, the church had followed what Wright called "a classic European (or New England Congregational) liturgical style." The new worship style incorporated African and African American as well as European elements, combining "the 'old-time religion' devotional services and prayer meetings with testimonies, public prayer, and congregational singing" and "songs from every imaginable quarter of the black experience, including spirituals, common meter, hymns, anthems, traditional gospel, and contemporary gospel." A church-sponsored dance ministry taught African and Caribbean dances to children and teenagers, who performed regularly during the worship services. On one Sunday of each month the one-hundred-voice Sanctuary Choir dressed in African clothing.[29]

The furnishings and ornamentation of the Trinity auditorium (Plate 78) also testified to the church's Afrocentric orientation. Kente cloth was used to cover the table in front of the preaching desk and for the curtain behind the choir loft. On either side of the platform were stained-glass windows, designed by Douglas Phillips and completed by Mona Phillips. The southeast window exhibited the Egyptian and African personages of the Old Testament, while the southwest window showed scenes from the New Testament. In the New Testament scenes most of the figures were brown-skinned, including Jesus, or black, like Simon the Cyrenian who was compelled to carry Jesus' cross. In the east window in the church lobby was another stained-glass window (Plate 79) that extended from ground level through the second floor, ending in a triangular apex. It traced the story of important black Christians from the early years of the Christian church through many centuries to the present day. Nineteenth-century personages included Richard Allen and Daniel Payne, as well as other famous African American men and women. Like the stained-glass windows of other megachurches, white as well as black, the Trinity Church windows were strongly didactic, designed, as Wright observed, to help "our children and grandchildren" understand "what it means to be unashamedly black and unapologetically Christian."[30]

Covenant Church, the Cathedral of the Holy Spirit, and Coral Ridge Presbyterian Church exhibited a much greater degree of ornamentation and used the visual arts much more extensively than other late-twentieth-century evangelical megachurches.[31] Whereas the ornamentation in most megachurch auditoriums served didactic purposes, the builders of Covenant Church used it to induce an affective experience in the worshipers—to "put the romance back into church" and to make the sanctuary look "churchly" (Plate 80). Although the neo-Gothic decor and furnishings did not express the beliefs or worship practices of Covenant's pentecostal congregation, they did testify to the builders' sense that the worship space was special, if not sacred, and therefore should look different from other spaces so as to inspire appropriate religious feelings.

The neo-Gothic furnishings and ornamentation in the auditorium of the Cathedral of the Holy Spirit (Plate 81) constituted a key component of Earl Paulk's plan to build a "Charismatic cathedral," a structure that would blend "liturgical tradition with the power of the Spirit." During the 1990s, while the worship center was under construction, Paulk introduced more liturgy and high church rituals into the worship services. To reinforce interest in historic, liturgical worship, he encouraged artists and artisans in the congregation to produce artwork and artifacts in the neo-Gothic idiom to be installed in the auditorium. "We're using the arts to build bridges between the traditional church and the charismatic community. We want to unite historic forms with pentecostal power," he explained.[32] The pews were decorated with carvings representing fleurs-de-lis. A white marble altar-table in front of the raised platform had a gold-painted altar railing and kneeling cushions. On the wall behind the choir loft were carved woodwork and stained glass in the neo-Gothic idiom. Oil paintings of biblical scenes decorated the sound and lighting pod. Banners, candles, and crosses, also in the neo-Gothic style, added to the profusion.

The furnishings, ornamentation, and architecture of the cathedral auditorium were designed not just for aesthetic or decorative purposes, but to reflect the worship practices of the cathedral, which ranged from contemporary-style pentecostal services to traditional liturgical services. Emphasizing the ecumenical orientation, Associate Pastor Dan Rhodes declared, "We reach across to the liturgical churches; we have charismatic masses using the table of the Lord, the Gregorian chants, the high liturgy." But, he quickly added, "in theology we're Reformed. The preaching of the Word takes precedence over the sacraments."[33] Indeed, the arrangement of the furnishings in the sanctuary provided a graphic illustration of his comment: the preaching desk stood at the center of the platform and higher than the altar-table.

The auditorium of the Coral Ridge Presbyterian Church, like the church exterior, featured some neo-Gothic elements. Harold Wagoner designed it in the shape of a cross, but with the transepts at 45-degree rather than 90-degree angles. At the same time, to give the effect of a "gathered church," he added fan-shaped seating.[34] The furnishings and ornamentation in the auditorium reflected the church's Reformed theology and traditional order of worship (Plate 82). The large wooden pulpit was emblazoned with a verse from Romans, "As it is written, the just shall live by faith," which a church leaflet termed "the birth text of the Protestant Reformation." Other carvings on the pulpit included the shields of Calvin and Luther and a long sword representing the Word of God. A metal sculpture of a dove affixed to a panel carved to represent rays of light symbolized the Holy Spirit as the giver of wisdom and understanding. A huge tester towered over the pulpit to give it visual prominence and to emphasize the importance of the preaching of the Word. Besides the pulpit, the platform ordinarily accommodated a large communion table in the center, a lectern on the north side, and, next to it, a baptismal font, all ornamented with wood carvings representing various religious images. Behind the communion table stood a large cross, ten feet tall and made of brass—an "empty cross" that symbolized "the risen and victorious Christ."[35]

Just as the exteriors of most megachurches revealed their continuity with earlier architectural forms, so did the worship centers reflect their antecedents. The Willow Creek auditorium recalled the austerity of the seventeenth-century meetinghouses, whereas the decor in most other megachurch worship centers bore a closer resemblance to that of the nineteenth- and early-twentieth-century auditorium churches. In this regard, the use of the visual arts in the megachurches was not so new as some commentators presumed. The builders of the auditorium churches had used them, and so had the builders of some fundamentalist and pentecostal churches. Think of the carved wood, the stained-glass windows and fresco-work, and the decorated baptisteries of the Lovely Lane Methodist Church, Trinity Methodist Episcopal Church, Mother Bethel A. M. E. Church, the Baptist Temple, Tremont Temple, and the Angelus Temple.

Other elements of the worship centers also reflected the megachurches' architectural antecedents: the amphitheater arrangement, the invitation stairways, the prominent placement of the baptisteries. The new platform designs and the sound, lighting, and video systems were innovations, but they reinforced the trend toward a performance-oriented, theater-like ambience in the auditorium that had begun in the early nineteenth century.

All of which suggests that the megachurches acclaimed as emblems of a "new reformation" or "new paradigm" were very much a product of the forms of church architecture that preceded them. Architecturally, they constituted an evolution, not a revolution.

Epilogue

The Everyday House of God

> Except the Lord build the house, they labour in vain that build it.—Psalm 127:1

Late-twentieth-century megachurch architecture provoked scathing criticism. Commentators objected that it failed to inspire awe or to "celebrate the transcendent nature of God," that its horizontal orientation de-emphasized "sacral associations." One critic declared that it seemed "determined to banish the sense of mystery and otherworldliness that has long been at the very heart of the architecture of Christianity." As his remark suggests, much of the criticism focused on the details and furnishings commentators missed in the megachurches (and which they associated with the iconic Federal- or Gothic-style church)—crosses, spires, hymnals, pipe organs, stained-glass windows, pews. Thus Charles Trueheart described Mariners Church as "an understated horizontal brick pile with barely a peak in its auditorium roof, let alone anything suggesting a spire." Its outdoor baptismal pool he dismissed as "a turquoise hot tub."[1]

Critics complained that megachurches lacked "architectural distinction." They disparaged the elevation of "function over worship—designing buildings to accommodate musicals, theater productions, potlucks, sporting events and education rather than constructing beautiful, symbol-filled, worship-orientated sanctuaries." Above all, they disapproved of their resemblance to secular, commercial buildings. Megachurch buildings, they said, looked more like warehouses, malls, theaters, convention centers or corporate headquarters than churches.[2]

Whatever its focus, much of the criticism of megachurches reflected an underlying, perhaps unconscious, assumption about the relation between "the sacred" and "the profane," that the two were absolutely separate from, and the opposite of, each other. The sacred constituted "an ideal and transcendental world . . . set apart from ordinary life," whereas the profane consisted of "the everyday and the utilitarian," the "commonplace" and the "familiar."[3] According to this way of thinking, a church should embody the sacred and eschew the profane.

Recently, a number of scholars in various fields have begun to question the rigid distinction drawn between the sacred and the profane, insisting that in some cultures they have often overlapped or mingled. In a seminal study of material Christianity in the United States, for example, Colleen McDannell found "little evidence that American Christians experience a radical separation of the sacred from the profane." Indeed, her research showed "the continual scrambling of the sacred and the profane" by Protestants as well as Catholics.[4]

Evangelical megachurches provide a particularly rich illustration of such scrambling. There *was* a great deal of the profane in the megachurches. Think of the sermons and ministries addressing individuals' personal and family needs and problems; the pervasive influence of popular culture, especially in music; the Fourth of July pageants, the sports leagues, the fitness centers, the economic development projects. In many cases, too, the architecture was frankly imitative of commercial designs, forms, and technology.

The megachurches were everyday churches built for and serving everyday people. And intentionally so. Megachurch pastors liked to say, "We meet people where they are." Rick Warren told a newspaper reporter, "Rather than dealing with the hereafter, we deal with what it means to be here right here and now." Wayne Skaff of the Community of Joy spelled out the architectural implications: "We asked the architect to design buildings that would meet the everyday thinking of the people."[5]

Whereas the critics disdained the megachurches for their emphasis on the profane and the mundane, megachurch people embraced them because of it—because it made the church relevant to their everyday lives. At the same time, however, and unlike the critics, megachurch people experienced a profound sense of the sacred in the megachurches. This was especially true during the worship service, when many individuals said they felt "the presence of God," meaning that they encountered a deity who was approachable, familiar, and palpable.[6]

Whether it provoked ecstatic pentecostal behaviors or more quietist feelings of joy, peace, gratitude, or love, megachurch worship introduced the individual to an immanent as opposed to a transcendent God, revealed in the person of Jesus Christ or during the baptism of the Holy Spirit. Obviously this kind of God, with whom an individual could enjoy a direct, intimate relationship, was very different from the distant, ma-

Plate 67. Auditorium, Southeast Christian Church, Louisville (1998). Photograph courtesy of the *Southeast Outlook.*

Plate 68. Auditorium, Brentwood Baptist Church, Houston (1986).

Plate 69. Auditorium, First Baptist Church, Jacksonville, Florida (1994). Photograph courtesy of Lynn Armstrong, Photographer.

Plate 70. Auditorium, Roswell Street Baptist Church, Marietta, Georgia (1979).

Plate 71. Auditorium, Prestonwood Baptist Church, Plano, Texas (1999).

Plate 72. Auditorium, Calvary Assembly of God, Winter Park, Florida (1985).

Plate 73. Auditorium, Apostolic Church of God, Chicago (1992).

Plate 74. Stained glass, Prestonwood Baptist Church, Plano, Texas (1999).

Plate 75. Revelation
Window, Second Baptist
Church, Houston (1986).

Plate 76. Auditorium, St. Luke "Community" United Methodist Church, Dallas (1993).

Plate 77. Stained-glass windows, St. Luke "Community" United Methodist Church.

Plate 78. Auditorium, Trinity United Church of Christ, Chicago (1994).

Plate 79. East Window, Trinity United Church of Christ. Depicted are, in top row, left to right, Henry McNeil Turner, a bishop of the African Methodist Episcopal Church, and John Jasper, a Baptist preacher from Virginia; in bottom row, left to right, Amos Beman, a Congregational minister and abolitionist from New Haven, Connecticut, John Chavis, a teacher and missionary, Nanny Helen Burroughs, a teacher and preacher, and Harriet Tubman, one of the leaders of the Underground Railroad.

Plate 80. Auditorium, Covenant Church, Carrollton, Texas (1995).

Plate 81. Auditorium, Cathedral of the Holy Spirit, Decatur, Georgia (1991).

Plate 82. Auditorium, Coral Ridge Presbyterian Church, Fort Lauderdale, Florida (1973).

jestic, awe-inspiring deity invoked in the liturgical churches. The notion of an immanent God gained credence in the megachurches as a result of the influence exerted by the pentecostal/charismatic movement, either directly, in the classical pentecostal and neo-pentecostal megachurches, or indirectly, through contemporary Christian worship and music, which was largely pentecostal/charismatic in origin and accent. The music, especially, became "the means for encounter with God." The songs emphasized "the emotion and experience of spirituality" rather than theological doctrine. Rather than being written *about* God, they were addressed *to* him, using second-person instead of third-person pronouns. They encouraged worshipers to seek a personal, intimate relationship with God.[7]

Among megachurch people, the notion of an immanent God combined with traditional doctrines of the Creation and the Incarnation to dissolve any rigid distinction between the sacred and the profane. Megachurch pastors and congregants believed that God was "present and active in the world," constantly intervening in the everyday lives of human beings. And he could be encountered anywhere, not just in church. That was the kind of deity megachurch pastors such as Bill Hybels described in their sermons. A reporter paraphrased one of his messages as follows: "The distant God isn't all that far away. He's not the presiding official in a court of law tallying wrongdoings and weighing them against works of wonder. He's waiting for you in the stands of the soccer field, between the rack of clothes at Field Days, or in the boardroom.

He wants to be your friend, and if you let him, it will change your life."[8]

The critics judged megachurch architecture to be profane. Megachurch people did not believe their church buildings were intrinsically sacred, but they did invest them with sacrality. Some pastors, for example, attributed the impulse to build a church or even its design to God. Frederick Price claimed, "It is God's will that we build that sanctuary." Earl Paulk declared, "God said 'Build a Church' and gave us blueprints." The pastor of Covenant Church took guidance from the prophecies of a minister-friend who spoke of "a mighty, mighty building so near to the highway being raised up in honor of God." Karl Strader also cited "prophecies" and "miracles," telling his congregation, "God has spoken to us to build a beautiful edifice that will be a classic architectural design to attract people . . . from throughout Central Florida."[9]

Megachurch people also invested their church buildings with sacred meaning by installing crosses on the exterior and inside the worship center and by using various forms of sacred art—paintings, murals, stained glass, and sculpture. Bishop Arthur Brazier of the Apostolic Church of God explained why the images of doves and the words "Jesus Christ is Lord" were carved into the brick walls above the choir loft in the worship center. He had considered simply hanging pictures there. But if someone wanted to turn the sanctuary into a theater, all he would have to do is take down the pictures. Carving the images and words into the walls—in effect, carving religious meaning into the walls—ensured that they would have to be torn out if the purpose of the building were changed.[10]

Three megachurch congregations employed more novel means of endowing the church building with sacral significance. When the Valley Cathedral worship center was being constructed, pieces of paper with Bible passages written on them were dropped into the holes dug for the supporting pillars, so that the church would be "truly built on the Word of God." During the renovation of the Hughes Aircraft facility—a profane space if ever there was one—members of Faith Community Church went through the building writing Scripture verses all over the floors. They were ultimately covered over by tiles or carpeting, but they symbolized the congregation's commitment to stand firmly on God's Word. Citing Deuteronomy 6:9, Southeast Christian staff and church members did the same thing in their church complex, and before any services were conducted in the worship center, hundreds of volunteers filled fifteen-minute time slots, reading the entire Bible aloud there, as if to imbue the space with the wisdom of the Scriptures.[11]

Megachurch lore offers still other illustrations of pastors' and congregants' propensity for investing their church buildings with sacred meaning. At a church picnic on the new site of Southeast Christian Church, groups touring the bare steel and concrete structure heard from a guide how the cross functioned as a structural component of the roof. "If you were to pull the cross out of the structure, it would fall apart," he declared. "So it's both significant in the design and symbolic for

[sic] how the church rests on Christ." A couple on the tour testified to their amazement at the revelation and the profound experience it evoked. "When he said it was holding the building together, we just cried," the husband said. The story spread through the congregation, gaining credence, until it was contradicted, more than a year later, by the architect.[12]

Southeast Christian pastor Bob Russell presented another reading of the church building that also invested it with spiritual significance. In the dedication sermon for the new worship center, he told about climbing onto the roof before it was finished so as to look out over the surrounding area. Glancing down, he noticed something that "put goosebumps on my arms." The company that supplied the waterproof material for the roof was the Grace Ice and Water Shield Co., Inc. "The insulation comes in six-foot sheets, and the word 'Grace' is printed in gold letters on each sheet," Russell explained. "I could see the word 'Grace, Grace, Grace, Grace,' hundreds of times covering the roof. The cross stands towering above, but this church is covered by grace."[13]

Believing that everything came from God—and that he often intervened in human affairs—megachurch builders frequently acknowledged that they could not have built a church unless he had enabled them to do so. The dedication sermons and publications produced for newly built megachurches were full of passages describing works of God that guided or facilitated their financing and construction: the effective ministry of the pastors, the growth of the congregation, the success of the fund-raising and building committees, the "raising up" of wealthy contributors. Referring to Dauphin Way's purchase of a strategically located site on I-65, the writer of a church brochure declared, "It is as if God has saved it for this church at this time." Lynn Cross also saw the hand of God in the events surrounding Fellowship Church's acquisition of property on which to build.[14]

The *Southeast Outlook* devoted considerable space to a story recounting God's influence on the design of the sound system of Southeast Christian Church. In it MGA consultant Mike Garrison described his difficulties in devising a sound system that would function effectively in the round worship center. He said that one afternoon he became "so frustrated that I walked out around the auditorium asking, 'Lord, why would You bring us all the way (from California) and leave us without the answers?' I then went up on the top of the building and sat down, right at the cross. The wind was blowing, and I was literally holding on to the cross and crying out to the Lord, 'Why is this so difficult? Why can't we come up with a solution?'" He climbed down an hour later and walked again around the worship center. "And then," according to reporter Steve Coomes, "an idea struck him. Using an unconventional design and simpler components," he created a system that worked. Garrison believed the sound system installed in the auditorium was the one God pointed out to him "after his rooftop hour of prayer," that it was "a heaven-sent solution."[15]

And then there was the account of divine intervention during the construction of Prestonwood Baptist Church, which was described in the church's informational leaflet on the three-hundred-foot band of stained glass in the atrium. When Roger Hogan and his team arrived on site and installed the first window, the wind was blowing 35 miles per hour. Then, according to Hogan, "it completely stopped and became very still. It stayed that way until we reached the final window, when it began to blow 35 mph again.'" The leaflet concluded the account with a pointed reference to Jesus as "the Miracle Worker."[16]

That a church building should communicate the faith of its congregation was the rule evangelical church builders inherited from the Puritans and maintained into the twentieth century. Late-twentieth-century megachurch builders were no less dedicated to the functionalist aesthetic. The forms they appropriated from earlier periods of evangelical church architecture proved remarkably well adapted to their new mode of worship and their new ideas about God, as well as their commitment to evangelism. Curved seating and the large platform, originally instituted in the nineteenth-century auditorium churches to improve the hearing of the Word, facilitated the megachurches' new emphasis on music and other performing arts. Invitation stairways aided the commitment to evangelism. So did the horizontal orientation of the megachurches, which recalled the tents, tabernacles, temples, and churches of the revivalists and nineteenth- and early-twentieth-century dissenting evangelicals. Extending outward rather than upward, the megachurches signaled that "the church's mission is to the world—not to itself." The horizontality also reflected megachurch people's discovery of an immanent deity. Under the comparatively flat ceilings of their worship centers, megachurch people encountered an immanent God, not the transcendent God of the heaven-pointing, liturgical churches. And, finally, like the revivalists and dissenting evangelicals, megachurch builders used modern, secular styles of architecture, which communicated megachurch people's conviction that "religion is not a thing apart from everyday life" and that the church was not a refuge from the world—it was not only in the world but of the world.[17]

In all of these ways, late-twentieth-century megachurch builders, pastors, and congregants kept the faith—in the functionalist aesthetic as well as in the tenets of their religion—and on a scale that doubtless would have amazed and gratified many of their predecessors.

Notes

Introduction: Building the Faith

1. ("New paradigm churches") Donald E. Miller, *Reinventing American Protestantism: Christianity in the New Millennium*, 1; Lyle E. Schaller, *The New Reformation: Tomorrow Arrived Yesterday*; Charles Trueheart, "Welcome to the Next Church"; Leith Anderson, *A Church for the 21st Century*; Ken Sidey, "So Long to Sacred Space," *Christianity Today*, November 8, 1993, p. 46. See also Paul Goldberger, "The Gospel of Church Architecture, Revised." On "shopping mall" and "supermarket churches," see, for example, Virginia Culver, "Changes Expected for Religion in the West," *Denver Post*, November 12, 1994 (from LexisNexis internet data base, hereinafter cited as LN); George W. Cornell, "Today's 'Megachurches' Able to Offer Younger Christians More Programs," *Commercial Appeal*, January 5, 1991 (LN). Michael S. Hamilton, in "Willow Creek's Place in History," *Christianity Today*, November 13, 2000, pp. 62–68, was one of the few commentators to put megachurches in historical perspective.

2. John Vaughan, publisher of *Church Growth Today*, quoted in Cathy Lynn Grossman, "Baby Boomers Flock to Full-Service Megachurches," *USA Today*, August 6, 1991 (LN); Vaughan cited in Gustav Niebuhr, "Where Religion Gets a Big Dose of Shopping-Mall Culture"; George Barna, *The Index of Leading Spiritual Indicators: Trends in Morality, Beliefs, Lifestyles, Religious and Spiritual Thought, Behavior, and Church Involvement* (Dallas: Word Publishing, 1996), 109.

3. On evangelicals as a subculture, see Paul K. Conkin, *The Uneasy Center: Reformed Christianity in Antebellum America*, 114–15, 117–18; Barbara G. Wheeler, "You Who Were Far Off: Religious Divisions and the Role of Religious Research," *Auburn Views* 4 (winter 1998): 1–7; Christian Smith, *American Evangelicalism: Embattled and Thriving* (Chicago: University of Chicago Press, 1998), 106–7, chap. 5. For a perceptive discussion of material culture and what it reveals about religious belief and behavior, see Colleen McDannell, *Material Christianity: Religion and Popular Culture in America*, 2–4.

4. Jhennifer Amundson, presentation at conference on "Evangelical Worship and Church Architecture," Judson College, Elgin, Illinois, October 13, 2001.

1. The Meetinghouse

1. Peter W. Williams, *Houses of God: Region, Religion, and Architecture in the United States,* 6.

2. Mather quoted in Marian C. Donnelly, *The New England Meeting Houses of the Seventeenth Century,* 101; Peter W. Williams, "Religious Architecture and Landscape," 1327. See also Peter W. Williams, "Metamorphoses of the Meetinghouse: Three Case Studies," in Paul Corby Finney, ed., *Seeing Beyond the Word: Visual Arts and the Calvinist Tradition* (Grand Rapids, Mich.: William B. Eerdmans Publishing Company, 1999), 479–84; Peter Benes and Philip Zimmerman, eds., *New England Meeting House and Church: 1630–1850,* 1; Donnelly, *New England Meeting Houses,* 107; Horton Davies, *The Worship of the American Puritans, 1629–1730,* 233.

3. Benes and Zimmerman, eds., *New England Meeting House and Church,* 4, 8; Davies, *Worship of the American Puritans,* 236; Charles A. Place, "From Meeting House to Church in New England, I. The Meeting House in the First Hundred Years," *Old-Time New England* 13 (October 1922): 69–77.

4. Mather quoted in Davies, *Worship of the American Puritans,* 19–20. According to Williams, "Religious Architecture and Landscape," 1328, the Puritans allowed nonpictorial wood carving and other ornamentation. The pulpit in the Puritan meetinghouses "was often elaborately carved and of fine wood, but bore no pictorial representations of religious subjects." On the meetinghouse interior, see also Williams, "Religious Architecture and Landscape," 1326–27; Dell Upton, *Holy Things and Profane: Anglican Parish Churches in Colonial Virginia* (Cambridge, Mass.: MIT Press, 1986), 97; Benes and Zimmerman, eds., *New England Meeting House and Church,* 35.

5. Place, "From Meeting House to Church in New England, I," 76, 77; Benes and Zimmerman, eds., *New England Meeting House and Church,* 37, 38–44; Charles A. Place, "From Meeting House to Church in New England, II. The Eighteenth Century Meeting House," *Old-Time New England* 13 (January 1923): 118, 123; Williams, *Houses of God,* 7. For photographs of capsule-type pulpits, see Upton, *Holy Things and Profane,* 134–36.

6. William H. Pierson, Jr., *American Buildings and Their Architects: The Colonial and Neo-Classical Styles,* 98, 68–69, 94–105, 131–35; Williams, *Houses of God,* 10, 12–13; Marilyn J. Chiat, *America's Religious Architecture: Sacred Places for Every Community,* 62.

7. Data pages, Meeting House, Sandown, New Hampshire, in Historic American Buildings Survey (HABS), Library of Congress, Prints and Photographs Division, Washington, D.C.; data pages, First Congregational Church, Bennington, Vermont, ibid.

8. John B. Boles, "Introduction," in Boles, ed., *Masters and Slaves in the House of the Lord: Race and Religion in the American South, 1740–1870* (Lexington: University Press of Kentucky, 1988), 15, and see also 9–14.

9. Carol V. R. George, *Segregated Sabbaths: Richard Allen and the Rise of Independent Black Churches, 1760–1840* (New York: Oxford University Press, 1973), 62; data pages, Abolition Church, Boston, HABS; data pages, First African Baptist Church, Savannah, Georgia, HABS; John Linley, *The Georgia Catalog: Historic American Buildings Survey: A Guide to the Architecture of the State* (Athens: University of Georgia Press, 1982), 84, 187; E[manuel] K[ing] Love, *A History of the First African Baptist Church, from Its Organization, January 20th, 1788, to July 1st, 1888* (Savannah, Ga.: The Morning News Print, 1888), 33–34, 143; Edgar Garfield Thomas, *The First African Baptist Church of North America* (Savannah, Ga.: n.p., 1925), 129.

2. Building for Revivalism

1. Richard Carwardine, *Transatlantic Revivalism: Popular Evangelicalism in Britain and America, 1790–1865* (Westport, Conn.: Greenwood Press, 1978), 45, dates "the period of the Second Great Awakening and its postscript" from 1790 to 1865. On the origins and development of revivalism, see Paul K. Conkin, *The Uneasy Center: Reformed Christianity in Antebellum America,* 119–30.

2. B. W. Gorham, *Camp Meeting Manual, A Practical Book for the Camp Ground,* 34.

3. Ibid., 30–31, 38–39.

4. Latrobe quoted in Talbot Hamlin, *Benjamin Henry Latrobe* (New York: Oxford University Press, 1955), 321; Roger Robins, "Vernacular

American Landscape: Methodists, Camp Meetings, and Social Responsibility," *Religion and American Culture* 4 (June 1994): 169; Charles A. Johnson, *The Frontier Camp Meeting: Religion's Harvest Time*, 41–48; Ellen Weiss, *City in the Woods: The Life and Design of an American Camp Meeting on Martha's Vineyard* (New York: Oxford University Press, 1987), 4, 9–19.

5. Johnson, *Frontier Camp Meeting*, 41–46, 132–33; Dickson D. Bruce, Jr., *And They All Sang Hallelujah: Plain-Folk Camp-Meeting Religion, 1800–1845*, 71.

6. Bruce, *And They All Sang Hallelujah*, 73–77, 80–81, 84–86, 90–91.

7. Gorham, *Camp Meeting Manual*, 18, 19, 33–35, 159, 167.

8. Malcom quoted in Edwin M. Long, *The Union Tabernacle; or, Movable Tent-Church: Showing in Its Rise and Success a New Department of Christian Enterprise* (Philadelphia: Parry and McMillan, 1859), 25–26; Gorham, *Camp Meeting Manual*, 38–40.

9. Malcom quoted in Long, *Union Tabernacle*, 25; "Home Missions—Western Fashion," *New York Evangelist*, December 13, 1834.

10. "Home Missions—Western Fashion." On the use of tents in camp meetings, see, for example, Gorham, *Camp Meeting Manual*, chap. 3.

11. "Home Missions—Western Fashion"; Marion L. Bell, *Crusade in the City: Revivalism in Nineteenth-Century Philadelphia* (Lewisburg, Pa.: Bucknell University Press, 1977), 186; Union Tabernacle Association quoted in Long, *Union Tabernacle*, 11–12, 91–92, 118.

12. Young Men's Christian Association (Philadelphia), *Pentecost; or, the Work of God in Philadelphia, A.D. 1858* (Philadelphia: Parry and McMillan, 1859), 23, 31; Long, *Union Tabernacle*, title page, 98, 107, 117–18; Bell, *Crusade in the City*, 186.

13. Long, *Union Tabernacle*, 15, 24, 98, 118, 119. An estimated 150,000 persons attended services at the tabernacle during its four months in Philadelphia. Young Men's Christian Association (Philadelphia), *Pentecost*, 24.

14. See, for example, Charles G. Finney, *The Memoirs of Charles G. Finney: The Complete and Restored Text*, 81; W. F. P. Noble, *A Century of Gospel-Work: A History of the Growth of Evangelical Religion in the United States* (Philadelphia: H. C. Watts and Co., 1876), 295–97, 300–301, 355–57, 386–87, 583–84.

15. Jonathan Greenleaf, *A History of the Churches of All Denominations in the City of New York, from the First Settlement to the Year 1846* (New York: E. French, 1846), passim. On halls, see, for example, T. Allston Brown, *A History of the New York Stage* (3 vols.; New York: Dodd, Mead and Company, 1903), vol. 1, 362–63, 423–25, vol. 3, 8, 115, 169, 222, 343, 516.

16. Jacob Knapp, *Autobiography of Elder Jacob Knapp* (New York: Sheldon, 1868), 216.

17. "The History of Western Theatre," in *The New Encyclopaedia* (Chicago: Encyclopaedia Britannica, Inc., 1985) 28: 534–35, 537, 539; John Russell Brown, ed., *The Oxford Illustrated History of Theatre* (New York: Oxford University Press, 1995), 66, 68–69, 75, 92, 295–96); Glynne Wickham, *A History of the Theatre* (Oxford, England: Phaidon Press Limited, 1985), 90–96; Phyllis Hartnoll, *The Theatre: A Concise History* (n.p.: Thames and Hudson, 1985), 37–50.

18. Edmund S. Morgan, "Puritan Hostility to the Theatre," *Proceedings of the American Philosophical Society* 110 (October 1966): 340, 343–45.

19. Harry S. Stout, *The Divine Dramatist: George Whitefield and the Rise of Modern Evangelicalism* (Grand Rapids, Mich.: William B. Eerdmans Publishing Company, 1991), 22–23, 24, 40, 42, 43, 44, 79, 236.

20. On evangelists' criticism of the theater, see R. Laurence Moore, *Selling God: American Religion in the Marketplace of Culture* (New York: Oxford University Press, 1994), 49, 50–51, 100; on other nineteenth-century religious critics, see David Grimsted, *Melodrama Unveiled: American Theater and Culture, 1800–1850* (Chicago: University of Chicago Press, 1968), 25, 26, 27, 30–31, 52–56, 85–86.

21. ("Stage techniques," "theatrics") Moore, *Selling God*, 45, 47–50; ("vernacular preaching," etc.) Nathan O. Hatch, *The Democratization of American Christianity*, 133–35.

22. Charles Grandison Finney, *Lectures on Revivals of Religion*, edited by William G. McLoughlin (Cambridge, Mass.: Belknap Press of Harvard University Press, 1960), 220.

23. Carwardine, *Transatlantic Revivalism*, 26–27; Charles C. Cole, Jr., "The Free Church Movement in New York City," *New York History* 34 (July 1953): 290–91.

24. Lewis Tappan, "History of the Free Churches in the City of New-York," in Andrew Reed and James Matheson, *A Narrative of the Visit to the American Churches of the Deputation from the Congregational Union of England and Wales* (2 vols.; New York: Harper and Brothers, 1835), vol. 2, 350.

25. Finney, *Memoirs*, 354.

26. (Seating capacity, dimensions, decor) George C. D. Odell, *Annals*

of the New York Stage (15 vols.; New York: Columbia University Press, 1927–1949), vol. 3, 119–20, 256, and see also 201; ("beauty and fashion") Brown, History of the New York Stage, vol. 1, 84, 86, 87; Bruce A. Mc-Conachie, Melodramatic Formations: American Theatre and Society, 1820–1870 (Iowa City: University of Iowa Press, 1992), 22; Mary C. Henderson, The City and the Theatre: New York Playhouses from Bowling Green to Times Square (Clifton, N.J.: James T. White and Company, 1973), 49, 58; ("pest," etc.) Finney, Memoirs, 354, 354n110.

27. Lewis Tappan to Charles Grandison Finney, March 16, 1832, in Charles Grandison Finney, Papers, 1817–1875 (microform; Oberlin College Library, Oberlin, Ohio), reel #3.

28. On the challenge urban revivalists faced, see Carwardine, Transatlantic Revivalism, 18–28.

29. Tappan to Finney, March 16, March 22, April 11, and April 19, 1832, in Finney, Papers, 1817–1875, reel #3.

30. ("Fitting up") Finney, Memoirs, 356n2, 360, 360n20. In addition to the seven thousand dollars, they spent two thousand for the lease, according to Cole, "Free Church Movement," 291. New York Evangelist quoted in Keith J. Hardman, Charles Grandison Finney, 1792–1875: Revivalist and Reformer, 252, and see also 251. Finney served the Chatham Street Chapel until he moved, in 1836, to the newly built Broadway Tabernacle, also in New York City; he remained there until April, 1837, when he became professor of theology at Oberlin College.

31. Noble, Century of Gospel-Work, 287. As Richard Carwardine has pointed out, the Methodists brought the altar call from the camp meeting to American towns and cities in the early nineteenth century, and it became "a standard feature of Methodist revivals." Beginning in the 1820s, some Calvinists adopted the Methodist practice or altered it slightly by developing a device known as "the anxious seat" or "mourners' bench." This was "a pew set aside at the front of the congregation to which those in a state of concern over their souls could go to be exhorted and prayed for at the close of the sermon, and there be encouraged by the minister and his zealous church members." Finney first made use of the anxious seat during a revival in Rochester, New York, in 1830. Carwardine, Transatlantic Revivalism, 13, 15; Richard Carwardine, "The Second Great Awakening in the Urban Centers: An Examination of Methodism and the 'New Measures,'" Journal of American History 59 (September 1972): 333, 339. According to Frank Grenville Beardsley, A History of American Revivals (New York: American Tract Society, 1912), 194–95, the anxious seat and the altar call enjoyed wide usage among antebellum evangelicals. In "History of the Free Churches," 349–50, Tappan observed that the invitation to the anxious seat was "the usual practice" in the free churches of New York City. On Finney's preaching, see Hardman, Charles Grandison Finney, 61, quoting Finney; and Finney, Lectures on Revivals of Religion, 212.

32. Leonard H. Rhodes, Brief History of Tremont Temple (Boston: n.p., [1917?]), 5; Edgar C. Lane, A Brief History of Tremont Temple, 1839 to 1950 (church booklet, [1950]), 1–2 (used with the permission of the American Baptist Historical Society [ABHS], Rochester, N.Y.); Justin D. Fulton, Memoir of Timothy Gilbert (Boston: Lee and Shepard, 1866), 10, 52, 53, 59, 62, 72, 158 (used with the permission of the ABHS); Knapp, Autobiography, 128, 129; William W. Clapp, Jr., A Record of the Boston Stage (Boston: James Munroe and Company, 1853), 274, 360.

33. Fulton, Memoir, 161, and see also 57; Clapp, Record of the Boston Stage, 386.

34. Fulton, Memoir, 158–60.

35. Ibid., 170, 188–89, 193–95, 199–200, 202; Greenleaf, History of the Churches of All Denominations, 359. Fulton served as pastor of Tremont Temple from 1864 to 1873. The architect of the 1853 building was William Washburn. Tremont was an early example of a church that housed offices and stores providing rental income, which it had done since 1842, when it renovated the Tremont Theatre. See Daniel Bluestone, Constructing Chicago, 96–98, regarding so-called combination church and business buildings in Chicago.

36. Fulton, Memoir, 189–92.

37. Kathryn Teresa Long, The Revival of 1857–58: Interpreting an American Religious Awakening (New York: Oxford University Press, 1998), 37; Beardsley, History of American Revivals, 225, 226; Russell E. Francis, "The Religious Revival of 1858 in Philadelphia," Pennsylvania Magazine of History and Biography 70 (January 1946): 66; Noble, Century of Gospel-Work, 420–21. For a picture of the exterior of Jayne's Hall, built in 1849, see Theo B. White, ed., Philadelphia Architecture in the Nineteenth Century (Philadelphia: University of Pennsylvania Press, 1953), Plate 45.

38. Henderson, City and the Theatre, 83; Cuyler quoted in "Burton's

Theater.—A Midday Prayer-Meeting," *New York Daily Tribune,* March 18, 1858.

39. "A Word to the Revivalists," *New York Daily Tribune,* March 24, 1858; "Yesterday at Burton's Theater," ibid., March 25, 1858.

40. YMCA leaders quoted in Bell, *Crusade in the City,* 185.

41. On the "radically innovative" methods used by early-nineteenth-century evangelists, see Hatch, *Democratization of American Christianity,* 57–58; on the "new measures" promoted by Finney and his followers, as well as Methodists and Baptists, see Carwardine, *Transatlantic Revivalism,* 4–18; on the rejection of traditional notions of ecclesiastical space, see John Brinckerhoff Jackson, *The Necessity for Ruins and Other Topics* (Amherst: University of Massachusetts Press, 1980), 84; on "revival motifs," see Conkin, *Uneasy Center,* 195.

42. Protestant church membership and church attendance had increased dramatically since the 1790s. See Carwardine, *Transatlantic Revivalism,* 45, 159–61; John B. Boles, *The Great Revival, 1787–1805: The Origins of the Southern Evangelical Mind* (Lexington: University Press of Kentucky, 1972), 184–86; Long, *Revival of 1857–58,* 48; Christine Leigh Heyrman, *Southern Cross: The Beginnings of the Bible Belt* (New York: Alfred A. Knopf, 1997), Appendix.

3. The Auditorium Church

1. One reason for the increase in the membership of black churches and denominations was the accession of large numbers of newly freed slaves in the South. Some left the white churches in which they had held membership before emancipation; others had never been members of a Christian congregation. The former slaves either joined existing black denominations such as the A.M.E. or A.M.E.Z. Churches, or helped increase the membership of newly organized denominations such as the Colored Methodist Episcopal Church (formed in 1870; changed its name in 1954 to Christian Methodist Episcopal Church) or of the independent black Baptist churches that proliferated after the Civil War.

The authoritative work on the nineteenth-century auditorium church is Jeanne Halgren Kilde, *When Church Became Theatre: The Transformation of Evangelical Architecture and Worship in Nineteenth Century America,* which was published after we had submitted the manuscript of this book for publication. During the research and writing of our book, we found Kilde's dissertation "Spiritual Armories: A Social and Architectural History of Neo-Medieval Auditorium Churches in the United States, 1869–1910" (Ph.D. diss., University of Minnesota, 1991) very helpful; but for the convenience of the reader we cite the much expanded published version. Our definition of the auditorium church is more inclusive than Kilde's. Whereas she limits the term to churches whose audience rooms had an inclined floor and curved seating (the amphitheater plan), we follow Pierson, Jr., *American Buildings and Their Architects,* in including churches with a level auditorium floor. Kilde also restricts the term to churches with "neo-medieval" exteriors, but we include churches with neoclassical exteriors as well. And, finally, following Pierson, we date the origins of the auditorium church in the United States earlier than Kilde—in the first and second decades of the nineteenth century rather than in the 1830s.

2. Pierson, Jr., *American Buildings and Their Architects,* 377; Williams, *Houses of God,* 110; Rhodri Windsor Liscombe, *Altogether American: Robert Mills, Architect and Engineer, 1781–1855* (New York: Oxford University Press, 1994), 19, 20, 45–46, 74; Rhodri Windsor Liscombe, *The Church Architecture of Robert Mills* (Easley, S.C.: Southern Historical Press, 1985), 1, 13.

3. Pierson, Jr., *American Buildings and Their Architects,* 384.

4. Ibid., 375–77; Mills quoted in Liscombe, *Altogether American,* 47, and see also 46; Liscombe, *Church Architecture of Robert Mills,* 1.

5. Finney, *Memoirs,* 367. On Finney's preaching tour in Philadelphia, see Hardman, *Charles Grandison Finney,* 159, 163–71.

6. L. Nelson Nichols, *History of the Broadway Tabernacle of New York City* (New Haven, Conn.: Tuttle, Morehouse and Taylor Co., 1940), 64; Greenleaf, *History of the Churches of All Denominations,* 179; Joseph P. Thompson, *The Last Sabbath in the Broadway Tabernacle: A Historical Discourse* (New York: Calkins and Stiles, 1857), 12; Finney, *Memoirs,* 364n35, 367n46; Susan Hayes Ward, *The History of the Broadway Tabernacle Church* (New York: Broadway Tabernacle Church, 1901), 28; "Opening of the

Broadway Tabernacle," *New York Evangelist,* April 16, 1836. The cost was $66,500, which included the land. Isaac M. Dimond and William Green, Jr., led the venture and contributed most of the necessary funds.

7. (Wren's tabernacles) C. Mark Hamilton, *Nineteenth-Century Mormon Architecture and City Planning* (New York: Oxford University Press, 1995), 54; Thompson, *Last Sabbath,* 13.

8. Twenty-five hundred is the capacity given by most historians, including Nichols, *History of the Broadway Tabernacle,* 59; Thompson, *Last Sabbath,* 13; Ward, *History of the Broadway Tabernacle Church,* 28. It was Thompson who asserted that it could accommodate up to four thousand. However, church historians, like church builders, are inclined to exaggerate seating capacity. In the 1850s, Henry C. Watson, music editor of the *New York Mirror,* fulminated against the inflated estimates of the seating in the tabernacle, which often hosted concerts and other musical performances. "The Tabernacle, when crammed, will not hold over thirty-one or [thirty-] two hundred; it will not seat over twenty-two hundred," he insisted. Vera Brodsky Lawrence, *Strong on Music: The New York Music Scene in the Days of George Templeton Strong* (2 vols.; Chicago: University of Chicago Press, 1988, 1995), vol. 1, 374. On the design of the Broadway Tabernacle, see Finney, *Memoirs,* 367, 378; Hardman, *Charles Grandison Finney,* 252–53, 301, 302; Ward, *History of the Broadway Tabernacle Church,* 29; Lawrence, *Strong on Music,* vol. 1, 15, 43, 49, 307; Nichols, *History of the Broadway Tabernacle,* 64; Charles E. Hambrick-Stowe, *Charles G. Finney and the Spirit of American Evangelicalism* (Grand Rapids, Mich.: William B. Eerdmans Publishing Company, 1996), 162; Keith J. Hardman, "Charles G. Finney, the Benevolent Empire, and the Free Church Movement in New York City," *New York History* 67 (October 1986): 432.

9. ("Plain even to bareness," "near together," etc.) William C. Beecher and Rev. Samuel Scoville, *A Biography of Rev. Henry Ward Beecher* (New York: Charles L. Webster and Company, 1888), 225, 226; ("never take it for a church," "mighty organ") J. T. Lloyd, *Henry Ward Beecher, His Life and Work* (London: Walter Scott, 1887), 65, 66; ("perfect auditorium") Lyman Abbott, *Henry Ward Beecher* (1903; reprt., New York: Chelsea House, 1980), 79–80, and see also 77–78, 88; and see also Clifford E. Clark, Jr., *Henry Ward Beecher: Spokesman for a Middle-Class America* (Chicago: University of Illinois Press, 1978), 88–89. According to Clark, the church cost thirty-six thousand dollars.

10. Talmage quoted in Charles Eugene Banks, *Authorized and Authentic Life and Works of Talmage* (Chicago: Henry Neil, 1902), 91; commentator quoted in John Rusk, *The Authentic Life of T. DeWitt Talmage, the Greatly Beloved Divine* (n.p.: L. G. Stahle, 1902), 54, and, for an illustration, 73. *New York Times* writer quoted by Banks, *Authorized and Authentic Life and Works of Talmage,* 95, and see also 92, 96. Designed by Leonard Vaux, the tabernacle was dedicated on September 25, 1870, and cost between forty and forty-five thousand dollars. According to Charles Francis Adams, *The Life and Sermons of Rev. T. DeWitt Talmage* (Chicago: M. A. Donohue and Co., 1902), 17, it "revolutionized" church architecture and was widely imitated, not only in Brooklyn and New York City but also in Montreal, Louisville, Chicago, and San Francisco.

11. ("Cathedral-like") Adams, *Life and Sermons of Talmage,* 17; ("wide and spacious aisles") Rusk, *Authentic Life of Talmage,* 64, and, for an illustration of the second tabernacle, 73. According to Banks, *Authorized and Authentic Life and Works of Talmage,* 125, 126, 127, the second church, built on the site of the first tabernacle, was dedicated in 1874 and cost $123,800. The architect was John Welch. The building and lot for the third tabernacle, dedicated in 1891, cost about $300,000.

12. Lloyd, *Henry Ward Beecher,* 64, 71, 95; Adams, *Life and Sermons of Talmage,* 41; ("boiling with energy") Banks, *Authorized and Authentic Life and Works of Talmage,* 45, and see also 94, 187.

13. "Prince Emmanuel Burroughs," in *Encyclopedia of Southern Baptists,* vol. 1, 210; John A. Lankford, *Report of Lankford's Artistic Church and Other Designs* (Atlanta: Byrd Print, Co., c. 1916); H. M. Dexter, *Meeting Houses: Considered Historically and Suggestively;* Rev. W[illiam] W[allace] Everts, *The House of God: or Claims of Public Worship* (New York: American Tract Society, 1872); W. T. Euster, *The Philosophy of Church Building: How to Build a Beautiful Modern Church or Parsonage at Half Price;* Mouzon William Brabham, *Planning Modern Church Buildings* (Nashville: Cokesbury Press, 1928); Rev. W. M. Patterson, *A Manual of Architecture for Churches, Parsonages, and School-Houses* (Nashville: Publishing House of the Methodist Episcopal Church, 1875); F. E. Kidder, *Churches and Chapels: Designs and Suggestions for Church-Building Committees, Architects and Builders;* F. E. Kidder, *Churches and Chapels: Their Arrangement, Construction and Equipment Supplemented by Plans, Interior and Exterior Views of Numerous Churches of Different Denominations, Arrangement and Cost;* Harry L. Strickland and J. E. Greene, *Churches, Buildings and Interi-*

or Equipment (Birmingham, Ala.: American Printing Co., 1915); George W. Kramer, *The What How and Why of Church Building.*

14. ("Modern" or "progressive") Kidder, *Churches and Chapels: Their Arrangement,* 41; Kramer, *What How and Why of Church Building,* 18–19, 26, 216; P. E. Burroughs, "Preface," *Church and Sunday-School Buildings.*

15. ("White, staring . . . edifices," "simple cross") Convention of Ministers and Delegates of the Congregational Churches of the United States, *A Book of Plans for Churches and Parsonages. Published under the Direction of the Central Committee, Appointed by the General Congregational Convention, October, 1852. Comprising Designs by Upjohn, Downing, Renwick, Wheeler, Wells, Austin, Stone, Cleveland, Backus, and Reeve,* 19, 11; ("churchly appearance") Brabham, *Planning Modern Church Buildings,* 18; ("overgrown barn") Dexter, *Meeting-Houses,* 4; Francine Haber, Kenneth R. Fuller, and David N. Wetzel, *Robert S. Roeschlaub: Architect of the Emerging West, 1843–1923,* 64, 66; White quoted in David Gilmore Wright and Calvin Correll, *The Restoration of the Lovely Lane Church, Baltimore City Station: The Mother Church of American Methodism,* 47. According to Ryan K. Smith, "The Cross: Church Symbol and Contest in Nineteenth Century America," *Church History* 70 (December 2001): 11, because of its association with Roman Catholicism, the use of the cross provoked controversy among American Protestants, but by the 1870s it was regarded as "the usual symbol of the Christian religion." The use of towers to give a "churchly" look to religious edifices was part of the "rage for towers" in the United States noted by Carroll L. V. Meeks, *The Railroad Station: An Architectural History* (New Haven, Conn.: Yale University Press, 1956), 94.

16. ("Beauty and impressiveness") P. E. Burroughs, *Let Us Build: A Practical Guide,* 19; Richard L. Bushman, *The Refinement of America: Persons, Houses, Cities,* 242–50; Convention of the Congregational Churches, *Book of Plans,* 4; "Methodist Church Architecture," *National Magazine,* December, 1855, 98; Methodist Episcopal Church Board of Church Extension, *Sample Pages of Catalogue of Architectural Plans for Churches and Parsonages furnished by the Board of Church Extension of the Methodist Episcopal Church for the Year 1884* (Philadelphia: Board of Church Extension, Methodist Episcopal Church, [1884?]), 1.

17. Bushman, *Refinement of America,* 341; Jay C. Henry, "Dallas Downtown Churches" (unpublished paper presented at Dallas Museum of Art symposium, "Downtown Dallas Churches," March 1997); C. A. Cummings quoted in "Modern Church Architecture," *American Architect and Building News,* December 8, 1877, 394.

18. For an idea of the variety of architectural styles, as well as the size and cost, of the large auditorium churches constructed in the late nineteenth and early twentieth century, see the architectural plans and perspectives in Kidder, *Churches and Chapels: Designs and Suggestions,* 42–44, and, on two-story churches, 5, 48; and P. E. Burroughs, *A Complete Guide to Church Building,* 97–103, 105, 107–10.

19. ("No adequate precedent") Kramer, *What How and Why of Church Building,* 62; Cummings quoted in "Modern Church Architecture," 393–94; ("no more affiliation") [J. A. F.?], "Modern Church Building. I," *American Architect and Building News,* February 15, 1879, 51–52.

20. ("Servile copyism," "fitness to use") J. A. F., "Modern Church Building, II.," *American Architect and Building News,* March 1, 1879, 67; [J. A. F.?], "Modern Church Building, I," 51; Kidder, *Churches and Chapels: Their Arrangement,* 35.

21. Kidder, *Churches and Chapels: Their Arrangement,* 29; P. E. Burroughs, *Building a Successful Sunday School* (New York: Fleming H. Revell Company, 1921), 69; Euster, *Philosophy of Church Building,* 25.

22. Dexter, *Meeting-Houses,* 24.

23. Daniel Bluestone, *Constructing Chicago,* 84, 85, 96; ("scientific principles") "A Church Burned," *Chicago Tribune,* January 17, 1873; "Dedication of the Union Park Congregational Church," *Chicago Tribune,* November 13, 1871.

24. J. A. F., "Modern Church Building, II," 66–67; Kramer, *What How and Why of Church Building,* 51–52.

25. Willard B. Robinson and Todd Webb, *Texas Public Buildings of the Nineteenth Century* (Austin: University of Texas Press, 1974), 142; Wright and Correll, *Restoration of the Lovely Lane Church,* 50, 51, 52; Haber, Fuller, and Wetzel, *Robert S. Roeschlaub,* 71–72.

Designed by Samuel G. T. Morsell, the eclectic red-brick, granite-trimmed Metropolitan A.M.E. Church cost seventy thousand dollars to build. It measured approximately 80 by 120 feet and featured a basement, a first story at grade level, and a second story housing the auditorium. Data pages, Metropolitan A.M.E. Church, Washington, D.C., Historic American Buildings Survey (HABS), Library of Congress, Prints and Photographs Division, Washington, D.C.; nomination form, Metropolitan African Methodist Episcopal Church, Washington, D.C.,

National Register of Historic Places (NRHP) Inventory, U.S. Department of the Interior, National Park Service, Washington, D.C. On the Mother Bethel A.M.E. Church, see Daniel A. Payne, *History of the African Methodist Episcopal Church*, 462–63. The second and third buildings constructed by the Mother Bethel congregation were meetinghouses with neoclassical detailing. For pictures of those structures, see Edward D. Smith, *Climbing Jacob's Ladder: The Rise of Black Churches in Eastern American Cities, 1740–1877*, 42.

A solid brick structure raised on a high basement, Antioch Baptist Church had curved seating in both the auditorium and the gallery. Nomination form, Antioch Baptist Church, Shreveport, La., NRHP Inventory, U.S. Department of the Interior, National Park Service, Washington, D.C. The Sixteenth Street Baptist Church, a tan brick structure with light stone trim, was designed by an African American architect, Wallace A. Rayfield, and built by an African American firm, Windham Brothers Construction Company. Nomination form, Sixteenth Street Baptist Church, Birmingham, Ala., NRHP Inventory, U.S. Department of the Interior, National Park Service, Washington, D.C.; Charles A. Brown, *W. A. Rayfield: Pioneer Black Architect of Birmingham, Ala.* (Birmingham: Gray Printing Company, 1972), in Tutwiler Collection, Birmingham Public Library, Birmingham, Ala.

26. "Dedication of the Union Park Congregational Church"; (secondary platform) Burroughs, *Church and Sunday-School Buildings*, 71. In smaller auditorium churches the platform was at least five feet deep and twelve feet across; larger auditorium churches had more platform space.

27. ("Very midst," "magnetism") Kramer, *What How and Why of Church Building*, 53; "Methodist Church Architecture," 499; Burroughs, *Church and Sunday-School Buildings*, 61–62 (italics in original). Depending on the size of the audience room and the incline of the floor, architectural commentators advised constructing platforms twelve to thirty inches high.

28. Conkin, *Uneasy Center*, 206–7; Kenneth G. Phifer, *A Protestant Case for Liturgical Renewal* (Philadelphia: Westminster Press, 1965), 151; Julius Melton, *Presbyterian Worship in America: Changing Patterns since 1787* (Richmond, Va.: John Knox Press, 1967), 35–36; Christopher H. Owen, "By Design: The Social Meaning of Methodist Church Architecture in Nineteenth-Century Georgia," *Georgia Historical Quarterly* 75 (summer 1991): 247–48; Payne, *History of the A.M.E Church*, 52–59, 458; Daniel Alexander Payne, *Recollections of Seventy Years* (1888; reprt., New York:

Arno Press and the *New York Times*, 1968), 233–37; Carter G. Woodson, *The History of the Negro Church*, 231–32; Kilde, *When Church Became Theatre*, 133–39.

29. ("Towered") James F. White, *Protestant Worship and Church Architecture: Theological and Historical Considerations*, 125; Kidder, *Churches and Chapels: Their Arrangement*, 64; Burroughs, *Church and Sunday-School Buildings*, 75.

30. Haber, Fuller, and Wetzel, *Robert S. Roeschlaub*, 76; Euster, *Philosophy of Church Building*, 77.

31. Kate Atkinson Bell, Christine Hall Ladner, and Joanna William Poor, eds., *A Church in the City Reaching the World*, 189. Sometimes the baptistery was located under the platform (covered by a movable floor) or under the choir loft.

32. On seating, see Kidder, *Churches and Chapels: Their Arrangement*, 57; Euster, *Philosophy of Church Building*, 97; Burroughs, *Church and Sunday-School Buildings*, 219–20. On lighting and heating/ventilating systems, see Burroughs, *Complete Guide*, 34; Burroughs, *Church and Sunday-School Buildings*, 67; Haber, Fuller, and Wetzel, *Robert S. Roeschlaub*, 68. On the development of lighting, heating, and ventilating systems in nineteenth- and early-twentieth-century America, see Merritt Ierley, *Open House: A Guided Tour of the American Home, 1637–Present* (New York: Henry Holt and Company, 1999), 166–75; Merritt Ierley, *The Comforts of Home: The American House and the Evolution of Modern Convenience* (New York: Clarkson N. Potter, 1999), 121–31, 200–213.

33. Convention of the Congregational Churches, *Book of Plans*, 22; Kramer, *What How and Why of Church Building*, 180.

34. Payne, *History of the A.M.E. Church*, 463.

35. ("Subdue" light) Convention of the Congregational Churches, *Book of Plans*, 26; ("strain") M. F. Cummings, "Modern Church Architecture," *American Architect and Building News*, April 13, 1878, 131; Methodist Episcopal Church Board of Church Extension, *Sample Pages*, 2.

36. On the decoration of auditorium churches, see Kilde, *When Church Became Theatre*, 153–56. On the Trinity and Lovely Lane churches, see Haber, Fuller, and Wetzel, *Robert S. Roeschlaub*, 67, 68, 72; A. A. Cox, "The First M. E. [sic] Church and Its Associated Buildings, Baltimore, Maryland," *American Architect and Building News*, June 11, 1892, 166; Wright and Correll, *Restoration of the Lovely Lane Church*, 31, 35.

37. ("Nothing") Convention of the Congregational Churches, *Book of*

Plans, 28; ("cobalt") Bluestone, *Constructing Chicago,* 90; ("rich and warm," etc.) Wright and Correll, *Restoration of the Lovely Lane Church,* 35.

38. Kilde, *When Church Became Theatre,* 151–56; Bushman, *Refinement of America,* 178–80; Bluestone, *Constructing Chicago,* 90; Russell Lynes, *The Tastemakers: The Shaping of American Popular Taste* (1954; reprt., New York: Dover Publications, Inc., 1980), 81–87. For illustrations and discussion of the interiors of late-nineteenth-century upper-class American homes, see, for example, *Artistic Houses: Being a Series of Interior Views of a Number of the Most Beautiful and Celebrated Homes in the United States, with a Description of the Art Treasures Contained Therein* (1883; reprt., New York: Benjamin Blom, Inc., 1971); and Katherine C. Grier, *Culture and Comfort: Parlor Making and Middle-Class Identity, 1850–1930* (Washington, D.C.: Smithsonian Institution Press, 1988).

39. ("Luxury," "extravagance," "ostentation") "Chicago," *The Standard,* February 24, 1876; Charles Grandison Finney, *Lectures on Revivals of Religion,* edited by William G. McLoughlin (Cambridge, Mass.: The Belknap Press of Harvard University Press, 1960), 237, italics in original.

40. Convention of the Congregational Churches, *Book of Plans,* 11–12.

41. "Dedication of the Union Park Congregational Church."

42. Matthew Anderson, *Presbyterianism. Its Relation to the Negro. Illustrated by the Berean Presbyterian Church, Philadelphia, with Sketch of the Church and Autobiography of the Author* (Philadelphia: John McGill White and Co., 1897), 65–67; Payne, *History of the A.M.E. Church,* 464; Allen quoted in Owen, "By Design," 251. See also Benjamin Elijah Mays and Joseph William Nicholson, *The Negro's Church* (1933; reprt., New York: Arno Press and the *New York Times,* 1969), 117, 280.

43. Kilde, *When Church Became Theatre,* 128–29. Haber, Fuller, and Wetzel, *Robert S. Roeschlaub,* 63, 71, 72, described the auditorium of the Trinity Methodist Episcopal Church in Denver as "conceived in circulation pattern and plan as a late Rococo theater" and asserted that "the spatial organization is borrowed from the prototype of small eighteenth-century opera houses." For photographs of nineteenth-century American theaters, opera houses, and concert halls, see David Naylor and Joan Dillon, *American Theaters: Performance Halls of the Nineteenth Century* (New York: John Wiley and Sons, Inc., 1997), and Simon Tidworth, *Theatres: An Architectural and Cultural History* (New York: Praeger Publishers, 1973).

44. Lawrence W. Levine, *Highbrow/Lowbrow: The Emergence of Cultural Hierarchy in America* (Cambridge, Mass.: Harvard University Press, 1988), 101, and see also 68, 104; Bushman, *Refinement of America,* 358; "A Church Burned," 4; *Rocky Mountain Christian Advocate* quoted in Haber, Fuller, and Wetzel, *Robert S. Roeschlaub,* 72.

45. Euster, *Philosophy of Church Building,* 21.

46. Burroughs, *Church and Sunday-School Buildings,* 67.

4. The Multipurpose Church

1. Convention of the Congregational Churches, *Book of Plans,* 16; ("new instrumentalities") Conwell quoted in Robert J. Burdette, *The Modern Temple and Templars: A Sketch of the Life and Work of Russell H. Conwell* (New York: Silver, Burdett and Company, 1894), 184. For statements by nineteenth- and early-twentieth-century architects and churchmen promoting the multipurpose church, see Dexter, *Meeting-Houses,* 25–26; Burroughs, *Complete Guide,* 13–14, 21–27; Burroughs, *Church and Sunday-School Buildings,* 9; Kramer, *What How and Why of Church Building,* 41, 49–50, 58–59, 69–72; "Modern Church Architecture," *American Architect and Building News,* December 8, 1877, 393; Cummings, "Modern Church Architecture," 131; J. A. F., "Modern Church Building, II," 67; Patterson, *Manual of Architecture,* 30–31; Brabham, *Planning Modern Church Buildings,* 28; Kidder, *Churches and Chapels: Designs and Suggestions,* 12–13; Kidder, *Churches and Chapels: Their Arrangement,* 29–30; Everts, *House of God,* 81; Burroughs, *Let Us Build,* 27–32. Evangelicals were not the only ones to build multipurpose churches; so did the more liberal, modernist Protestant denominations, as well as Roman Catholics and Jews. See, for example, Jean Miller Schmidt, *Souls or the Social Order: The Two-Party System in American Protestantism* (Brooklyn, N.Y.: Carlson Publishing Inc., 1991), 66–68, 119–20; Williams, *Houses of God,* 17; David Kaufman, *Shul with a Pool: The "Synagogue-Center" in American Jewish History* (Hanover, N.H.: Brandeis University Press, 1999). On African American multipurpose church buildings, see Mays and Nicholson, *The Negro's Church,* 116–17.

2. Anne M. Boylan, *Sunday School: The Formation of an American Institution, 1790–1880* (New Haven, Conn.: Yale University Press, 1988), 12–13, 20, 39–40, 152.

3. On the Akron Plan, see Kidder, *Churches and Chapels: Their Arrangement*, 45–50; Kramer, *What How and Why of Church Building*, 56–57, 60, 216–20; Ellwood Hendrick, *Lewis Miller: A Biographical Essay* (New York: G. P. Putnam's Sons, 1925); Willard B. Robinson, *Reflections of Faith: Houses of Worship in the Lone Star State*, 81–83, 99, 132*n*18, 166, 177. On Pilgrim Congregational Church, see Chiat, *America's Religious Architecture*, 109.

4. Burroughs, *Church and Sunday-School Buildings*, 68, 123.

5. See, for example, ibid., 9–10, chaps. 4–6; Burroughs, *Let Us Build*, 13–14, chap. 5; Burroughs, *Complete Guide*, chap. 5; Robinson, *Reflections of Faith*, 176.

6. On Bethany Presbyterian Church Sabbath School, see Herbert Adams Gibbons, *John Wanamaker* (2 vols.; New York: Harper and Brothers Publishers, 1926), vol. 1, 187–89. Gibbons, 169–92, 189–90, attributes Wanamaker's "new kind of Sunday School" (referring to the building that housed it as well as the way the school was organized) to the same innovating impulse that guided the design of the "new kind of store" Wanamaker opened in the Grand Depot, two years later, in 1877. On the educational buildings constructed by First Baptist, Dallas, and First Baptist, Jacksonville, see Leon McBeth, *The First Baptist Church of Dallas: Centennial History (1868–1968)* (Grand Rapids, Mich.: Zondervan Publishing House, 1968), 167; B. S. Wall, Jr., "History of First Baptist Church, Jacksonville, Florida, 1838–1968" (mimeographed typescript, [1968?], courtesy of First Baptist Church, Jacksonville); and, for drawings and floor plans, Brabham, *Planning Modern Church Buildings*, 173, 226–29.

7. Burroughs, *Complete Guide*, 12–13; Adam Clayton Powell, "The Church in Social Work," *Opportunity* 1 (January 1923): 15; Lankford, *Report*.

8. On the Chautauqua Association and YMCA, see Moore, *Selling God*, 116, 150, 152–54. On holiness camp meetings and "Christian resorts," see Kenneth O. Brown, *Holy Ground: A Study of the American Camp Meeting* (New York: Garland Publishing, Inc., 1992), 32; Charles A. Parker, "Ocean Grove, NJ: Queen of the Victorian Methodist Camp Meeting Resorts," *Nineteenth Century* (spring 1984): 21–25; Troy W. Messenger, "Holy Leisure: The Camp Meeting at Ocean Grove, New Jersey" (Ph.D. diss., New York University, 1997), 13–14, 38–39, 54–57; Weiss, *City in the Woods*.

9. On the Broadway Tabernacle, see Nichols, *History of the Broadway Tabernacle*, 64, 97–98; Lawrence, *Strong on Music*, vol. 1, 15, 43, 49, 307.

Although Finney judged the acoustics of the tabernacle excellent for preaching, George Templeton Strong pronounced it "the worst possible room for an orchestra or a chorus," noting that "the reverberation from the absurd little dome and skylight muddles everything up and produces the same effect on concerted [*sic*] music that a crape veil does on a picture." Lawrence, *Strong on Music*, vol. 1, 307. On social events in other auditorium churches, see *The Work in Tremont Temple* (Boston: Union Temple Baptist Church, [1871?]), 23 (used with the permission of the American Baptist Historical Society, American Baptist-Samuel Colgate Library, Rochester, N.Y.); Clarence Taylor, *The Black Churches of Brooklyn* (New York: Columbia University Press, 1994), 23; Linda K. Kirby, *Heritage of Heroes: Trinity United Methodist Church, 1859–1988*, 104–6.

10. Burroughs, *Complete Guide*, 12–13. See also Kidder, *Churches and Chapels: Their Arrangement*, 40–41; Lankford, *Report*, n.p.

11. Haber, Fuller, and Wetzel, *Robert S. Roeschlaub*, 151*n*32; Kirby, *Heritage of Heroes*, 187–88.

12. Gibbons, *John Wanamaker*, vol. 2, 324, 337–38; *Church Building Quarterly*, 1896, quoted in Kidder, *Churches and Chapels: Their Arrangement*, 50, 52.

13. Marilee Munger Scroggs, *A Light in the City: The Fourth Presbyterian Church of Chicago* (Chicago: Fourth Presbyterian Church of Chicago, 1990), 75–81.

14. Ralph E. Luker, *Social Gospel in Black and White: American Racial Reform, 1885–1912* (Chapel Hill: University of North Carolina Press, 1991), 174, 177, 184, 190; Robert Gregg, *Sparks from the Anvil of Oppression: Philadelphia's African Methodists and Southern Migrants, 1890–1940* (Philadelphia: Temple University Press, 1993), 58, 61; Allan H. Spear, *Black Chicago: The Making of a Negro Ghetto, 1890–1920* (Chicago: University of Chicago Press, 1967), 92, 95, 177; Elisabeth Lasch-Quinn, *Black Neighbors: Race and the Limits of Reform in the American Settlement House Movement, 1890–1945* (Chapel Hill: University of North Carolina Press, 1993), 68, 69; Milton C. Sernett, *Bound for the Promised Land: African American Religion and the Great Migration* (Durham, N.C.: Duke University Press, 1997), 119, 133, 134, 144, 158; Anderson, *Presbyterianism. Its Relation to the Negro*, 250–51.

15. Burroughs, *Complete Guide*, 10; *Chicago Defender* quoted in Sernett, *Bound for the Promised Land*, 158, and see also 119, 143–44, 157; Spear,

Black Chicago, 92, 177–78; Lasch-Quinn, *Black Neighbors,* 68; Woodson, *History of the Negro Church,* 254.

16. *Southwestern Christian Advocate* quoted in Sernett, *Bound for the Promised Land,* 158.

17. On Pilgrim Congregational Church, see Eric Johannesen, *Cleveland Architecture, 1876–1976* (Cleveland: Western Reserve Historical Society, 1979), 51–52; Foster Armstrong, Richard Klein, and Cara Armstrong, *A Guide to Cleveland's Sacred Landmarks* (Kent, Ohio: Kent State University Press, 1992), 227. On Bethany Presbyterian Church, see William R. Glass, "Liberal Means to Conservative Ends: Bethany Presbyterian Church, John Wanamaker, and the Institutional Church Movement," *American Presbyterians* 68 (fall 1990): 183, 186, 187, 188, 189; Aaron I. Abell, *The Urban Impact on American Protestantism, 1865–1900* (Cambridge, Mass.: Harvard University Press, 1943), 155–56.

18. The origins of the Baptist Temple date from 1870, when it was a mission Sunday school of the Tenth Baptist Church of Philadelphia, holding classes in Bethune Hall, which was located on the second floor of a grocery store. In 1871, the church was organized with fifty-six charter members. Between 1872 and 1874, the congregation worshiped in a large tent that accommodated about five hundred persons. It had a board floor, pews with cushions, gas lighting, and was heated by several large stoves. The building dedicated in 1891 was the congregation's second. The first was a neo-Gothic structure with an auditorium featuring amphitheater seating for between six and seven hundred persons and the ornate decoration and furnishings characteristic of so many late-nineteenth-century auditorium churches—a frescoed ceiling, stained-glass windows, and "handsomely upholstered" pews. Edward O. Elliott, *Tent to Temple: A History of the Grace Baptist Church, Philadelphia, Pa., 1870 to 1895* (Philadelphia: n.p., 1946), 6, 9, 23, and, for drawings of the tent and the first church building, 4, 24 (courtesy of Baptist Temple, Blue Bell, Pa.). On the design of the temple, see Edmund K. Alden, "Progressive Methods of Church Work. XV.—The Temple, Philadelphia," *Christian Union,* March 18, 1893, 508, 509; Agnes Rush Burr, *Russell H. Conwell, Founder of the Institutional Church in America, The Man and the Work* (Philadelphia: John C. Winston Company, 1908), 153–55; Burdette, *Modern Temple and Templars,* 206–7. The architect who designed the temple was Thomas Lonsdale, according to John Milner Associates, Inc., "An Historic Inventory of The Auditorium of

The Baptist Temple, Temple University" (typescript; Philadelphia, 1984), in Conwellana-Templana Collection, Central Library System, Temple University, Philadelphia.

19. Alden, "Progressive Methods," 509; Burdette, *Modern Temple and Templars,* 206, 208, 209, 213–14, 222; Burr, *Russell H. Conwell,* 153; Elliott, *Tent to Temple,* 63; John Milner Associates, "Historic Inventory."

20. Burr, *Russell H. Conwell,* 208; Alden, "Progressive Methods," 509.

21. Burr, *Russell H. Conwell,* 203, 207; Burdette, *Modern Temple and Templars,* 206–7; Alden, "Progressive Methods," 508.

22. Burr, *Russell H. Conwell,* 177–80.

23. Elliott, *Tent to Temple,* 50, 77–78; Burdette, *Modern Temple and Templars,* 227, 230–31; Frances L. Kraus, "Years of Grace" (church brochure, 1967, courtesy of Baptist Temple, Blue Bell, Pa.).

24. See, for example, Burroughs, *Building a Successful Sunday School,* 126, 127; Brabham, *Planning Modern Church Buildings,* 26, 27.

25. Burr, *Russell H. Conwell,* 178–79.

26. On this point, see Anderson, *Presbyterianism,* 249; Sernett, *Bound for the Promised Land,* 119.

27. ("Going over to the world") Burdette, *Modern Temple and Templars,* 310–11; ("coldness and forgetfulness") Burr, *Russell H. Conwell,* 180–81.

28. Conwell quoted in Burr, *Russell H. Conwell,* 159, 178.

5. Building for Mass Evangelism

1. The new generation of evangelicals rejected the liberal theological doctrines that had gradually gained acceptance, to a greater or lesser degree, in the mainline evangelical churches. Fundamentalists, for example, held fast to the five tenets formulated at the Niagara Bible Conference of 1895: the inerrancy of Scripture, the deity and virgin birth of Christ, the substitutionary atonement of Christ, the physical resurrection of Christ, and the imminent Second Coming of Christ. Holiness and pentecostal groups added other doctrines to produce what they called a "full gospel." Holiness churches and denominations emphasized entire sanctification (the "second blessing"), a second work of grace subse-

quent to the initial conversion experience. Pentecostals emphasized the "baptism of the Holy Spirit," an experience following, and distinct from, conversion, and evidenced by, among other things, speaking in tongues.

2. ("One hundred thousand dollar churches") Bruce L. Shelley, *Evangelicalism in America* (Grand Rapids, Mich.: William B. Eerdmans Publishing Company, 1967), 56; Vick quoted in Louis Entzminger, *The J. Frank Norris I Have Known for 34 [sic] Years* (Fort Worth: n.p., 1946), 260–61.

3. Edith L. Blumhofer, *Restoring the Faith: The Assemblies of God, Pentecostalism, and American Culture* (Urbana: University of Illinois Press, 1993), 96; Joel A. Carpenter, *Revive Us Again: The Reawakening of American Fundamentalism,* 57–58, 76; Vick quoted in Entzminger, *J. Frank Norris,* 260–61.

4. Beardsley, *A History of American Revivals,* 283; E. Ray Tatum, *Conquest or Failure? Biography of J. Frank Norris* (Dallas: Baptist Historical Foundation, 1966), 129; C. Allyn Russell, *Voices of American Fundamentalism: Seven Biographical Studies* (Philadelphia: Westminister Press, 1976), 29; Entzminger, *J. Frank Norris,* 266, 267; Blumhofer, *Restoring the Faith,* 167.

5. On Moody's and Sunday's tabernacles, see Rev. W. H. Daniels, "The New Revival Hall," *Northwestern Christian Advocate,* September 27, 1876, 1; Homer Rodeheaver, *Twenty Years with Billy Sunday* (Winona Lake, Ind.: Rodeheaver Co., 1936), 75; Elijah P. Brown, *The Real Billy Sunday: The Life and Work of Rev. William Ashley Sunday, D.D., the Baseball Evangelist* (New York: Fleming H. Revell Company, 1914), 138, picture caption facing p. 189. On the use of secular buildings, see Beardsley, *History of American Revivals,* 268, 269, 282; Noble, *A Century of Gospel-Work,* 455–56; Rodeheaver, *Twenty Years,* 99, 114–15.

6. William R. Moody, *The Life of Dwight L. Moody* (New York: Fleming B. Revell Company, 1900), 268; James F. Findlay, Jr., *Dwight L. Moody, American Evangelist, 1837–1899* (Chicago: University of Chicago Press, 1969), 200; Herbert Adams Gibbons, *John Wanamaker* (2 vols.; New York: Harper and Brothers Publishers, 1926), vol. 1, 137.

7. (Moody tabernacle) Daniels, "New Revival Hall," 1; (Sunday tabernacles) William T. Ellis, *"Billy" Sunday: The Man and His Message* (Philadelphia: John C. Winston Company, 1914), 66; Larry K. Eskridge, "Only Believe: Paul Rader and the Chicago Gospel Tabernacle, 1922–1933" (Master's thesis, University of Maryland, 1985), 59, 61, 62–63,

65–66, 98n32. For a drawing of the exterior of the Chicago Gospel Tabernacle, see Carpenter, *Revive Us Again,* n.p.; for a photo of the interior, see Michael S. Hamilton, "Willow Creek's Place in History," *Christianity Today,* November 13, 2000, 63. On barns featuring a broken-gable or clerestory roof, also known as a monitor roof, see Allen G. Noble and Richard K. Cleek, *The Old Barn Book: A Field Guide to North American Barns and Other Farm Structures* (New Brunswick, N.J.: Rutgers University Press, 1995), 39; and Stanley Schuler, *American Barns: In a Class by Themselves* (Exton, Pa.: Schiffer Publishing Ltd., 1984), 46–55.

8. Better known as Ryman Auditorium, the Union Gospel Tabernacle was financed by a converted riverboat captain named Thomas Green Ryman and the popular southern revivalist Sam Jones. Designed by architect A. T. Thompson and completed in 1892, it cost about one hundred thousand dollars. See Thomas B. Brumbaugh, Martha I. Strayhorn, and Gary G. Gore, eds., *Architecture of Middle Tennessee: The Historic American Buildings Survey* (Nashville: Vanderbilt University Press, 1974), 40, 46; Ellen Beasley, "The End of the Rainbow," *Historic Preservation* 24 (January–March 1972): 21; William U. Eiland, *Nashville's Mother Church: The History of the Ryman Auditorium* (Nashville: Opryland USA, 1992), 17.

9. Ellis, *"Billy" Sunday,* 66, illustration facing p. 301; Brumbaugh, Strayhorn, and Gore, eds., *Architecture of Middle Tennessee,* 42; Daniels, "New Revival Hall," 1.

10. (Moody tabernacle) Daniels, "New Revival Hall," 1; (Chicago Gospel Tabernacle) Eskridge, "Only Believe," 62; (Sunday's platforms) Rodeheaver, *Twenty Years,* 75, 121. For descriptions of Sunday (used every inch of platform) Brown, *Real Billy Sunday,* 140; ("50 per cent," "constant movement," *Louisville Herald*) Rodeheaver, *Twenty Years,* 22, 100; ("people understand," "impossible for him to stand up") Ellis, *"Billy" Sunday,* 138, 139.

11. Eskridge, "Only Believe," 63; Rodeheaver, *Twenty Years,* 122.

12. Carpenter, *Revive Us Again,* 75; Everett L. Perry, "The Role of Socio-Economic Factors in the Rise and Development of American Fundamentalism" (Ph.D. diss., University of Chicago Divinity School, 1959), 67, 68, 98–99; Brown, *Real Billy Sunday,* 139; "Moody and Sankey," *Chicago Tribune,* October 2, 1876; Daniels, "New Revival Hall," 1.

13. William G. McLoughlin, "Is There a Third Force in Christendom?" *Daedalus* 96 (winter 1967): 53; ("intelligent sermonizing" and refined

music) Woodson, *History of the Negro Church*, 228–31; ("corn-field ditties") Payne, *Recollections of Seventy Years*, 253–57.

14. Timothy L. Smith, *Called Unto Holiness: The Story of the Nazarenes: The Formative Years* (Kansas City, Mo.: Nazarene Publishing House, 1962), 268; Taylor, *Black Churches of Brooklyn*, 90; ("self-expression," "emotional release") Perry, "Role of Socio-Economic Factors," 69, and see also 67, 71, 74, 100.

15. Rodeheaver, *Twenty Years*, 73, 78; Ellis, *"Billy" Sunday*, 264.

16. On the invitation, see Carpenter, *Revive Us Again*, 77; David Bennett, *The Altar Call: Its Origins and Present Usage* (New York: University Press of America, Inc., 2000).

17. The wooden tabernacle was built in 1898. Its auditorium reportedly held twenty-two hundred chairs, and the platform accommodated a choir of sixty persons and a twenty-piece orchestra. "Bible Conference to Begin Tonight," *Atlanta Constitution*, March 6, 1899; "Sixty-Fifth Anniversary: The Baptist Tabernacle, Atlanta, Georgia, 1898–1963," in Special Collections, Mercer University Main Library, Macon, Ga.

18. On the Bible conferences, see William R. Glass, "The Ministry of Leonard G. Broughton at Tabernacle Baptist Church, 1898–1912: A Source of Southern Fundamentalism," *Baptist Quarterly* 4 (March 1985): 39–41. On the 1911 structure, see Greta Barrett, "The Baptist Tabernacle Story" (church bulletin, n.d.), in Special Collections, Mercer University Main Library, Macon, Ga. Hunt designed a number of Methodist, Presbyterian, and Baptist churches in Texas, Alabama, and other southern states. See "Reuben Harrison Hunt," in Henry Withey and Elsie R. Withey, *Biographical Dictionary of American Architects* (Los Angeles: New Age Publishing Co., 1956), 309–10. On the dedication week services, see "Sixty-Fifth Anniversary: The Baptist Tabernacle, Atlanta, Georgia, 1898–1963"; "Many Thousands Attend Opening of Tabernacle," *Atlanta Constitution*, September 11, 1911.

19. "Organ Dedicated at Tabernacle," *Atlanta Constitution*, September 13, 1911; Fuzzy Woodruff, "Dr. G. Campbell Morgan, England's Most Eminent Divine as Seen by Fuzzy Woodruff, the South's Cleverest Sporting Writer," *Atlanta Constitution*, September 17, 1911. The Baptist Tabernacle was unusual among the churches built by dissenting evangelicals in that, like most auditorium churches, it functioned as a multipurpose church. It operated "mission stations" in various parts of Atlanta, and its church complex included a Bible and Missionary Training Institute, an infirmary, a Young Ladies dormitory for working-class girls, and a Tabernacle Employment Department. Two other structures built by dissenters offered programs and facilities similar to those of the auditorium churches, but on a smaller scale. Paul Rader's Chicago Gospel Tabernacle presented concerts and pageants and provided recreational facilities for adults and children, including a summer camp on Lake Michigan. Aimee Semple McPherson's Angelus Temple in Los Angeles had nurseries for children too young to attend Sunday school, an employment service, a commissary for the needy, and a training institute for evangelists and missionaries. Glass, "Ministry of Leonard Broughton," 42–43; Vivian Perkins and William F. Doverspike, "The Baptist Tabernacle," in James L. Baggot, ed., *History of Atlanta Baptist Church* (Atlanta: privately published, [1962?]), 5; "Work of the Tabernacle Baptist and Its Pastor," *Atlanta Constitution*, October 12, 1902; Eskridge, "Only Believe," 79, 81, 88–92, 94; Hamilton, "Willow Creek's Place in History," 62–63; "Aimee Semple McPherson," in Charles H. Lippy, ed., *Twentieth Century Shapers of American Popular Religion* (New York: Greenwood Press, 1989), 266; Daniel Mark Epstein, *Sister Aimee: The Life of Aimee Semple McPherson* (New York: Harcourt Brace Jovanovich, Publishers, 1993), 249; Edith L. Blumhofer, *Aimee Semple McPherson: Everybody's Sister* (Grand Rapids, Mich.: William B. Eerdmans Publishing Company, 1993), 256.

20. Woodruff, "Dr. G. Campbell Morgan."

21. Russell, *Voices of American Fundamentalism*, 29.

22. For descriptions of the 1888 and 1912 churches, see "The First Baptist Church," *Fort Worth Daily Gazette*, June 17, 1888; Robinson and Webb, *Texas Public Buildings*, 142, 143; Tatum, *Conquest or Failure?* 96, 169–70. On the third First Baptist structure (1933), see Tatum, *Conquest or Failure?* 255, 261, 282; "Seminary Grows Up," *Fort Worth Star-Telegram*, June 15, 1947 (clipping courtesy of the Fort Worth Public Library, Fort Worth, Texas).

23. Tatum, *Conquest or Failure?* 261. See also [J. Frank Norris?], *Inside History of First Baptist Church Fort Worth and Temple Baptist Church Detroit: Life Story of Dr. J. Frank Norris* ([Fort Worth, Texas?]: n.p., [1937?]), 8, 304. For pictures of the interior, see [Norris?], *Inside History*, 4, 304; Entzminger, *J. Frank Norris*, 28, 29; Tatum, *Conquest or Failure?* 299.

24. Tatum, *Conquest or Failure?* 271. See also "New Temple Baptist Sunday School Building," *Detroit News*, February 27, 1937 (clipping supplied by the Detroit Public Library). After nine months in the Temple Baptist

pulpit, Norris reported 1,145 additions. By 1943, Temple Baptist claimed a membership of about 8,500. In 1946, Norris boasted a combined membership of 25,000 in his two churches, which he claimed was the largest congregation ever pastored by a single individual in the history of the church. Tatum, *Conquest or Failure?* 281. For a picture of Temple Baptist church, see Entzminger, *J. Frank Norris,* 62.

25. Vick quoted in Entzminger, *J. Frank Norris,* 260–61.

26. "New Temple Baptist Sunday School Building"; Tatum, *Conquest or Failure?* 282.

27. On the development of the skyscraper, see Bluestone, *Constructing Chicago,* chap. 4; Spiro Kostof, *A History of Architecture: Settings and Rituals,* 2d ed. (New York: Oxford University Press, 1995), 661–66, 708.

28. On Massee, see Russell, *Voices of American Fundamentalism,* 111, 114, 118. On the design of Tremont Temple, see "Tremont Temple, Boston, Mass. Messrs. Blackall & Newton, Architects, Boston, Mass.," *American Architect and Building News* 45 (July 14, 1894): 19.

29. "Tremont Temple," 19; Boston Landmarks Commission Building Information Form, in "Central Business District Preservation Study," prepared by Pamela W. Fox and Mickail Koch, pt. 1, vol. 4, n.p., from collection of the Boston Athenaeum, Boston.

30. William R. De Plata, *Tell It from Calvary* (New York: Calvary Baptist Church, 1972), 56–57, 65, 91.

31. George A. Lane, *Chicago Churches and Synagogues: An Architectural Pilgrimage* (Chicago: Loyola University Press, 1981), 172; Blumhofer, *Aimee Semple McPherson,* 245, 246, 247; Eskridge, "Only Believe," 98*n32.*

32. Blumhofer, *Aimee Semple McPherson,* 99, 234, 235, 245, 259–62. McPherson had visited the Hippodrome while living in New York City in 1911. Built by the circus king P. T. Barnum in the early 1870s, the Hippodrome was a giant wooden building 425 feet long and 200 feet wide, which accommodated as many as eight thousand spectators, and which had a stage measuring 98 feet long and 110 feet deep. Neil Harris, *Humbug: The Art of P. T. Barnum* (Chicago: University of Chicago Press, 1973), 243–44, and, for a picture of the exterior and interior of the Hippodrome, 260.

33. Blumhofer, *Aimee Semple McPherson,* 234, 236, 246.

34. Ibid., 245, 246, 249, 251; "Pray without Ceasing," *Foursquare Crusader,* January 1940, 29, supplied by the Heritage Department, International Church of the Foursquare Gospel, Los Angeles.

35. Guide to Collection 330, Records of Moody Memorial Church, in Billy Graham Center Archives, Wheaton, Ill., from Web site, bgcarc @wheaton.edu, June 10, 1999; Eskridge, "Only Believe," 33; Perry, "Role of Socio-Economic Factors," 302. The architects were Fugard and Knapp.

36. Eskridge, "Only Believe," 40; Guide to Collection 330; Lane, *Chicago Churches and Synagogues,* 172.

37. According to Chiat, *America's Religious Architecture,* 291, Mason Temple replaced the National Temple, a frame structure built in 1924, which burned down in 1936. On the design of Mason Temple, see *History and Formative Years of the Church of God in Christ with Excerpts from the Life and Works of Its Founder—Bishop C. H. Mason* (Memphis: Church of God in Christ Publishing House, 1969), 71, 110, 111; registration form, Mason Temple, Memphis, Tenn., National Register of Historic Places (NRHP) Inventory, U.S. Department of the Interior, National Park Service, Washington, D.C.

38. *History and Formative Years,* 73; registration form, Mason Temple, NRHP Inventory.

39. Tatum, *Conquest or Failure?* 254.

6. The Gathered Church

1. On the church building boom, see Robert Wuthnow, *The Restructuring of American Religion: Society and Faith since World War II* (Princeton, N.J.: Princeton University Press, 1988), 27, 35–36; John R. Scotford, "The Aftermath of the Church Building Boom," *Christian Century* 84 (December 27, 1967): 1650. "Revolution" was the term many commentators used. See, for example, "The New Look in Architecture," *Christian Century* 71 (January 27, 1954): 103. It was part of the international movement known as modernism that had developed earlier in the United States and Europe and involved secular as well as ecclesiastical architecture. On the European phase of the revolution, see Paul Thiry, Richard M. Bennett, and Henry L. Kamphoefner, *Churches and Temples* (New York: Reinhold Publishing Corporation, 1953), 11P–13P; James F. White, *Protestant Worship and Church Architecture: Theological and Historical Con-*

siderations, 147–67. Numerous books treating innovative religious buildings constructed in Europe were available to American architects, pastors, and congregations. See, for example, Albert Christ-Janer and Mary Mix Foley, *Modern Church Architecture: A Guide to the Form and Spirit of 20th Century Religious Buildings* (New York: McGraw-Hill Book Company, Inc., 1962).

On the architectural reformers, see, for example, Paul Tillich, "Contemporary Protestant Architecture"; E. A. Sövik, *Architecture for Worship* (Minneapolis: Augsburg Publishing House, 1973); Mark Allen Torgerson, "Edward Anders Sövik and His Return to the 'Non-Church'" (Ph.D. diss., University of Notre Dame, September, 1995), 17. Before establishing his own office in Philadelphia in 1944, Harold E. Wagoner had been a staff member of the Bureau of Architecture of the Methodist Church; in the years following World War II, he served as president of the Church Architectural Guild of America and of the Philadelphia chapter of the American Institute of Architects. "From Blueprint to Building" (information sheet in the collection of the Coral Ridge Presbyterian Church library, Fort Lauderdale, Fla.). John R. Scotford wrote *When You Build Your Church,* 2d ed. (Great Neck, N.Y.: Channel Press, 1958). Pastor and church consultant C. Harry Atkinson published *How to Get Your Church Built* (Garden City, N.Y.: Doubleday and Company, Inc., 1964). A professor of worship at Southern Methodist University, James F. White authored several books, including *Protestant Worship and Church Architecture.* See also Thiry, Bennett, and Kamphoefner, *Churches and Temples;* Victor Fiddes, *The Architectural Requirements of Protestant Worship* (Toronto: Ryerson Press, 1961); Donald J. Bruggink and Carl H. Droppers, *Christ and Architecture: Building Presbyterian/Reformed Churches* (Grand Rapids, Mich.: William B. Eerdmans Publishing Company, 1965); Donald J. Bruggink and Carl H. Droppers, *When Faith Takes Form: Contemporary Churches of Architectural Integrity in America* (Grand Rapids, Mich.: William B. Eerdmans Publishing Company, 1971).

On the organizations and journals promoting architectural reform, see Fiddes, *Architectural Requirements,* 65–66; *Encyclopedia of Associations: National Organizations of the U.S.,* vol. 1 (Detroit: Gale Research Company, 1961), 282; James Hudnut-Beumler, "The Many Mansions of God's House: The Religious Built Environment as Assimilation and Differentiation" (from Material History of American Religion Project Web site, www.materialreligion.org, March 1998).

2. Harold E. Wagoner, "A New Religiosity? Sensate Chaos? or What the Heck Is Happening to Church Building?" *Faith and Form* 8 (spring 1975): 8–9. On the Gothic Revival of the early twentieth century, see Kilde, *When Church Became Theatre,* 203–11. Even Southern Baptists were unable to resist the Gothic spell. William A. Harrell, who succeeded P. E. Burroughs as head of the Southern Baptist Convention's Department of Church Architecture, published a guide to church building in 1947 in which he promoted auditoriums in the shape of a narrow rectangle, with a level rather than a sloping floor, straight rather than curved pews, and a platform no more than twenty-four inches high. Harrell, *Planning Better Church Buildings,* 18–20, 23.

3. ("Real and true") Edward A. Sövik, "What Is Religious Architecture?" 9; ("imitative-traditional") Tillich, "Contemporary Protestant Architecture," 125; ("suited aesthetically") Atkinson, *How to Get Your Church Built,* 171; ("express the beliefs") Scotford, "Aftermath," 1651. For references to Sullivan's dictum, see Scotford, "Aftermath," 1651; White, *Protestant Worship and Church Architecture,* 198; Fiddes, *Architectural Requirements,* 58; Marvin Halverson, "On Getting Good Architecture for the Church," in John Knox Shear, ed., *Religious Buildings for Today* (n.p.: F. W. Dodge Corporation, 1957), 3. On the "gathered church" and the mid-twentieth-century reformers' interest in the early Christians, the Protestant Reformers, and the English Nonconformists, see, for example, Fiddes, *Architectural Requirements,* 28, 32, 35; White, *Protestant Worship and Church Architecture,* chap. 4, 143–47; Williams, "Religious Architecture and Landscape," 1338.

4. Edward A. Sövik, "Church Design and the Communication of Religious Faith," *Architectural Record,* December 1960, 138; Torgerson, "Edward Anders Sövik," 81; ("religiously inadequate") Tillich, "Contemporary Protestant Architecture," 123; White, *Protestant Worship and Church Architecture,* 140–41.

5. Sövik, "Church Design," 139; White, *Protestant Worship and Church Architecture,* 126; Bruggink and Droppers, *When Faith Takes Form,* 24, 60; Scotford, "Aftermath," 1652.

6. Bruggink and Droppers, *Christ and Architecture,* 400, 401–2, 403, 408–11, 415.

7. ("Aware of the presence") White, *Protestant Worship and Church Architecture,* 191; ("mere decoration") Atkinson, *How to Get Your Church Built,* 199, 204, 206.

8. ("Honest expression") Tillich, "Contemporary Protestant Architecture," 125; ("witness") White, *Protestant Worship and Church Architecture*, 200. See also White, p. 199; Sövik, *Architecture for Worship*, 55–57; Fiddes, *Architectural Requirements*, 69.

9. "New Look in Church Architecture," 103–4; Carole Rifkind, *A Field Guide to Contemporary American Architecture* (New York: Penguin Putnam, 1998), 191; Hudnut-Beumler, "Many Mansions," 16; Williams, "Religious Architecture and Landscape," 1338; Wuthnow, *Restructuring of American Religion*, 36.

10. Fiddes, *Architectural Requirements*, 73–74; Bruggink and Droppers, *Christ and Architecture*, 564, 580, 586–87, 638–43; Halverson, "On Getting Good Architecture for the Church," 6; Thiry, Bennett, and Kamphoefner, *Churches and Temples*, 23P, 31P.

11. Christ-Janer and Foley, *Modern Church Architecture*, 252–54.

12. Saarinens quoted in Thiry, Bennett, and Kamphoefner, *Churches and Temples*, 59P.

13. Bruggink and Droppers, *When Faith Takes Form*, 96–104.

14. See especially Edward Sövik's idea of the "non-church," discussed in Torgerson, "Edward Anders Sövik."

7. Building for Church Growth

1. On Willow Creek Association, see Jeffrey Weiss, "Willow Creek," *Orange County Register*, July 18, 1998 (LN); on Vineyard and Calvary, C. M. Robeck, Jr., "Calvary Chapel," in Stanley M. Burgess and Gary B. McGee, eds., *Dictionary of Pentecostal and Charismatic Movements*, 106; on Full Gospel Baptist Fellowship, Teresa Hairston, "What a Fellowship," *Gospel Today*, July 1996, 18–22, and Gayle White, "'A Movement . . . to Wake Up the Denomination,'" *Atlanta Journal and Constitution*, January 16, 1944 (LN); on Fellowship of Inner City Word of Faith Ministries, John Dart, "Themes of Bigness, Success Attract Independent Churches," *Los Angeles Times*, July 20, 1991. "Back to that Oldtime Religion," *Time*, December 26, 1977, 53, estimated the number of evangelicals, "after a generation of steady growth," at 45.5 million. On the growth, numbers, and socioeconomic status of evangelicals in the late twentieth century, see also "Born Again! The Year of the Evangelicals," *Newsweek*, October 25, 1976, 68–70, 73, 76, 78; James Davison Hunter, *American Evangelicalism: Conservative Religion and the Quandary of Modernity* (New Brunswick, N.J.: Rutgers University Press, 1983), 49, chap. 4; Brad Edmondson, "Bringing in the Sheaves," *American Demographics*, August, 1998, 31; Christian Smith, *American Evangelicalism: Embattled and Thriving* (Chicago: University of Chicago Press, 1998), 76–77.

2. Elmer L. Towns, "Big Churches?" *Christianity Today*, October 5, 1971, 6; Elmer Towns and Jerry Falwell, *Church Aflame* (Nashville: Impact Books, 1971), 37; Elmer Towns, *Capturing a Town for Christ* (Old Tappan, N.J.: Fleming H. Revell Company, 1969); Elmer L. Towns, *World's Largest Sunday School* (Nashville: Thomas Nelson, Inc., 1974).

3. Carpenter, *Revive Us Again*, 161–62, describes the post–World War II evangelistic efforts of Billy Graham and various parachurch groups, which he says constituted a "revival of revivalism" that was "much more daring and innovating than their predecessors'." See also 164–67, 223–29. On Billy Graham's crusades, see William Martin, *A Prophet with Honor: The Billy Graham Story* (New York: William Morrow and Company, Inc., 1991), 239, 233, 385. On Graham's 1957 crusade in Madison Square Garden, see "God in the Garden," *Time*, May 27, 1957, 46–47.

4. Our term "church growth experts" includes fellow travelers as well as bona fide members of the so-called Church Growth Movement, started in the 1950s by Donald McGavran, author of *The Bridges of God* (1955) and founder of the School of World Mission and Institute of Church Growth at Fuller Theological Seminary, Pasadena, California. Elmer L. Towns, John N. Vaughan, and David J. Seifert, *The Complete Book of Church Growth*, 100–101, defined the strategy of the Church Growth Movement as follows: "to locate and evangelize winnable populations or 'peoples' already established as homogeneous units." The emphasis was on converting groups within populations rather than isolated individuals. Since it employed social science techniques in locating and measuring the "winnability" of groups, the experts considered it a science. On Wagner and Wimber, see G. B. McGee, "Charles Peter Wagner"; C. P. Wagner, "John Wimber"; and C. P. Wagner, "Church Growth," in Burgess and McGee, eds., *Dictionary of Pentecostal and Charismatic Movements*, 875, 889, 187. Lyle E. Schaller was a United Methodist minister who joined the staff of the Yokefellow Institute in 1971 as parish con-

sultant and wrote numerous books in subsequent decades. John N. Vaughan was director of the International Megachurch Research Center, Bolivar, Missouri, editor of *Church Growth Today,* and author of several books on church growth and megachurches. George Barna was president of the Barna Research Group, Glendale, California, and wrote numerous books on marketing and church growth.

5. Robert H. Schuller, *Your Church Has Real Possibilities!* 6, 10, 71; Anderson, *A Church for the 21st Century.*

6. Wade Clark Roof, *A Generation of Seekers: The Spiritual Journey of the Baby Boom Generation* (New York: HarperSan Francisco, 1993). See also Leith Anderson, *Dying for Change: An Arresting Look at the New Realities Confronting Church and Para-Church Ministries,* 52.

7. ("High schools") Anderson, *Dying for Change,* 51–52; Warren quoted in Dana Parsons, "New-Time Religion: Megachurches Master the Art of Marketing for the Masses," *Los Angeles Times,* December 24, 1987 (LN); Schaller quoted in George W. Cornell, "The Bigger the Better, Church Consultant Says," ibid., January 5, 1991 (LN). On the decline of denominational loyalty, see "'User Friendly' Services Blur Denominational Distinctions," *Christian Science Monitor,* April 11, 1997 (LN); Bill J. Leonard, "Do American Denominations Have a Future?" *News and Observer* (Raleigh, N.C.), November 8, 1996 (LN).

8. Lynne Hybels and Bill Hybels, *Rediscovering Church: The Story and Vision of Willow Creek Community Church,* 32.

9. Elmer L. Towns, *An Inside Look at 10 of Today's Most Innovative Churches,* 196, 17; C. Peter Wagner, *Church Planting for a Greater Harvest: A Comprehensive Guide* (Ventura, Calif.: Regal Books, 1990), 57, 58, 78–95; Cathleen Ferraro, "Churches Turning to Marketing to Increase Size of Their Flocks," *Investor's Daily,* February 7, 1991 (LN); Marc Spiegler, "Scouting for Souls," *American Demographics,* March 1996 (LN); George Barna, "The Church of the '90s: Meeting the Needs of a Changing Culture," *RTS Ministry* 9 (fall 1990): 10.

10. Schaller, *The New Reformation,* 73.

11. Schuller, *Your Church,* 123, italics in original.

12. Ibid., 112–14, 115, 160.

13. Ibid., 119, 144–45; G. A. Pritchard, *Willow Creek Seeker Services: Evaluating a New Way of Doing Church,* 50.

14. Schuller, *Your Church,* 77, 117, 124, 125.

15. Susan Borchardt, *Religious Architecture in America, 1632–1976*

(Washington, D. C.: St. John's Church, 1976), 53; *Great Churches of Today: Outstanding Congregations, Their Leaders, Their Program, Their People, by the Staff of Decision* (Minneapolis: World Wide Publications, 1970), 72; Towns, Vaughan, and Seifert, *Complete Book,* 39. According to Williams, *Houses of God,* 271–72, Neutra's son Dion designed the Tower of Hope. On the idea behind the structure, see Schuller, *Your Church,* 173–74.

16. *Great Churches of Today,* 71; Towns, Vaughan, and Seifert, *Complete Book,* 38, 40.

17. Hybels and Hybels, *Rediscovering Church,* 69, and see also 51. Charles Blake, pastor of the West Angeles Church of God in Christ, Los Angeles, also acknowledged Schuller's influence. He recalled that in 1971, while visiting the Garden Grove Church, "my mind was suddenly opened to the possibility of pastoring a big church.... all of the boundaries were removed. I could conceive of being as big as God would make me." Blake quoted in Joe Maxwell, "Church Growth in the 'Hood,'" *Christianity Today,* April 8, 1996, 27.

18. Except where noted otherwise, information on Willow Creek Community Church is based on authors' research visit and interview with Barbara Blegen, May 19, 1996. In *Megachurches and America's Cities: How Churches Grow,* 31–32, John Vaughan ranked Willow Creek Community Church, along with First Baptist Church in Hammond, Indiana, "as one of the two largest churches in the United States in week-by-week attendance." Hybels and Hybels, *Rediscovering Church,* 123, reported that in February 1992 the church hit its highest nonholiday weekend attendance ever, 17,010 persons, but attendance dropped somewhat after that. In 1996 worship attendance at three weekend services was about 16,000. In the Elk Grove telephone directory yellow pages, Willow Creek advertised its services under three headings: "Churches-Community," "Churches-Non-Denominational," and "Churches-Interdenominational." *Pages Plus 1995–96: Elk Grove Village* (Chicago, Ill.: DonTech, 1995). Pritchard, *Willow Creek,* 295–96, contends that Hybels followed Schuller's example in calling Willow Creek a community church. In the mid 1990s, Willow Creek offered three identical seeker services, Saturday at 6 P.M. and Sunday at 9 and 11:15 A.M. For "believers" the church held two midweek "New Community" evening worship and teaching services.

For references to Willow Creek as a prototype, see Larry Witham, "'Seeker' Churches Targeting Boomers," *Washington Times,* August 12,

1995 (LN); Angela Winter Ney, "Young Adults Make a Leap of Faith to Nondenominational Megachurches," *Baltimore Sun,* March 27, 1994 (LN); Michael G. Maudlin and Edward Gilbreath, "Selling Out the House of God?" *Christianity Today,* July 18, 1994, 25; John Seel, *The Evangelical Forfeit: Can We Recover?* (Grand Rapids, Mich.: Baker Books, 1993), 91; Deirdre Sullivan, "Targeting Souls," *American Demographics,* October 1991 (LN); Stewart M. Hoover, "The Cross at Willow Creek: Seeker Religion and the Contemporary Marketplace," in Bruce David Forbes and Jeffrey H. Mahan, eds., *Religion and Popular Culture* (Berkeley: University of California Press, 2000), 145.

On Hybels's marketing orientation, see Gustav Niebuhr, "The Minister as Marketer: Learning from Business"; Hybels quoted in Hybels and Hybels, *Rediscovering Church,* 173; Pritchard, *Willow Creek,* 61–62, 67–68, chap. 3; ("one of the most innovative") Towns, *Inside Look,* 44.

19. Hybels and Hybels, *Rediscovering Church,* 104. The architectural firm for the first phase was O'Donnell, Wicklund, Pigozzi, Architects, of Northbrook, Illinois. Guy Fishman of S. Guy Fishman Associates, of Northbrook, was the architect for the second building phase.

20. Towns, *Inside Look,* 44; ("corporate headquarters . . . business park") Anthony B. Robinson, "Learning from Willow Creek Church," 68; ("community college") Harvard Business School, *Willow Creek Community Church* (Boston: Harvard Business School Publishing, 1991), 10.

21. "Marketing the Message," *Asbury Park Press* (Neptune, N.J.), November 25, 1995 (LN); William Langley, "Review: God's Shopping Mall," *Sunday Telegraph,* June 4, 1995 (LN).

22. Hybels and Willow Creek staffers quoted in Pritchard, *Willow Creek,* 81–82.

23. Hybels and Hybels, *Rediscovering Church,* 59. According to Russell Chandler, "'Customer' Poll Shapes a Church," *Los Angeles Times,* December 11, 1989 (LN), after the service, Hybels "worked the bullpen," an area below the right front corner of the stage, conversing with anyone who wished to talk with him. On why he did not give the invitation, see Pritchard, *Willow Creek,* 50.

24. Debra Hale, "Megachurches Favor Videos and Sermons," *Charleston Gazette,* December 2, 1995 (LN); Langley, "Review: God's Shopping Mall."

25. Adelle M. Banks, "Megachurches at Center of Black Middle Class," *Stuart News/Port St. Lucie News,* May 25, 1996 (LN); Cecile Holmes White, "Booming Brentwood," *Houston Chronicle,* July 6, 1991; Deborah Kovach Caldwell, "More than Worship," *Dallas Morning News,* May 11, 1997; Joan Connell, "Reaching Out to Black Men," *Cleveland Plain Dealer,* April 6, 1994 (LN); Steve Brunsman, "Booming Churches," *Houston Post,* November 4, 1994 (LN); "Black Megachurches Surge," 686; Karen M. Thomas, "Church Home," *Dallas Morning News,* March 6, 1993 (LN); Robert M. Franklin, *Another Day's Journey: Black Churches Confronting the American Crisis,* 59–61; Lawrence H. Mamiya, "A Social History of the Bethel African Methodist Church in Baltimore: The House of God and the Struggle for Freedom," in James P. Wind and James W. Lewis, eds., *American Congregations, Volume 1: Portraits of Twelve Religious Communities* (Chicago: University of Chicago Press, 1994), 266–67, 269; Michael A. Battle, Sr., ed., *The African-American Church at Work,* 62–63.

26. Except where noted otherwise, information on Ebenezer African American Methodist Church is based on authors' research visit and interview with Melvin Clay, October 3, 1997; and telephone conversation with Clay, September 29, 2000. Sherry Sherrod DuPree, *African-American Holiness Pentecostal Movement: An Annotated Bibliography,* 347, listed Ebenezer as a "Charismatic Methodist" church and, with more than eight thousand members in 1995, the largest A.M.E. church in the world. See also "Ebenezer African American Methodist Episcopal Church History," in *47th Session, Washington Annual Conference, Second Episcopal District, African Methodist Episcopal Church . . . April 16–20, 1997* (n.p., [1997]), n.p.

27. Author's telephone conversation with Stan Britt, October 2, 2000. His architectural firm, Sultan, Campbell, Britt, was based in Washington, D.C. Churches represented about a third of its practice, according to Britt, and Ebenezer was the largest of the churches the firm had designed. On Allen, see George, *Segregated Sabbaths,* 54–55; church member quoted in "Black Megachurches Surge," 686.

28. "Black Megachurches Surge," 686.

29. Except where noted otherwise, information on Trinity United Church of Christ is based on Jeremiah A. Wright, Jr., to Anne C. Loveland, May 8, 1996; authors' research visit and interview with Lela Mooney, May 24, 1996; and authors' research visit and interview with Marie A. Merriweather, October 11, 2001. The 1994 worship center was designed by a Chicago architectural firm, Wendell P. Campbell and Associates.

30. Jeremiah A. Wright, Jr., "Defining and Living Out Your Identity," in Lyle E. Schaller, *Center City Churches: The New Urban Frontier*, 87–90. See also Jeremiah Wright, "The African Centered Church," *Gospel Today*, September/October 1995, 41.

8. The Megachurch

1. ("Tool for ministry") Warren quoted in Anna Cekola, "Orange County Focus: Mega-Church to be a 'Spiritual Oasis,'" *Los Angeles Times*, December 30, 1992 (LN); Towns and Falwell, *Church Aflame*, 169; Hybels and Hybels, *Rediscovering Church*, 192; ("God deserves") Ninie O'Hara, "A Kodak Moment," *Southeast Outlook*, October 3, 1997.

2. Gwenn E. McCormick, *Designing Worship Centers*, 23–25.

3. Joel Garreau, *Edge City: Life on the New Frontier* (New York: Doubleday, 1991), 3, 4, 11, 422–38; Richard O. Davies, *The Age of Asphalt: The Automobile, the Freeway, and the Condition of Metropolitan America* (Philadelphia: J. B. Lippincott Company, 1975), 28; Kenneth T. Jackson, *Crabgrass Frontier: The Suburbanization of the United States* (New York: Oxford University Press, 1985), 163, 246.

4. Except where noted otherwise, information on First Baptist Church of Jacksonville, Florida, is based on authors' research visit and interview with J. Dudley Freeman, Construction Administrator, December 8, 1996. The church's main auditorium, completed in 1994, was designed and built by KBJ Architects, who worked with the Crown Division of McDevitt-Street, headquartered in Charlotte, North Carolina. In 1996, attendance at First Baptist's Sunday morning service averaged about 8,000 persons; at the evening service, about 6,500. A Wednesday evening worship service averaged about 5,000. First Baptist, Jacksonville, was affiliated with the Southern Baptist Convention.

5. *Together We Build* (church booklet [1987?]), 5.

6. Mary Beth Sammons, "Full-Service Church," *Chicago Tribune*, April 3, 1994 (LN); authors' research visit to Saddleback Church, Lake Forest, California, and interview with Karen Kelly, February 19, 1999.

7. Hundreds of zoning controversies erupted in the 1980s and 1990s, as megachurch builders sought to construct new churches or expand existing ones. The controversies pitted pastors and congregations against local government planning boards and zoning commissions, as well as homeowners in affected residential areas. At issue were such matters as zoning regulations, tax revenues, property values, and problems relating to drainage, noise, traffic congestion, and environmentally sensitive land, not to mention First Amendment guarantees of freedom of religion. For a general overview, see John W. Kennedy, "Permission Denied," *Christianity Today*, April 28, 1997, 72–76.

8. Graham quoted in Christine Wicker, "Casting a Large Vision," *Dallas Morning News*, September 19, 1996 (LN). Other megachurches that located in undeveloped or newly developing areas include the following: Bellevue Baptist Church, which moved from midtown Memphis to the small community of Cordova, Tennessee, in 1989; Southeast Christian Church, which chose a 105-acre site on the outskirts of Louisville in eastern Jefferson County, Kentucky, for its new church complex; and Saddleback Church, Lake Forest, California, built on a site accessing the 241 Toll Road as well as five other major highways in a newly developing area of large office parks, shopping malls, and upscale residences. Bellevue Baptist's experience in its new location suggested that Prestonwood had good reason to hope for new growth in Plano. Between 1989 and 1995, the Cordova church expanded its membership from 18,852 to 25,140, and its worship attendance increased by about one thousand, to almost 7,000 persons. Dan Lester Greer, "Bellevue Baptist Church as an Example of the Megachurch Model in Church Growth" (D.Min. project, Fuller Theological Seminary, 1995), 218, 220; David Waters, "Fellowship Boom Town," *Commercial Appeal*, December 4, 1995 (LN); David Waters, "After Soul-Searching, Many Churches Leave City," ibid., March 7, 1993; Veda Morgan, "Further Development of Blankenbaker, I-64 Just 'A Matter of When,'" *Courier-Journal*, November 15, 1995 (LN); authors' research visit to Saddleback Church, Lake Forest, California, and interview with Karen Kelly, February 19, 1999.

9. Hunter, dean of the School of World Missions and Evangelism at Asbury Theological Seminary, Wilmore, Kentucky, quoted in Cary McMullen, "Colossal Churches Attract Masses," *The Ledger* (Lakeland, Fla.), April 26, 1998 (LN); "Prestonwood Baptist Church," HH Architects Web site, www.hharchitects.com, June 7, 2000.

10. On the evolution of the shopping mall, and for some good illus-

trations of its architecture, see Richard Longstreth, *City Center to Regional Mall: Architecture, the Automobile, and Retailing in Los Angeles, 1920–1950* (Cambridge, Mass.: MIT Press, 1997), especially chap. 11; Richard Longstreth, "The Perils of a Parkless Town," in Martin Wachs and Margaret Crawford, eds., *The Car and the City: The Automobile, the Built Environment, and Daily Urban Life* (Ann Arbor: University of Michigan Press, 1992), 143, 148, 150, 152; Jackson, *Crabgrass Frontier*, 257–60.

11. Except where noted otherwise, information on Faith Community Church is based on authors' research visit and interviews with Jim Hayford and Mike Keys, February 17, 1999. Faith Community Church was an independent pentecostal church with a mostly blue-collar, ethnically diverse congregation. Debora Vrana, "Religion: Designing a Mall-Like Ambience for Worship," *Los Angeles Times*, November 8, 1997 (LN). In 1999, the worship attendance at its three weekend services totalled about six thousand. David Miller designed the auditorium, which occupied one quadrant of the structure. David Gilmore of LPA Inc., in Irvine (the firm that designed the terminal at Orange County's John Wayne Airport), designed the main entrance and the remaining three quadrants.

12. Dirk Sutro, "Prayers and Pasta," *Los Angeles Times*, August 18, 1996; Vrana, "Religion: Designing a Mall-Like Ambience for Worship."

13. Except where noted otherwise, all information on A Community of Joy (formerly Community Church of Joy) is based on authors' research visits and interviews with Kenn Sanders, Wayne Skaff, and Dianne Eggum, April 2 and 4, 1996, and March 30, 2000; and telephone conversation with David A. Price of David A. Price Associates, Tustin, California, June 10, 1996. In 1998, the church estimated its "constituency" at approximately ten thousand. *Grand Opening and Dedication, April 19, 1998* (church booklet, 1988). The weekend worship attendance in 2000 was between twenty-eight hundred and three thousand, not including children attending Sunday school. A Community of Joy was affiliated with the Evangelical Lutheran Church in America and was one of its fastest-growing churches.

14. Mark Gottdiener, *The Theming of America: Dreams, Visions, and Commercial Spaces* (Boulder, Colo.: Westview Press, 1997), 76, 109–12, 79–80, 85. See also William Severini Kowinski, *The Malling of America: An Inside Look at the Great Consumer Paradise* (New York: William Morrow and Company, Inc., 1985). The comparison between A Community of Joy and Disneyland is not so far-fetched as one might think. David Price, the architect who designed the Joy complex, also worked on Disneyland. In 2000, the church's Leadership Center held a four-day conference entitled "The Imaginative Church" at the Walt Disney World Resort in Orlando, Florida. Two of the general sessions featured speakers from the Disney Institute. A brochure advertising the conference promised that participants would "learn strategies and tactics used at Walt Disney World Resort for ensuring customer loyalty" and how to develop "a guest-friendly environment that invites, excites and delights." *The Imaginative Church* (church brochure, [2000]). On the shopping mall ambience of A Community of Joy, see Walt Kallestad, *Entertainment Evangelism: Taking the Church Public*, 7, 8; "Worship Services at Joy," *Joy Alive!* March 2000, 2; *A Community of Joy: Groundbreaking, March 24, 1996* (church brochure, [1996]); *Grand Opening and Dedication*.

15. Except where noted otherwise, information on Midwest Christian Center is based on authors' research visit and interview with Joan Cieslak, May 22, 1996; and telephone interview with a staff member, August 2, 2000. The architect for the church, which opened July 4, 1989, was Dave Richenour. In the mid-1990s, the weekend worship attendance (at three Sunday services) was three thousand.

Except where noted otherwise, information on Oak Cliff Bible Fellowship is based on authors' research visit, October 29, 1998. The church's main building, called the worship center, was built at a cost of $7 million and dedicated in October 1995. In 1997, Oak Cliff Fellowship had fifty-five hundred members.

Except where noted otherwise, information on Calvary Church is based on authors' research visit, May 18, 1996. Affiliated with the Assemblies of God, Calvary Church became a regional church after moving to its 116-acre site on Route 59 in the early 1990s. Its multipurpose church complex, which included a twenty-five-hundred-seat auditorium, cost $13.1 million to build. The auditorium opened in December 1993; the other facilities were completed the following year. "Calvary Church: Who We Are" (church leaflet, n.d.); Casey Banas, "Growing with the Gospel," *Chicago Tribune*, March 6, 1994.

16. Richard Longstreth, *The Buildings of Main Street: A Guide to American Commercial Architecture* (New York: AltaMira Press, 2000), 16, 126–29.

17. Except where noted otherwise, information on the Vineyard Chris-

tian Fellowship is based on authors' research visit and interview with Ross Hoult, February 20, 1999. The Vineyard Christian Fellowship of Anaheim, California, was the mother church of the Association of Vineyard Churches organized by John Wimber, who also founded the Anaheim church (in 1977). Most Vineyard Fellowships were small (the median congregation had 150 members), but the Anaheim church had a three-thousand-seat sanctuary and its worship attendance qualified it as a megachurch. Russell Chandler, "Vineyard Fellowship Finds Groundswell of Followers," *Los Angeles Times,* October 5, 1990, reported that the congregation numbered five thousand. See also Miller, *Reinventing American Protestantism,* 19, 46–50.

Except where noted otherwise, information on Mariners Church is based on authors' research visit and interview with Jan Lynn and Kyle Webb, February 22, 1999. Mariners Church was the product of the merger, in 1996, of South Coast Community Church in Irvine and Mariners Church in Newport Beach. "Kenton," *Access Mariners Church,* January 1999. In that year the new congregation moved into a complex of buildings in Irvine that had housed the South Coast church and Liberty Baptist Church. It renovated the South Coast auditorium for use as a worship center and turned the Baptist building, which had a large, open room with a stage, into a "community center." The weekend worship attendance at Mariners in 1998 and early 1999 averaged about forty-five hundred.

Except where noted otherwise noted, information on Fellowship Church is based on authors' research visit and interview with Lynn Cross, November 3 and 4, 1999. Urban Architecture, a Dallas firm, designed the two-story, $16 million structure, which housed a forty-one-hundred-seat worship center, an atrium, a bookstore, a nursery, and various educational and administrative offices. Formerly known as the Fellowship of Las Colinas, the Fellowship Church moved in 1997 to a new 137-acre site (later expanded to 162 acres) on Highway 121, which it purchased from the Resolution Trust Corporation. It was affiliated with the Southern Baptist Convention. In November 1999 the church reported a weekend worship attendance of between eight thousand and nine thousand persons.

18. Except where noted otherwise, information on First Baptist Church, Houston, is based on authors' research visit and interview with Steve Seelig, June 28, 1996. In 1996, the weekend worship attendance of this Southern Baptist church was six thousand. For an aerial view of First Baptist, see Bell, Ladner, and Poor, eds., *A Church in the City,* 176.

Except where noted otherwise, information on the First Evangelical Free Church is based on authors' research visit and interview with Dr. Stanley Bill Olson, May 20, 1996. Associated with the Evangelical Free Church of America, the Rockford church had a membership in the mid 1990s of about twenty-five hundred. For an aerial perspective see Marilyn McDonald, ed., *Our Godly Heritage . . . A Foundation for the Future* (Rockford, Ill.: Johnson Press, 1984), 30.

Except where noted otherwise, information on Second Baptist Church, Houston, is based on authors' research visit and interview with Libby Kelton, June 27, 1996. In 1996, the total worship attendance at two identical Sunday morning services was nine thousand; for the evening service, between one and two thousand. Second Baptist, Houston, was affiliated with the Southern Baptist Convention. The dome resembled the one that had adorned Second Baptist's downtown facility, a neoclassical auditorium. For a drawing of the downtown church, see *For Such a Time as This* (church booklet, [1986]). Edwin Young quoted in Zoe Heller, "The Mall of God," *The Independent,* June 2, 1991 (LN).

19. Except where noted otherwise, information on Saddleback Church is based on authors' research visit and interviews with Lance Collins and Karen Kelly, February 19, 1999. The architect for the Saddleback complex was David Gilmore, of LPA, Inc., in Irvine, California, who was also one of the architects who designed the Faith Community Church. Vrana, "Religion: Designing a Mall-Like Ambience for Worship." Sherri Brown, "The Search for Saddleback Sam," *MissionsUSA,* July–August 1988, 6, reported that 70 percent of Saddleback's members were "new Christians." In 1999, the total weekend worship attendance (including children attending Sunday school) was thirteen to fourteen thousand. Saddleback was affiliated with the Southern Baptist Convention. On the "Saddleback Strategy," see Brown, "Search for Saddleback Sam," 13–14, 16–17; Rick Warren, *The Purpose Driven Church: Growth without Compromising Your Message and Mission* (Grand Rapids, Mich.: Zondervan Publishing House, 1995). Warren quoted in Cekola, "Orange County Focus: Mega-Church to be a 'Spiritual Oasis.'"

20. Carol McGraw, "Houses of the Spirit," *Orange County Register,* August 31, 1997 (LN).

21. Except where noted otherwise, information on Prestonwood Bap-

tist Church is based on authors' research visit to the church at its north Dallas location and interview with Valerie Weaver, October 28, 1998, and to the new church in Plano and interview with Elaine Peveto, November 2, 1999. Founded in 1977, and affiliated with the Southern Baptist Convention, Prestonwood had a long history of successful evangelism. Before it moved to the 138-acre location in Plano, it was reputed to have the largest worship attendance in Dallas. Christine Wicker, "Fishers of Men," *Dallas Morning News,* September 17, 1995 (LN), reported the membership to be thirteen thousand. By 1998, before the move to Plano, it had risen to fifteen thousand. On the design of the church, see Susan Williamson, "Planning for Numbers," 53; Bentley Systems, Inc., "HH Architects Designs Texas-size Church in Dallas," from HH Architects Web site, www.hharchitects.com, June 7, 2000. HH Architects, based in Dallas, was a multidisciplinary firm known for its large religious projects, as well as designs for schools and universities, municipal and state governments, and corporate and commercial clients.

22. Except where noted otherwise, information on Brentwood Baptist Church is based on authors' research visit and interview with Tina Davis, June 17, 1996. Brentwood Baptist Church was a predominantly African American church affiliated with the Southern Baptist Convention. In the mid 1990s it claimed a membership of seventy-five hundred. The Brentwood dome opened in May 1986. According to a church brochure, it was the "unique design" of the pastor, Dr. Joe S. Ratliff. *Brentwood Baptist Church* (church brochure, [1996?]). The architect was George H. Smart of Smart and Whitehead, AIA, Houston.

Except where noted otherwise, information on Crenshaw Christian Center is based on authors' research visit, February 21, 1999. The Faith-Dome was built in 1989, at a cost of $9 million, after Rev. Frederick K. C. Price moved his predominantly African American congregation onto the twenty-eight-acre campus that formerly housed Pepperdine University. Constructed of white alumninum, the arc of the dome harmonized with the geometric form of the white, Bauhaus-style Pepperdine buildings. John Dart, "Pastor Frederick Price's 'FaithDome,'" *Los Angeles Times,* September 9, 1989 (LN), quoted Price as saying that the idea for the dome came in a vision he had while visiting Howard Hughes' *Spruce Goose* in Long Beach, California. "When we walked in that building to see the airplane, I said, 'This is what we need.'" In 1989, when the Faith-

Dome opened, the Crenshaw congregation was thought to be the largest predominantly black congregation in southern California. John N. Vaughan, *Megachurches and America's Cities: How Churches Grow,* Appendix C, recorded Crenshaw's worship attendance for 1991 as sixty-five hundred. On the interior of the FaithDome, see Dart, "Pastor Frederick Price's 'FaithDome.'"

23. Except where noted otherwise, information on the World Changers Ministries Christian Center is based on authors' research visit, June 10, 1998. A church leaflet described World Changers, pastored by Creflo A. Dollar, Jr., as "a Word of Faith, non-denominational, Christ-centered ministry." "Changing Your World!" (church leaflet, n.d.). Vaughan, *Megachurches,* Appendix C, listed it as one of the twelve fastest-growing churches in the United States during 1989–1990. In 1996, when it opened its new structure, the congregation numbered nine thousand–plus. Kent Kimes, "World Changers Make a Sort of Peace With Dome's Opponents," *Atlanta Journal and Constitution,* January 4, 1996 (LN).

24. Except where noted otherwise, information on North Phoenix Baptist Church is based on authors' research visit and interview with Rick Hooten, April 6, 1996. The weekend worship attendance at North Phoenix in 1996 was about thirty-five hundred. Ben Winton, "Valley Megachurches Light the Way to 21st Century," *Arizona Republic,* February 18, 1996 (LN). The church was affiliated with the Southern Baptist Convention.

Except where noted otherwise, information on the Family Worship Center, part of the World Ministry Center of Jimmy Swaggart Ministries, is based on authors' conversation with Robert Coleman, February 5, 1996, and research visit to the World Ministry Center, February 1, 2000. Designed by Robert M. Coleman and Partners, Architects, of Baton Rouge, the six-thousand-seat Family Worship Center was the centerpiece of a huge complex built on a one-hundred-acre tract near Interstate 10. In 1985, the year it opened, Swaggart estimated worship attendance at his church at about twenty-five hundred. Doug LeBlanc, "New Church for Easter Dedication," *Morning Advocate,* April 8, 1985; Mark Ballard, "Jimmy Swaggart Goes for It All," *Gris Gris,* September 18, 1985; Mike Dunne, Curt Eysink, Doug LeBlanc, "Swaggart Subject of Church Probe," *Morning Advocate,* February 20, 1988; all three clippings in Vertical File, Goodwood Library, Baton Rouge, Louisiana. Formerly affiliated with the Assemblies of God, the World Ministry Center became an independent pentecostal church in 1988, after Swaggart was dismissed by the denomination for sexual misconduct.

25. Except where noted otherwise, information on Southeast Christian Church is based on authors' research visit, May 19 and 20, 1999. The church complex, dedicated in 1998, was located on a 105-acre site alongside I-64. Southeast was nondenominational but had roots in the Christian Churches/Churches of Christ. "Welcome to Southeast!" (church leaflet, n.d.); Bob Russell, "Reflections," *Southeast Outlook,* April 22, 1999. In 2000, the membership numbered 17,949. Steve Coomes, "New 'Assimilation Strategy' Helps Newcomers Plug Into Southeast," ibid., January 21, 1999. On the dimensions of the worship center, see "Southeast Christian Church Relocation Project Facts and Figures" (church information sheet, n.d.); "Southeast Relocation Project Fun Facts and Figures" (church information sheet, n.d.). Architect David Miller was an Orange, California, architect who had designed Southeast Christian's former facility and the auditorium of Faith Community Church in West Covina, California, as well as other churches. Jack Brammer, "Architect Sees Church He Envisioned," *Southeast Outlook,* October 22, 1998. Construction manager Clark Esser was also an evangelical from California. A member of Calvary Church in Santa Ana, he had built more than two dozen churches in his home state. Ninie O'Hara, "Esser Ready to Finish Southeast, Head Home," ibid., June 10, 1999.

26. Except where noted otherwise, information on the Crystal Cathedral is based on authors' research visit, February 24, 1999. See Paul Goldberger, *On the Rise: Architecture and Design in a Postmodern Age,* 185; Schuller quoted in David Singer, "The Crystal Cathedral: Reflections of Schuller's Theology," *Christianity Today,* August 8, 1980, 28; ("image making skyscrapers") Carleton Knight, III, "Introduction," in *Philip Johnson/John Burgee: Architecture, 1979–1985* (New York: Rizzoli International Publications, Inc., 1985), 6; Johnson quoted in Hilary Lewis and John O'Connor, *Philip Johnson: The Architect in His Own Words* (New York: Rizzoli International Publications, Inc., 1994), 101.

27. On Schuller's evangelistic orientation, see "Hard Questions for Robert Schuller About Sin and Self-Esteem," *Christianity Today,* August 10, 1984, 16. The description of Schuller's reaction to Johnson's and Burgee's design is a composite of four accounts: Franz Schulze, *Philip*

Johnson: Life and Work (New York: Alfred A. Knopf, 1994), 338–39; Knight, "Introduction," 7–8; "Hard Questions for Robert Schuller," 15; Lewis and O'Connor, *Philip Johnson,* 98.

28. "Hard Questions for Robert Schuller," 14.

29. Quoted descriptions in Schulze, *Philip Johnson,* 339; *Philip Johnson/John Burgee,* 16; Carol Flake, *Redemptorama: Culture, Politics, and the New Evangelicalism* (Garden City, N.Y.: Anchor Press/Doubleday and Company, Inc., 1984), 57. See also Goldberger, *On the Rise,* 183. For drawings of the floor plan, see *Philip Johnson/John Burgee,* 16; Lewis and O'Connor, *Philip Johnson,* 98.

30. Johnson quoted in Lewis and O'Connor, *Philip Johnson,* 98, 101, 102; and in Singer, "The Crystal Cathedral," 28. The auditorium accommodated 2,890 persons. Goldberger, *On the Rise,* 183.

31. Schuller's "possibility" theology was a version of positive thought, probably influenced by Dr. Norman Vincent Peale. ("Flowing energy") Goldberger, *On the Rise,* 184; Schuller quoted in "Hard Questions for Robert Schuller," 15.

32. Schuller quoted in John Dart, "Schuller's New Center Faulted for its Secular Look," *Los Angeles Times,* November 25, 1989 (LN); Johnson quoted in Lewis and O'Connor, *Philip Johnson,* 102, and see also 101.

33. Willow Creek Community Church Web site quoted in Scott L. Thumma, "The Kingdom, the Power, and the Glory: The Megachurch in Modern American Society," 490.

34. Williams, *Houses of God,* 184. The populist ethos of twentieth-century evangelicals may have contributed to their rejection of avant-garde modernism in architecture, as in other areas of high culture. See Hatch, *Democratization of American Christianity,* 219. Two commentators on the Crystal Cathedral quoted in Lewis and O'Connor, *Philip Johnson,* 97.

35. Per Olof Berg and Kristian Kreiner, "Corporate Architecture: Turning Physical Settings into Symbolic Resources," in Pasquale Gagliardi, ed., *Symbols and Artifacts: Views of the Corporate Landscape* (New York: Walter de Gruyter, 1990), 43, 45; Alan Phillips, *The Best in Science, Office and Business Park Design* (London: B. T. Batsford Ltd., 1993), 16.

36. Except where noted otherwise, information on the Apostolic Church of God is based on authors' research visit and interviews with Bishop Arthur M. Brazier and Patti Caire, May 22, 1996. The Apostolic Church of God was a member of the Pentecostal Assemblies of the

World; Brazier became pastor of the church in 1960, and in 1976 was elevated to Bishop of the Sixth Episcopal District of the denomination, which included seventy-two churches in the state of Illinois. "The Apostolic Church of God Celebrates 66 Years of Grace Proclaiming the Gospel," 7. Kate N. Grossman, "'Megachurches' Cross Racial Line," *Saturday* (*Baton Rouge Advocate*), October 16, 1999, reported the membership of the Apostolic Church of God to be more than fourteen thousand. In 1996, the average weekend worship attendance in the Dorchester sanctuary was about six thousand. The Dorchester sanctuary and tower, dedicated in 1992, were designed by a member of the church, Elbert G. Ray of Ray/Dawson P.C., Architects and Engineers, whose father had been an elder in the church. A forty-thousand-square-foot, two-level addition to the sanctuary, which included banquet facilities for up to five hundred persons, a lecture hall, offices, and fifteen meeting rooms, was also designed by Ray and completed in 1998. Construction was done by II in One Contractors, Inc., and II in One Rebar, Inc., and financing was provided by the Highland Community Bank, all minority-owned enterprises. "Apostolic Church of God Celebrates 66 Years," 8–9.

37. Brazier quoted in "Apostolic Church of God Celebrates 66 Years," 11–12.

38. Including the cross, the total height of the worship center was 150 feet. Tim and Jennifer Byrd, "Solid-Rock Faith and Perfectly Fit Steel Form New Church's Structure," *Southeast Christian: Where He Leads . . . We Will Follow* (Louisville: *Southeast Outlook*, 1998), 68; ("evangelizing the lost") "Welcome to Southeast!"

39. Tara Dooley, "Church Aims Message to Sky," *Fort Worth Star-Telegram*, November 17, 1998 (newspaper Web site printout courtesy of Lynn Cross of Fellowship Church).

40. Except where noted otherwise, information on Valley Cathedral is based on authors' research visit and interview with Randy Sukow, April 4, 1996. The congregaton purchased its former church building (with the traditional cross and spire) from North Phoenix Baptist Church in 1978. It built the new worship center in 1990–1991. In 1996, plans were being formulated to renovate the former worship center and make it a chapel "with a sacred feel for more intimate worship settings, for weddings, etc." Pastor Dan Scott, "What About the Master Plan?" *Valley News*, April, 1996.

Except where noted otherwise, information on Carpenter's Home Church is based on authors' research visit and interview with Stephen Strader, December 11, 1996. The Carpenter's Home church building was completed in 1985, and was the fourth house of worship for the congregation, originally known as the First Assembly of God. When it moved from downtown Lakeland to the new location in the 1980s, it adopted the name of the recently vacated home for retired carpenters on the site. The builder of the new worship center was Roe Messner, a design-build contractor well known in the evangelical community in the 1960s, 1970s, and 1980s, who constructed many churches for his own denomination (Assemblies of God) and also for the Southern Baptist Convention. Doug Wead and Bill Wead, *Church Builder: The Roe Messner Story* (Springfield, Mo.: Restoration Fellowship, 1981). Carpenter's Home advertised itself as a "family church" and had a racially integrated membership. In 1996 the average worship attendance on Sunday morning was twenty-five hundred, and on Sunday evening, one thousand.

Except where noted otherwise, information on Phoenix First Assembly of God is based on authors' research visits, April 2, 1996, and March 19, 2000, and interview with Kenn Sanders, April 2, 1996. The Phoenix First complex occupied sixty-five acres. It, too, was built by Roe Messner. In 1985, when the worship center was dedicated, Phoenix First was one of the fastest-growing churches in the United States, primarily as a result of the drawing power of its pastor, Tommy J. Barnett, and the programs he implemented. By 1996, the weekend worship attendance at the church totaled about twelve thousand. John N. Vaughan, "America's 500 Fastest Growing Churches," *Church Growth Today* 2 (April 1987): 1; "Glitz, Outreach Help Church to Grow," *News-Leader* (Springfield, Mo.), April 7, 1993; S. M. Burgess, "Tommy J. Barnett," in Burgess and McGee, eds., *Dictionary of Pentecostal and Charismatic Movements*, 50; Winton, "Valley Megachurches Light the Way to the 21st Century."

Except where noted otherwise, information on Elmbrook Church is based on authors' research visit and interview with Fred Snyder, May 23, 1996; and telephone interviews with Chuck Weathers, September 27, 2000, and Ken Stock, September 28, 2000. Elmbrook Church was a nondenominational, "seeker-friendly" and family-oriented church whose congregation was made up largely of young adults (average age between thirty-three and thirty-four). It moved to its forty-acre site in 1975, after holding services in the Ruby Isle Theater, among other temporary accommodations. As of 1996, it had gone through four building phases, which produced a sprawling multilevel building encompassing a gymnasium, a combination nursery and day school for infants and preschool children, a fellowship hall, a chapel (the original sanctuary), and a new auditorium. Architect William Wenzler planned the first three phases, which included the main building. The fourth phase, which involved building the new, $12 million, three-thousand-seat auditorium, completed in February 1994, was under the direction of Ken Stock, supervising architect-engineer for Oliver Construction, a design-build firm based in Oconomowoc, Wisconsin, which also made use of design assistance from Ware Associates, a Chicago group that specialized in churches. Deborah Locke, "Curtain Raised on Elmbrook Church," *Milwaukee Journal*, February 28, 1994. In 1996, the average weekend worship attendance at Elmbrook was sixty-eight hundred.

41. Except where noted otherwise, information on West Angeles Church of God in Christ is based on authors' research visit, February 21, 1999. Constructed in 1987, the church building extended the length of a city block on Crenshaw Boulevard. According to Vaughan, *Megachurches*, Appendix C, the West Angeles COGIC was one of the twelve fastest-growing churches in the United States during 1990–1991 (of which eight were African American churches). By the early 1990s, with a worship attendance of more than sixty-four hundred, West Angeles had outgrown its current building and was planning a much larger facility a few blocks away, which would include an auditorium seating eight thousand persons. DuPree, *African-American Holiness Pentecostal Movement*, 348, reported the West Angeles membership in 1995 to be more than twenty-nine thousand. In August 2000, construction of the new West Angeles Cathedral, as it was called, was well under way. West Angeles Cathedral Web site, www.westa.org/cath, August 14, 2000.

42. McGraw, "Houses of the Spirit"; Tim Stafford, "God Is in the Blueprints," 78, which also features an excellent photo of the wall.

43. Stafford, "God Is in the Blueprints," 79.

44. On Southern Baptists and the Federal-style church, see Robinson, *Reflections of Faith*, 198, 199, 200, 227, 278, 279. Except where noted otherwise, information on Roswell Street Baptist Church is based on authors' research visit and interview with Anna Conley, June 12, 1998. In 1998 the membership of this Southern Baptist church was about nine thousand, and the average worship attendance at the Sunday morning service was about three thousand.

45. Except where noted otherwise, information on Dauphin Way Baptist Church is based on authors' research visit and interview with Troy Powell, June 5, 1997. The Dauphin Way church is a good example of a center city church that responded to demographic shifts by moving to a more advantageous location, a nineteen-acre site adjacent to the main traffic arteries of the city. It was designed by Hatfield and Halcomb Architects of Dallas (the same firm that designed Prestonwood Baptist Church in Plano), and The Architects Group, Inc., based in Mobile, Alabama. In addition to the worship center, a preschool educational building was also part of the first phase of the building campaign; the total cost of the two structures was about $13 million. The church was affiliated with the Southern Baptist Convention. ("Classic beauty") *Together We Build*, 6, and see also 13; *A Celebration of Faith* (church booklet, [1988]), 7, 16.

46. Information on First Baptist Church of Raytown is based on authors' research visit and interview with Steve Cowart, September 16, 2000, and telephone conversation with David Williams, September 26, 2000. HH Architects and a local firm, Hansen, Midgley, Niemackl based in Overland, Kansas, designed this Southern Baptist megachurch.

47. Except where noted otherwise, information on Bellevue Baptist Church is based on authors' research visit, August 6, 2000. The pastors and congregation of this Southern Baptist megachurch decided in the mid 1980s to move to the suburbs, leaving the downtown Memphis location the church had occupied for some eighty years. Randall Balmer, "Churchgoing: Bellevue Baptist Church Near Memphis," 484, reported the cost of the Cordova building, completed in 1989, to be $34 million. In 1995, the membership was 25,140, and worship attendance was almost 7,000 persons. Greer, "Bellevue Baptist Church," 218, 220. See also Robert Kerr, "Rev. Rogers Rolls On," *Commercial Appeal*, September 29, 1991.

48. Except where noted otherwise, information on the Cathedral of the Holy Spirit is based on authors' research visit and interview with Associate Pastor Dan Rhodes, June 9, 1998. An indispensable source of information on Earl Paulk and the Cathedral of the Holy Spirit is Thumma, "The Kingdom, the Power, and the Glory." The Cathedral of the Holy Spirit was an independent, multiracial pentecostal church. In 1998, blacks constituted about 75 percent of the congregation. Paulk quoted in Thumma, "The Kingdom, the Power, and the Glory," 159, 165, 278–79,

325. Paulk dedicated the Cathedral at the pinnacle of his ministry, when the church claimed some twelve thousand members. Soon afterward, the church experienced mounting debts and a serious decline in membership caused by racial tensions in the congregation and extensive media publicity regarding alleged sexual misconduct on the part of several of the pastors, including Paulk. See, for example, "A Church in Turmoil," *Atlanta Journal and Constitution*, May 28, 1992 (LN); Gayle White, "Paulk Church Files Lawsuit Over 'Rumors,'" ibid., November 13, 1992 (LN). Thumma, "The Kingdom, the Power, and the Glory," 465–66, reported that during the period 1991–1992, the church's average weekly worship attendance decreased from seven thousand to two thousand, and its membership, income, and ministries, as well as Paulk's authority, were greatly diminished.

49. "The Cathedral of the Holy Spirit at Chapel Hill Harvester Church" (church leaflet, [1995?]). In planning the new building, Paulk had sent Associate Pastor Dan Rhodes and an Argentina-born architect, Norbert Senftleben, around the country to look at various church buildings. After visiting Phoenix First Assembly of God and Carpenter's Home Church, among others, they chose Roe Messner to design their church building. According to Rhodes, they had already formulated the "design parameters," and they "wanted to be in total control." Once Messner presented his design, they "massaged" it: Senftleben added details and ornamentation to transform Messner's structure into a neo-Gothic edifice.

50. Except where noted otherwise, information on Covenant Church is based on authors' research visit and interviews with Jerry Parsons and Kelly Berard, November 4, 1999, and author's telephone conversation with Nick Cade of Nc-A Architects, Dallas, January 31, 2001. Covenant Church was a nondenominational, "Spirit-filled," multiracial church. In 1999, the weekend worship attendance totaled approximately 3,060. African Americans constituted about 30 percent of the congregation; the church also offered services in Portuguese, Korean, and Spanish.

51. *Covenant Church: 20 Years of Memories and Victories* (church booklet, [1995?]), 81. Once the auditorium opened, it became obvious that the church's musical program, which featured contemporary music performed by a full band and an eighty-voice choir, produced too much reverberation. To solve the problem, the church had to hang sound-absorbing panels, recommended by an acoustician, on the auditorium walls.

52. Except where noted otherwise, information on Coral Ridge Presbyterian Church is based on authors' research visit and interview with D. James Kennedy, December 13 and 14, 1996. Affiliated with the Presbyterian Church in America, the Coral Ridge Church was founded in 1959. Kennedy became its pastor in July 1960, and the congregation moved to its current site on North Federal Highway in the early 1970s. Designed by Harold E. Wagoner, the church building was completed in 1973. Two wings were added in 1990; Schwab, Twitty and Hanser Architectural Group, Inc., designed them to be compatible with the original architecture. See Patty Doyle, "A Heavenly Restoration," 24–25. During the winter season of 1995, the weekend worship attendance averaged between four and five thousand persons. On the design of the church, see anonymous, undated description of the church, in "Picture Portfolio of the History of Coral Ridge Presbyterian Church" (scrapbook, n.d., in the Coral Ridge Presbyterian Church library); Herbert Lee Williams, *D. James Kennedy: The Man and His Ministry*, 99–111, 140–41, 150–53; *Great Churches of Today*, 21. On the use of the fish in church design see Fiddes, *Architectural Requirements*, 70; White, *Protestant Worship and Church Architecture*, 193. The faceted windows were fabricated by Henry Lee Willet and E. Crosby Willet of Willet Stained Glass Studios, Philadelphia.

53. Except where noted otherwise, information on Calvary Assembly of God is based on authors' research visit and interview with Facilities Manager Bill Gray, January 7, 2000, and Gray to authors, January 23, 2001. The main building was designed by Schweizer Associates, Inc., of Orlando, Florida (now defunct) and completed in 1985. Calvary Assembly of God experienced considerable growth in the 1970s and early 1980s, reaching an all-time high of some seven thousand members. The membership plunged to around seventeen hundred in the late 1980s, but began growing again. In 1999–2000, the average weekend worship attendance was about twenty-five hundred.

54. Estimates of seating capacity are based on a sample of some fifty megachurches, including most of those discussed in this book, for which it was possible to determine the seating capacity of the auditorium, and on the twenty-plus auditorium churches discussed in chapter 3 for

which it was possible to find or estimate the seating capacity of the auditorium.

55. Price quoted in John Dart, "Themes of Bigness, Success Attract Independent Churches," *Los Angeles Times,* July 20, 1991. On Second Baptist, see Elmer L. Towns, *An Inside Look at 10 of Today's Most Innovative Churches,* 138; on Southeast Christian, see "Southeast Christian Church Year at a Glance—An Analysis of Growth" (church information sheet, February 1, 1999); Bob Russell, "Reflections," *Southeast Outlook,* February 4, 1999; Joseph Grove, "20,761 Worshippers Make SECC Easter Weekend Largest Ever," ibid., April 8, 1999; author's telephone conversation with Patty Anderson, March 14, 2001.

56. Roswell Street Baptist Church pamphlet quoted in Scott Thumma, "Exploring the Megachurch Phenomena: Their Characteristics and Cultural Context," from Hartford Institute for Religion Research Web site, www.hartfordinstitute.org, March 28, 2001.

9. The "Full Service" Church

1. Trueheart, "Welcome to the Next Church," 39. This chapter is based on research into the full service ministries of some one hundred late-twentieth-century megachurches (including those described in previous chapters), of which approximately one third were predominantly black or multiracial churches. Except where noted otherwise, information is based on authors' research visits to the various churches, as cited in previous chapters.

2. Towns, *Capturing a Town for Christ,* 82; Kallestad quoted in Beverly Medlyn, "Thousands of Unchurched Take New Approach to Joy," *Arizona Republic,* August 27, 1994 (LN); ("multiple entry points") Wicker, "Fishers of Men"; ("side doors") Sam Kiley, "US Feeds Its Souls with Snacks and Salvation," *Sunday Times* (Times Newspapers Limited), February 17, 1991 (LN). In the megachurches, therapeutic ministries treated a wide range of personal and emotional problems, offering support groups for, among others, individuals recovering from abortion, divorce, or a death in the family, or suffering from alcohol, drug, or sexual addictions.

3. Lyle E. Schaller, *The Seven-Day-A-Week Church;* Kallestad quoted in Medlyn, "Thousands of Unchurched Take New Approach to Joy"; Harvard Business School, *Willow Creek Community Church,* 26; "February Willow Creek" (church calendar, [1996]); Brazier quoted in "Apostolic Church of God Celebrates 66 Years," 5. See also Caldwell, "More Than Worship."

4. *Great Churches of Today,* 42. Except where noted otherwise, information on First Baptist Church of Dallas is based on authors' research visit and interview with Mary Anne Schmidt, October 28, 1998. Besides the original nineteenth-century auditorium (refurbished and enlarged in the early twentieth century), various other buildings made up the First Baptist complex, which occupied five city blocks. Several modern multistory buildings housed a very large Sunday school, a Christian academy, a radio station, a five-hundred-bed shelter, a multistory parking facility, and administrative offices, conference rooms, a library, bookstore, and other facilities. Recreational facilities included two gymnasiums, a skating rink, bowling alleys, racquetball courts, and a sauna. In the mid-1990s, the church had a worship attendance of around seventy-seven hundred and claimed a membership of some twenty-nine thousand. Vaughan, *Megachurches,* Appendix D; "Pulpit Temptation," *Houston Chronicle,* September 24, 1994 (LN); John N. Vaughan, *The World's Twenty Largest Churches,* 127, 132–33; Adelle M. Banks, "Ex-Pastor Raises Question About Megachurches' Future," *Orlando Sentinel,* October 1, 1994 (LN); Charles Reagan Wilson, *Judgment and Grace in Dixie: Southern Faiths from Faulkner to Elvis* (Athens: University of Georgia Press, 1995), 14.

5. A sign in one of the Kid Kountry classrooms at A Community of Joy defined the "vision" of the church's children's ministries as follows: "To create the most innovative and imaginative children's ministry, bringing the love of Christ to a new generation and leaving an eternal imprint of God's love on their lives." Jack DeBartolo, Jr., of DeBartolo Architects, in Phoenix, designed Small World Village. He had been hired by Pastor Tommy Barnett to oversee a renovation and building campaign called Vision 2000. Small World Village, an assemblage of white metal buildings arranged at various angles so as to enclose shaded, protected play areas, was the first of several new facilities completed by 2000. The oth-

ers, still in the planning stage, included an amphitheater, a youth outreach and fellowship center, and an adult education and banquet/convention facility with a five-thousand-square-foot commercial kitchen and a large "food court." DeBartolo was also working on another of Barnett's projects—the "Dream Center" of the Los Angeles International Church, part of the preacher's "vision for taking the church to the inner city." Authors' interview with Jack DeBartolo, Jr., Phoenix, March 30, 2000; and telephone conversation, April 24, 1996; *Fact Sheet: Important Information about the VISION 2000 Campaign* (church brochure, [1998]); Michael J. O'Connor, "Shaping Modern Religion," *Architecture Magazine,* January 1999, n.p.; Lawrence W. Cheek, "Jack DeBartolo 3: The Rising Son," ibid., May 1999, n.p.; Laurie Goodstein, "A Church Center For Those in Need Draws Bush's Eye," *New York Times,* February 18, 2001. On children's facilities at Prestonwood Baptist and Southeast Christian, see "Prestonwood Baptist Church," *Dallas Morning News Special Advertising Supplement,* June 18, 1999; Joseph Grove, "New Youth Center Gets Off to a God Start," *Southeast Outlook,* March 18, 1999.

6. See, for example, Williams, *D. James Kennedy,* 169; Roger Hines and Donna Rypel, *Roswell Street Baptist Church 50th Anniversary History, 1943–1993,* 26; Bell, Ladner, and Poor, eds., *A Church in the City,* 124–31.

7. Cay Hunter, comp., *Twenty-fifth Anniversary, Coral Ridge Presbyterian Church, 1960–1985* (church booklet, [1985]), n.p.

8. "Bellevue Today" (church bulletin, August 27, 2000).

9. *Excitement!* (Second Baptist church booklet, June, 1996), 7; Balmer, "Churchgoing: Bellevue Baptist Church Near Memphis," 487; Mary Jo Griffith, "Main Event Holidays 1992," *Orange County Register,* December 17, 1992 (LN); Barnett quoted in "Glitz, Outreach Help Church to Grow," *Springfield* (Mo.) *News-Leader,* April 7, 1993; Ratliff quoted in *Black Nativity* (church booklet, [1995]). Burgess, "Tommy J. Barnett," 50, reported that the pageants at Phoenix First drew as many as 130,000 over a period of a week to ten days. According to Lloyd Billingsley, "A Crystal Cathedral Spectacular," *Christianity Today,* January 22, 1982, 34, the 1982 Christmas pageant scheduled forty performances.

10. Ben Winton, "Valley Megachurches Light the Way to 21st Century," *Arizona Republic,* February 18, 1996 (LN); Ninie O'Hara, "Southeast Easter Pageant Will Be Different, Bigger, Better," *Southeast Outlook,* February 4, 1999. Ironically, the great expenditure of money required for the Southeast Christian pageant forced the church to compromise its evangelistic purpose by charging admission. See Bob Russell, "Reflections," ibid., February 25, 1999.

11. On the range of meetings in dining or fellowship halls, see, for example, *Great Churches of Today,* 42; Bell, Ladner, and Poor, eds., *A Church in the City,* 150. On the Coral Ridge, Roswell Street, and Southeast Christian fellowship halls, see Patty Doyle, "A Heavenly Renovation: Coral Ridge Presbyterian Church Renovation and Addition," 24, 25; Hines and Rypel, *Roswell Street Baptist Church 50th Anniversary History,* 26; Joseph Grove, "Fellowship Hall to be Open for Leadership Conference in May," *Southeast Outlook,* April 22, 1999.

12. Bell, Ladner, and Poor, eds., *A Church in the City,* 150; *For Such a Time as This* (church booklet, [1986]); Mark G. Toulouse, "W. A. Criswell," in Charles H. Lippy, ed., *Twentieth-Century Shapers of American Popular Religion* (New York: Greenwood Press, 1989), 98.

13. Thumma, "The Kingdom, the Power, and the Glory," 6, 337; Paul Thigpen, "Restoring the Arts to the Church," *Charisma and Christian Life* 16 (June 1990): 53, 56.

14. Late-nineteenth-, early-twentieth-century urban evangelical churches, it will be recalled, offered physical recreation programs and provided playgrounds, gymnasiums, bowling alleys, billiard and pool tables, even swimming pools. Fundamentalist, pentecostal, and holiness tabernacles and churches generally refrained from sponsoring such programs; the Chicago Gospel Tabernacle and the Baptist Tabernacle in Atlanta were exceptions. On the expansion of evangelical churches' recreation programs, see Agnes Durant Pylant, "Recreation, Church," *Encyclopedia of Southern Baptists,* vol. 2, 1135–36; Robert M. Boyd, "Recreation, Church," *Encyclopedia of Southern Baptists,* vol. 3, 1935; Ray Conner, "Recreation, Church," *Encyclopedia of Southern Baptists,* vol. 4, 2434.

15. *For Such a Time as This;* "Sports, Fitness, and Fun! Family Life Center, Second Baptist Church" (church leaflet, [1996]). Southeast Christian Church built an Activities Center comparable in scope to Second Baptist's Family Life Center, but even larger. Steve Coomes, "Grand Opening of Activities Center Set for Friday, Feb. 5," *Southeast Outlook,* January 28, 1999; "Southeast Christian Activities Center" (church leaflet, [1999]).

16. *Experiencing the Victory . . . Finishing the Race, Special Edition, Touch-*

ing Eternity (Prestonwood Baptist Church brochure, October 30–November 12), 5.

17. ("Through sports") "Exercising Our Faith," *Profile,* September/October, 1999, 8–9; ("we want") Ellen A. Wolkensperg, "New Activities Center Scores a Win with Opening Crowd," *Southeast Outlook,* February 11, 1999. The emphasis on evangelizing the unchurched led some megachurches, for example, Oak Cliff Bible Fellowship, North Phoenix Baptist Church, and First Baptist Church of Houston, to open their family life centers to the public at no cost. Other megachurches charged fees, and if non–church members were admitted, they paid slightly more than church members. Still other megachurches (for example, Second Baptist Church of Houston and Southeast Christian Church) made use of the centers a privilege of members and those who regularly attended the worship service. Author's telephone conversations with Oak Cliff staff member, April 30, 2001, with North Phoenix Baptist Church staff member, April 30, 2001, and with David Wise, Director, Christian Life Center, First Baptist Church, Houston, May 8, 2001; "Sports, Fitness, and Fun!"; "Who Can Use the Family Life Center?" *Southeast Outlook,* October 22, 1998; Coomes, "Grand Opening of Activities Center Set for Friday, Feb. 5."

18. "Vineyard Christian Fellowship of Anaheim" (church bulletin, February 21, 1999). On community service programs at other megachurches, see Russell Chandler, "Man of His Word," *Los Angeles Times,* March 21, 1992 (LN); Adelle M. Banks, "Megachurches at Center of Black Middle Class," *Stuart News/Port St. Lucie News* (Stuart, Fla.), May 25, 1996 (LN).

19. (Vineyard church) "Compassion Ministry," *Vinelife,* Winter, 1999, 6, 7; (New Birth Missionary Baptist Church) Sabrina Murphy, "Resurrection '98 Embracing the Community," *New Birth Voice* (Resurrection Sunday '98 edition). See also Bell, Ladner, and Poor, eds., *A Church in the City,* 174; Paul Thigpen, "What's the Fuss About 'Kingdom Now'?" *Ministries Today* 6 (July/August 1988): 36; *Ministry Opportunity Handbook* (Faith Community Church booklet, [1999?]), 43; "Choices: Prestonwood Pregnancy Center" (church leaflet, [1999?]); Christine Wicker, "Ministries Designed to Address Problems Inside and Out," *Dallas Morning News,* September 18, 1995 (LN); "Window on Southeast," *Southeast Outlook,* June 13, 1997.

20. C. Eric Lincoln and Lawrence H. Mamiya, "The Black Church and Social Ministry in Politics and Economics: Historical and Contemporary Perspectives," in Carl S. Dudley, Jackson W. Carroll, and James P. Wind, eds., *Carriers of Faith: Lessons from Congregational Studies* (Louisville: John Knox Press, 1991), 77, 80; Franklin, *Another Day's Journey,* 103–7. Two national interdenominational organizations involved in economic development were the Revelation Corporation of America, headquartered in Memphis, and the Congress of National Black Churches, based in Washington, D.C. Richard Vara, "Grass-roots Religion," *Houston Chronicle,* August 17, 1996 (LN).

21. "Apostolic Church of God Celebrates 66 Years," 10; James Traub, "Floyd Flake's Middle America," *New York Times Magazine,* October 19, 1997, 102–3; Joyce Shelby, "In Good Faith," *Daily News* (New York), February 11, 1996 (LN); (Windsor Village United Methodist Church) Steve Brunsman, "Booming Churches," *Houston Post,* November 5, 1994 (LN); (St. Agnes Baptist Church) Vara, "Grass-roots Religion."

22. "Apostolic Church of God Celebrates 66 Years," 4, 10, 11.

23. Price quoted in Hines and Rypel, *Roswell Street Baptist Church 50th Anniversary History,* 27; ("very non-Christian") D. James Kennedy quoted in Dan Nicholas, "Being Christ's Agent in a Fallen World: The Perspective of D. James Kennedy," *Religious Broadcasting,* November, 1986, 25. See also Patricia Leigh Brown, "Megachurches as Minitowns," *New York Times,* May 9, 2002.

24. Second Baptist, Houston, pastor quoted in Towns, *Inside Look,* 141; ("Christ-centered") "Prestonwood Christian Academy" (church advertising flyer, 1998); ("Christian environment") *For Such a Time as This.* A reporter for *Maclean's,* who talked with some of the people enjoying the athletic facilities at Second Baptist Church, Houston, quoted one member as saying, "There's always something fun going on. Aerobics or ball games are followed by prayer, so that everything has a deeper purpose." Diane Brady, "Churches Shun Tradition to Attract Young Adults," *Maclean's,* June 3, 1991 (LN).

25. ("Inward-turning") Ron Wilson, "'Feed My Sheep' Has New Meaning to Some Megachurches," *San Antonio Express-News,* October 31, 1998 (LN); ("Christian cocooning") Brown, "Megachurches as Minitowns"; ("lifestyle enclaves") sociologist Nancy Ammerman quoted in Cathleen Ferraro, "Churches Turning to Marketing to Increase Size of

Their Flocks," *Investor's Daily,* February 7, 1991 (LN); pastor of Mariners Church quoted in Trueheart, "Welcome to the Next Church," 40.

26. ("Refuge") E. Franklin Frazier, *The Negro Church in America,* 50. See also C. Eric Lincoln and Lawrence H. Mamiya, *The Black Church in the African American Experience,* 157–63; Melvin D. Williams, *Community in a Black Pentecostal Church: An Anthropological Study* (Pittsburgh: University of Pittsburgh Press, 1974); Samuel G. Freedman, *Upon This Rock: The Miracles of a Black Church* (New York: HarperCollins Publishers, Inc., 1993); Caldwell, "More Than Worship"; Adelle M. Banks, "Worship Service," *Chicago Tribune,* August 18, 1996 (LN); Andrew Herrmann, "Black Professionals Find Their Places in Church," *Chicago Sun-Times,* June 26, 1993 (LN); "Black Megachurches Surge," 686.

27. Robert Michael Franklin, "The Safest Place on Earth: The Culture of Black Congregations," in James P. Wind and James W. Lewis, eds., *American Congregations, Volume 2, New Perspectives in the Study of Congregations* (Chicago: University of Chicago Press, 1994), 258; ("spiritual, emotional . . . center") Franklin, *Another Day's Journey,* 52. See also Shelby, "In Good Faith"; Joan Connell, "Reaching Out to Black Men"; Susan Parrott, "Dallas Church Gets High-Tech Worship," *Saturday (Baton Rouge Advocate),* November 4, 2000; Wright, Jr., "Defining and Living Out Your Identity," 88–90.

10. The Worship Center

1. Ellen A. Wolkensperg, "Welcome Center Radiates Southeast Hospitality to 'Guests,'" *Southeast Outlook,* January 7, 1999. Tim Stafford observed that "older churches . . . were built with no concern whatsoever for the transition between sidewalk and sanctuary. Today's churches assume that people come with far less confidence and need a clear message from outside spaces that they are welcome, will feel comfortable, and can find friends if they want them." Stafford, "God Is in the Blueprints," 79. Except where noted otherwise, information in this chapter is based on authors' research visits to the megachurches cited in previous chapters. Megachurch builders and congregations generally employed the term "worship center" to designate the space used for corporate worship. However, a few pastors and church members continued to use the older terms "sanctuary" and "auditorium." For a comment on the validity of "worship center," see McCormick, *Designing Worship Centers,* 7.

2. Ellen A. Wolkensperg, "Seating Fills Sanctuary as Worship Center Gets Cozy," *Southeast Outlook,* November 26, 1998.

3. Jack Coffee, "Church Construction Now an Inside Job," ibid., May 23, 1997; "Fact Sheet" (Carpenter's Home Church information sheet, n.d.); "The Cathedral of the Holy Spirit at Chapel Hill Harvester Church" (church leaflet, [1995?]); John Dart, "Pastor Frederick Price's 'FaithDome,'" *Los Angeles Times,* September 9, 1989 (LN).

4. Megachurches with rectangular or square auditoriums included First Baptist Church, Dallas, Midwest Christian Center, Oak Cliff Bible Fellowship, Fellowship Church, Saddleback Church, and Willow Creek Community Church. The shapes chosen for the Covenant Church and Coral Ridge Presbyterian Church auditoriums were atypical. The builders of Covenant Church designed the auditorium in the shape of a Y, with the pews arranged in what the architect called a "fan-shape." Author's telephone conversation with Nick Cade, January 31, 2001. Harold Wagoner designed the Coral Ridge auditorium in the shape of a cross, but with the transepts at 45-degree rather than 90-degree angles. Williams, *D. James Kennedy,* 151.

5. Southeast Christian Church architect quoted in Jack Brammer, "Architect Sees Church He Envisioned," *Southeast Outlook,* October 22, 1998. On the sight lines in various megachurches, see Jack Coffee, "Southeast's New Sanctuary Is a Very Big Room with a Clear View," *Southeast Outlook,* June 13, 1997; "The Cathedral of the Holy Spirit at Chapel Hill Harvester Church"; Hines and Rypel, *Roswell Street Baptist Church 50th Anniversary History,* 24.

6. ("'Sight-sound-sensation' generation") Schaller, *The New Reformation,* 107. Robert Webber, *Worship Old and New: A Biblical, Historical, and Practical Introduction,* 121–22, discusses changing worship practices among evangelicals as part of a larger worship renewal movement that also affected Roman Catholics and mainline Protestants. For recommendations regarding worship forms and practices, see Frank C. Senn, "'Worship Alive': An Analysis and Critique of 'Alternative Worship Services,'" *Worship,* May 1995, 195; Wagner, *Church Planting for a Greater Harvest,* 137; Anderson, *A Church for the 21st Century,* 44.

7. On the Jesus People and neo-pentecostals, see David Di Sabatino, "The Ongoing Impact of Revival: The Music of the Jesus Movement and Its Influence," *Worship Leader,* July/August 1999, 23–27; Margaret Poloma, *The Charismatic Movement: Is There a New Pentecost?* (Boston: Twayne Publishers, 1982), chap. 1, 194–95, 243, 246; Lincoln and Mamiya, *The Black Church in the African American Experience,* 385–88; Paul Thigpen, "The New Black Charismatics," *Charisma and Christian Life,* November 1990, 58–59. On the music produced by the worship revitalization movement, see Larry L. Myers, "John Wimber's Legacy of Worship," *Voice of the Vineyard,* fall 1998, 16–23; Bruce Shelley and Marshall Shelley, *The Consumer Church* (Downers Grove, Ill.: InterVarsity Press, 1992), 135–39, 177; Miller, *Reinventing American Protestantism,* 80–85; Michael S. Hamilton, "The Triumph of the Praise Songs," *Christianity Today,* July 12, 1999, 29–35.

8. For descriptions of contemporary worship services, see Gustav Niebuhr, "The High Energy Never Stops"; Paul Basden, *The Worship Maze: Finding a Style to Fit Your Church* (Downers Grove, Ill.: InterVarsity Press, 1999), chaps. 7, 8; Miller, *Reinventing American Protestantism,* 44–46, 85–86; Don S. Browning, *A Fundamental Practical Theology: Descriptive and Strategic Proposals* (Minneapolis: Fortress Press, 1991), 28–29; Robert Michael Franklin, "Church and City: Black Christianity's Ministry," *Christian Ministry* 20 (March–April 1989): 18–19.

9. "Counting the Congregation," *Economist,* June 1, 1991 (LN); Beverly Medlyn, "Thousands of Unchurched Take New Approach to Joy," *Arizona Republic,* August 27, 1994 (LN); Zoe Heller, "The Mall of God," *Independent,* June 2, 1991 (LN); Pritchard, *Willow Creek,* 83; John Gerome, "Worship in a Big Way," *Chattanooga Times,* January 4, 1997 (LN); Freedman, *Upon This Rock,* 182; Dart, "Pastor Frederick Price's 'FaithDome.'"

10. John D. Witvliet, "The Blessing and Bane of the North American Megachurch: Implications for Twenty-First Century Congregational Song," 7.

11. For a general discussion of the praise and worship movement see Webber, *Worship Old and New,* 128–32.

12. The discussion of megachurch builders' use of theater designs is based on author's consultations with Gresdna A. Doty, Alumni Professor Emerita of Theatre, Louisiana State University, Baton Rouge, June 2001. Professor Doty provided invaluable insights regarding the history of theater design. On little-theater groups and experimental theaters, see Mary C. Henderson, *The Theater in America* (New York: Harry N. Abrams, Inc., Publishers, 1986), 257–58; Gresdna A. Doty and Billy J. Harbin, eds., *Inside the Royal Court Theatre, 1956–1981: Artists Talk* (Baton Rouge: Louisiana State University Press, 1990), 180–81.

13. Henderson, *Theater in America,* 258–59.

14. Ninie O'Hara, "Loft Is Expanded to Accommodate Worship Choir," *Southeast Outlook,* December 10, 1998. On the thrust stage, see Tyrone Guthrie, *A New Theatre* (New York: McGraw-Hill Book Company, 1964), 68; Christos G. Athanasopulos, *Contemporary Theater: Evolution and Design* (New York: John Wiley and Sons, 1983), 176–92.

15. Tyrone Guthrie, "Theatre at Minneapolis," in Stephen Joseph, ed., *Actor and Architect* (Toronto: University of Toronto Press, 1964), 46–47; Guthrie, *A New Theatre,* 69–70. For references to "intimacy," see, for example, O'Hara, "Loft Is Expanded to Accommodate Worship Choir"; Ninie O'Hara, "Southeast Pageant Will Be Different, Bigger, Better," *Southeast Outlook,* February 4, 1999; Timothy Wright, *A Community of Joy: How to Create Contemporary Worship* (Nashville: Abingdon Press, 1994), 20, 34; Thumma, "The Kingdom, the Power, and the Glory," 512; Deborah Locke, "Curtain Raised on Elmbrook Church," *Milwaukee Journal,* February 28, 1994; W. A. Harrell, "Architecture, Church," in *Encyclopedia of Southern Baptists,* vol. 3, 1572. On the platform steps, see Jerry A. Privette, *Auditorium Planning Guide for Southern Baptist Churches,* 17; McCormick, *Designing Worship Centers,* 38; *The Altar Call with Pastor Tommy Barnett,* videocassette produced by Keith Buchanan, Keith Buchanan Media Ministries, 1999.

16. Guthrie, "Theatre at Minneapolis," 33, 38; Athanasopulos, *Contemporary Theater,* 190.

17. Author's telephone conversation with Stephen Strader, June 25, 2000.

18. "Self-Guided Worship Center Tour" (Prestonwood Baptist Church information sheet, [1999?]); Ellen A. Wolkensperg, "Expanded Use of Video Prepared Congregation for New Sanctuary," *Southeast Outlook,* November 5, 1998.

19. O'Hara, "Loft Is Expanded to Accommodate Worship Choir"; Robinson, "Learning from Willow Creek Church," 69.

20. ("Less exalted") Ronald J. Allen, "Noted Teachers of Preaching on Preaching: The Place of Preaching in Emerging Trends in Worship," *Pulpit Digest,* September/October 1995, 76; Southeast Christian worship

minister quoted in O'Hara, "Loft Is Expanded to Accommodate Worship Choir"; Wright, *Community of Joy,* 106; author's telephone conversation with Stephen Strader, June 25, 2000.

21. "Self-Guided Worship Center Tour." See also McCormick, *Designing Worship Centers,* 52.

22. Stafford, "God Is in the Blueprints," 79–80; (acoustical difficulties) Steve Coomes, "You Ain't Heard Nothin' Yet," *Southeast Outlook,* January 7, 1999. On megachurch acoustics, see also Harold E. Wagoner, "Electronic Utopia?" *Faith and Form* 2 (April, 1969): 17; Ann Yoho, "Sound Investments," *Southeast Christian: Where He Leads . . . We Will Follow* (Louisville: *Southeast Outlook,* 1998), 76; Pamela Schaeffer, "Computer Bug Hits Churches," *St. Louis Post-Dispatch,* May 12, 1990 (LN); Jason Sickles, "Building Up, Trading Out," *Dallas Morning News,* December 14, 1996 (LN).

23. ("One-of-a-kind," Allen quote) O'Hara, "Loft Is Expanded to Accommodate Worship Choir"; (solving acoustical problems) Coomes, "You Ain't Heard Nothin' Yet."

24. (First Baptist, Houston, baptistery) Bell, Ladner, and Poor, eds., *A Church in the City,* 189; (Second Baptist, Houston, baptistery) *For Such a Time as This* and "Story of the Windows" (Second Baptist Church information sheet, [1996?]); ("come into the body of Christ') Robert E. Webber, "Church Buildings: Shapes of Worship," 20. On the "enhanced" baptismal ceremony, see Bob Russell, "Reflections," *Southeast Outlook,* May 20, 1999. A few megachurches held the baptismal ceremony outdoors in a pool constructed alongside or near the worship center. Fellowship Church used a circular pool that served as a fountain when not being used for baptism. Mariners Church and Saddleback Church had larger, irregularly shaped pools located on the church patios. The Willow Creek Community Church had no baptistery. The church offered baptism twice a year, in June and December, by sprinkling rather than immersion; individuals could participate in an immersion service at the pond in June if they wished. Author's telephone conversation with David Staal, March 22, 2001.

25. Webber, *Worship Old and New,* 211–12; Davin Seay, "Eye Has Not Seen: Flourishing Ministries Nurture a Christian Arts Renaissance," *Worship Leader* 8 (January/February 1999): 25. See also Robert Webber, *The Worship Phenomenon* (Nashville: Star Song Publishing Group, 1994),

85–88, 97. On the factors that contributed to evangelicals' interest in the visual arts, see Webber, *Worship Old and New,* 89.

26. "The Story of Faith in Stained Glass," *Dallas Morning News Advertising Supplement,* June 18, 1999; "The Meaning of the Oak Cliff Bible Fellowship 'Stained Glass'" (church information sheet, [1998?]); "Story of the Windows."

27. Robert M. Franklin, "Afrocentric Icons" (typescript of a National Public Radio commentary aired April 13, 2001), courtesy of Robert M. Franklin.

28. Except where noted otherwise, information on St. Luke "Community" United Methodist Church is based on authors' research visit, November 4, 1999. The St. Luke congregation added the word "community" to the church name to emphasize its ministry to the surrounding neighborhood. See Karen M. Thomas, "Church Home," *Dallas Morning News,* March 6, 1993 (LN); Holmes quoted in Caldwell, "More Than Worship." The fabricator of the stained-glass windows was Robert Foster of Foster Stained Glass, Bryan, Texas.

29. Wright, Jr., "Defining and Living Out Your Identity," 90, 91, 92, 97.

30. Jeremiah A. Wright, Jr., "History of Stained Glass: Trinity United Church of Christ" (Trinity United Church of Christ, n.d., videocassette). The Trinity Church stained-glass windows were produced and fabricated by Phillips Stained Glass, Inc., of Cleveland. The preliminary designs were done by Douglas Phillips, who began work on the project in the early 1990s. After he died of cancer in 1995, his wife, Mona Phillips, completed the project. The southeast and southwest windows were installed in 2000; the east window in 2001. The project also included a west window to be installed in 2002. Mona Phillips to authors, September 4, 2001; Jeremiah A. Wright, Jr., "Our Stained Glass Windows are *'One of a Kind!,'* *Trumpet* 2 (October 2001): 4–5; John W. Fountain, "Church's Window on the Past, and the Future," *New York Times,* February 9, 2001. On the use of the visual arts in two other black megachurches, see George O. Mc-Caleb, Jr., "The Greenforest Baptist Church," in Michael A. Battle, Sr., ed., *The African-American Church at Work,* 63; Mamiya, "A Social History of the Bethel African Methodist Episcopal Church," 221, 266–67.

31. The discussion of neo-Gothic elements in the auditoriums of the Cathedral of the Holy Spirit and Covenant Church is based on author's consultation with Marchita B. Mauck, Baton Rouge, Louisiana, January

18, 2001. A church consultant and Professor of Art History, College of Design, Louisiana State University, Mauck provided invaluable instruction regarding Gothic art, architecture, and iconography. For helpful illustrations of the medieval Gothic forms imitated by the two megachurches, see Maria Christina Gozzoli, *How to Recognize Gothic Art* (New York: Penguin Books, 1979), 20, 21; Wim Swann, *The Late Middle Ages: Art and Architecture from 1350 to the Advent of the Renaissance* (Ithaca, N.Y.: Cornell University Press, 1977), Figs. 34, 35, 49, 225.

32. ("A Charismatic cathedral") Paulk quoted in Thumma, "The Kingdom, the Power, and the Glory," 382; ("using the arts") Paulk quoted in Thigpen, "Restoring the Arts to the Church," 54. See also Scott Lee Thumma, "Megachurches of Atlanta," in Gary Laderman, ed., *Religions of Atlanta: Religious Diversity in the Centennial Olympic City* (Atlanta: Scholars Press, 1996), 209.

33. Author's telephone conversation with Associate Pastor Dan Rhodes, January 23, 2001.

34. Williams, *D. James Kennedy,* 151.

35. On Wagoner's design, see ibid., 151. On the furnishings and ornamentation in the auditorium, see "The Sanctuary of Coral Ridge Presbyterian Church" (church leaflet, n.d.); "Picture Portfolio." The photographs of the Coral Ridge church were taken during the Christmas season when the platform was arranged for a concert; as a result, some of the platform furnishings had been removed and the apron of the stage covered the marble steps leading up to the platform.

Epilogue. The Everyday House of God

1. ("Celebrate") Mark Alden Branch, "Inquiry: Religious Buildings," *Progressive Architecture,* December 1990 (LN); ("sacral associations") Williams, *Houses of God,* 185; ("determined") Paul Goldberger, "The Gospel of Church Architecture, Revised"; ("understated brick pile") Trueheart, "Welcome to the Next Church," 38, 39.

2. ("Architectural distinction") Branch, "Inquiry: Religious Build-

ings"; ("function over worship") Kurt Snow, "From the Warehouse to God's House: A Look at Present-Day Compromises in Church Architecture," *Chalcedon Report,* October 1995, 16. On the resemblance to secular, commercial buildings, see Goldberger, "Gospel of Church Architecture, Revised"; Trueheart, "Welcome to the Next Church," 53; Os Guinness, *Dining with the Devil: The Megachurch Movement Flirts with Modernity* (Grand Rapids, Mich.: Baker Book House, 1993), 77; Snow, "From the Warehouse to God's House," 16.

3. McDannell, *Material Christianity,* 4–5.

4. Ibid., 4.

5. ("Meet people") Kristin Campbell, "Divine Plans," *Austin American-Statesman,* June 20, 1998 (LN); Joe Heller, "The Mall of God," *Independent,* June 2, 1991 (LN); Bellevue Baptist Web site, www.bellevue.org; Warren quoted in Dana Parsons, "New-Time Religion," *Los Angeles Times,* December 24, 1987 (LN); authors' interview with Wayne Skaff, Phoenix, March 31, 2000.

6. Miller, *Reinventing American Protestantism,* 86–90. See also Mark A. Torgerson, "Enjoying God in a Crowd: Worship Space and the Megachurch," *Doxology* 19 (2002): 61–84.

7. On the notion of an immanent God, see Bernhard Lang, *Sacred Games: A History of Christian Worship* (New Haven, Conn.: Yale University Press, 1997), 419–31; McDannell, *Material Christianity,* 5–6. On music, see ("means for encounter") Witvliet, "The Blessing and Bane of the North American Megachurch," 8; ("emotion and experience") Di Sabatino, "The Ongoing Impact of Revival," 27; Myers, "John Wimber's Legacy of Worship," 16–23; Steve Rabey, "The Profits of Praise," *Christianity Today,* July 12, 1999, 33; Franklin, "The Safest Place on Earth," 260–61; Miller, *Reinventing American Protestantism,* 90–91.

8. ("Present and active") Pritchard, *Willow Creek,* 258, and see also 46–47, 259–63; (intervening) Miller, *Reinventing American Protestantism,* 124–25; ("distant God") Mary Beth Sammons, "Full Service Church," *Chicago Tribune,* April 3, 1994 (LN).

9. Price quoted in John Dart, "Pastor Frederick Price's 'FaithDome,'" *Los Angeles Times,* September 9, 1989 (LN); Paulk quoted in Thumma, "The Kingdom, the Power, and the Glory," 243; ("mighty building") *Covenant Church: 20 Years of Memories & Victories,* 28; ("prophecies") *Upon this Rock . . .* (Lakeland, Fla.: First Assembly Ministries, [1981?]), 2.

10. Authors' conversation with Bishop Arthur M. Brazier and Patti Caire, Apostolic Church of God, Chicago, May 22, 1996.

11. Authors' conversations with Randy Sukow, Valley Cathedral Church, Phoenix, April 3, 1996, and Mike Keys, Faith Community Church, West Covina, California, February 17, 1999; Ninie O'Hara, "9E's Notes," *Southeast Outlook,* November 26, 1998; "To God Be the Glory," ibid., December 31, 1998, photo insert.

12. Steve Coomes, "Boy It's Big! Congregation Tours New Facility at Picnic," *Southeast Outlook,* July 23, 1997; Jack Brammer, "Architect Sees Church He Envisioned," ibid., October 22, 1998.

13. Russell quoted in Ninie O'Hara, "More than 15,000 Attend Dedication Weekend," ibid., December 31, 1998.

14. *A Celebration of Faith* (church booklet, [1998]), 2, 10; *Together We Build* (church booklet, [1987?]), 5; authors' interview with Lynn Cross, Grapevine, Texas, November 3, 1999.

15. Steve Coomes, "'Heaven Sent' Solution Came After Prayer Over Acoustic Nightmares," *Southeast Outlook,* October 31, 1997.

16. "Guide to Stained Glass Windows" (Prestonwood Church leaflet, [1999?]).

17. ("Church's mission") McCormick, *Designing Worship Centers,* 28, 30; ("not a thing apart") Goldberger, "Gospel of Church Architecture, Revised."

Selected Bibliography

Anderson, Leith. *A Church for the 21st Century.* Minneapolis: Bethany House Publishers, 1992.

————. *Dying for Change: An Arresting Look at the New Realities Confronting Church and Para-Church Ministries.* Minneapolis: Bethany House Publishers, 1990.

"The Apostolic Church of God Celebrates 66 Years of Grace Proclaiming the Gospel." Special Supplement, *Chicago Sun-Times,* April 19, 1998.

Balmer, Randall. "Churchgoing: Bellevue Baptist Church Near Memphis." *Christian Century* 110 (May 5, 1993): 484–88.

Battle, Michael A., Sr., ed. *The African-American Church at Work.* St. Louis: Hodale Press, Inc., 1994.

Bell, Kate Atkinson, Christine Hall Ladner, and Joanna William Poor, eds. *A Church in the City Reaching the World.* Houston: First Baptist Church, 1985.

Benes, Peter, and Philip Zimmerman, eds. *New England Meeting House and Church: 1630–1850.* Boston: Boston University and the Currier Gallery of Art, 1979.

"Black Megachurches Surge." *Christian Century* 113 (July 3, 1996): 686–87.

Bluestone, Daniel. *Constructing Chicago.* New Haven, Conn.: Yale University Press, 1991.

Bruce, Dickson D., Jr. *And They All Sang Hallelujah: Plain-Folk Camp-Meeting Religion, 1800–1845.* Knoxville: University of Tennessee Press, 1974.

Burgess, Stanley M., and Gary B. McGee, eds. *Dictionary of Pentecostal and Charismatic Movements.* Grand Rapids, Mich.: Zondervan Publishing House, 1988.

Burroughs, P. E. *Church and Sunday-School Buildings.* Nashville: Sunday School Board, Southern Baptist Convention, 1920.

———. *A Complete Guide to Church Building.* Nashville: Sunday School Board, Southern Baptist Convention, 1923.

———. *Let Us Build: A Practical Guide.* Nashville: Broadman Press, 1938.

Bushman, Richard L. *The Refinement of America: Persons, Houses, Cities.* New York: Alfred A. Knopf, 1992.

Carpenter, Joel. *Revive Us Again: The Reawakening of American Fundamentalism.* New York: Oxford University Press, 1997.

Casey, Edward S. *Getting Back Into Place: Toward a Renewed Understanding of the Place-World.* Bloomington: Indiana University Press, 1993.

Chiat, Marilyn J. *America's Religious Architecture: Sacred Places for Every Community.* New York: John Wiley and Sons, Inc., 1997.

Conkin, Paul K. *The Uneasy Center: Reformed Christianity in Antebellum America.* Chapel Hill: University of North Carolina Press, 1995.

Conn, Harvie M. *The American City and the Evangelical Church: A Historical Overview.* Grand Rapids, Mich.: Baker Books, 1994.

Convention of Ministers and Delegates of the Congregational Churches in the United States. *A Book of Plans for Churches and Parsonages. Published under the Direction of the Central Committee, Appointed by the General Congregational Convention, October, 1852. Comprising Designs by Upjohn, Downing, Renwick, Wheeler, Wells, Austin, Stone, Cleveland, Backus, and Reeve.* New York: D. Burgess and Co., 1853.

Davies, Horton. *The Worship of the American Puritans, 1629–1730.* New York: Peter Lang, Publishing, 1990.

Dexter, H. M. *Meeting-Houses: Considered Historically and Suggestively.* Boston: J. H. Tilton and Co., 1859.

Donnelly, Marian C. *The New England Meeting Houses of the Seventeenth Century.* Middletown, Conn.: Wesleyan University Press, 1968.

Doyle, Patty. "A Heavenly Renovation: Coral Ridge Presbyterian Church Renovation and Addition." *Florida Architecture* 38 (September/October 1991): 24–25.

DuPree, Sherry Sherrod. *African-American Holiness Pentecostal Movement: An Annotated Bibliography.* New York: Garland Publishing Co., 1996.

Encyclopedia of Southern Baptists. Vols. 1–2. Nashville: Broadman Press, 1958.

———. Vol. 3. Nashville: Broadman Press, 1971.

———. Vol. 4. Nashville: Broadman Press, 1982.

Euster, W. T. *The Philosophy of Church Building: How to Build a Beautiful Modern Church or Parsonage at Half Price.* Pendleton, Oreg.: Pendleton Printery, 1908.

Finney, Charles G. *The Memoirs of Charles G. Finney: The Complete and Restored Text.* Edited by Garth M. Rosell and Richard A. G. Dupuis. Grand Rapids, Mich.: Academie Books, 1989.

Franklin, Robert M. *Another Day's Journey: Black Churches Confronting the American Crisis.* Minneapolis: Fortress Press, 1997.

Frazier, E. Franklin. *The Negro Church in America.* New York: Schocken Books, Inc., 1974.

Goldberger, Paul. "The Gospel of Church Architecture, Revised." *New York Times,* April 20, 1995.

———. *On the Rise: Architecture and Design in a Postmodern Age.* New York: Viking Penguin Inc., 1983.

Gorham, B. W. *Camp Meeting Manual, A Practical Book for the Camp Ground.* Boston: H. V. Degen, 1854.

Great Churches of Today: Outstanding Congregations, Their Leaders, Their Program, Their People, by the Staff of Decision. Minneapolis: World Wide Publications, 1970.

Haber, Francine, Kenneth R. Fuller, and David N. Wetzel. *Robert S. Roeschlaub: Architect of the Emerging West, 1843–1923.* [Denver:] Colorado Historical Society, 1988.

Hardman, Keith J. *Charles Grandison Finney, 1792–1875: Revivalist and Reformer.* Syracuse, N.Y.: Syracuse University Press, 1987.

Harrell, William A. *Planning Better Church Buildings.* Nashville: Convention Press, 1957.

Hatch, Nathan O. *The Democratization of American Christianity.* New Haven, Conn.: Yale University Press, 1989.

Hines, Roger, and Donna Rypel. *Roswell Street Baptist Church 50th Anniversary History, 1943–1993.* [Marietta, Ga.: Roswell Street Baptist Church, 1993].

Hybels, Lynne, and Bill Hybels. *Rediscovering Church: The Story and Vision of Willow Creek Community Church.* Grand Rapids, Mich.: Zondervan Publishing House, 1995.

Johnson, Charles A. *The Frontier Camp Meeting: Religion's Harvest Time.* Dallas: Southern Methodist University Press, 1955.

Kallestad, Walt. *Entertainment Evangelism: Taking the Church Public.* Nashville: Abingdon Press, 1996.

Kidder, F. E. *Churches and Chapels: Designs and Suggestions for Church-Building Committees, Architects and Builders.* New York: William T. Comstock, 1895.

———. *Churches and Chapels: Their Arrangement, Construction and Equipment Supplemented by Plans, Interior and Exterior Views of Numerous Churches of Different Denominations, Arrangement and Cost.* New York: William T. Comstock, 1906.

Kilde, Jeanne Halgren. *When Church Became Theatre: The Transformation of Evangelical Architecture and Worship in Nineteenth-Century America.* New York: Oxford University Press, 2002.

Kirby, Linda K. *Heritage of Heroes: Trinity United Methodist Church, 1859–1988.* Denver: Trinity United Methodist Church, 1988.

Kramer, George W. *The What How and Why of Church Building.* New York: n.p., 1897.

Lincoln, C. Eric. *The Black Church since Frazier.* New York: Schocken Books, 1974.

——— and Lawrence H. Mamiya. *The Black Church in the*

African American Experience. Durham, N.C.: Duke University Press, 1990.

McCormick, Gwenn E. *Designing Worship Centers.* Nashville: Convention Press, 1988.

McDannell, Colleen. *Material Christianity: Religion and Popular Culture in America.* New Haven, Conn.: Yale University Press, 1995.

Miller, Donald E. *Reinventing American Protestantism: Christianity in the New Millennium.* Berkeley: University of California Press, 1997.

Niebuhr, Gustav. "The High Energy Never Stops." *New York Times,* April 16, 1995.

———. "The Minister as Marketer: Learning from Business." *New York Times,* April 18, 1995.

———. "Where Religion Gets a Big Dose of Shopping-Mall Culture." *New York Times,* April 16, 1995.

Payne, Daniel A. *History of the African Methodist Episcopal Church.* 1891. Reprt., New York: Arno Press and the *New York Times,* 1969.

Pierson, William H., Jr. *American Buildings and Their Architects: The Colonial and Neo-Classical Styles.* Garden City, N.Y.: Anchor Books, 1976.

Pritchard, G. A. *Willow Creek Seeker Services: Evaluating a New Way of Doing Church.* Grand Rapids, Mich.: Baker Books, 1996.

Privette, Jerry A. *Auditorium Planning Guide for Southern Baptist Churches.* Nashville: Convention Press, 1975.

Robinson, Anthony B. "Learning from Willow Creek Church." *Christian Century* 108 (January 23, 1991): 68–70.

Robinson, Willard B. *Reflections of Faith: Houses of Worship in the Lone Star State.* Waco, Texas: Baylor University Press, 1994.

Savage, Beth L. *African American Historic Places.* Washington, D.C.: Preservation Press, 1994.

Schaller, Lyle E. *Center City Churches: The New Urban Frontier.* Nashville: Abingdon Press, 1993.

———. *The New Reformation: Tomorrow Arrived Yesterday.* Nashville: Abingdon Press, 1995.

———. *The Seven-Day-A-Week Church.* Nashville: Abingdon Press, 1992.

Schuller, Robert H. *Your Church Has Real Possibilities!* Glendale, Calif.: Regal Books, 1974.

Smith, Edward D. *Climbing Jacob's Ladder: The Rise of Black Churches in Eastern American Cities, 1740–1877.* Washington, D.C.: Smithsonian Institution Press, 1988.

Sövik, Edward. "What Is Religious Architecture?" *Faith and Form* 1 (1967 Special Issue): 8–9, 22–26.

Stafford, Tim. "God Is in the Blueprints." *Christianity Today* (September 7, 1998): 77–82.

Thumma, Scott L. "The Kingdom, the Power, and the Glory: The Megachurch in Modern American Society." Ph.D. diss., Emory University, 1996.

Tillich, Paul. "Contemporary Protestant Architecture." In *Modern Church Architecture: A Guide to the Form and Spir-*

it of 20th Century Religious Buildings. New York: Mc-Graw-Hill Book Company, Inc., 1962.

Towns, Elmer L. An Inside Look at 10 of Today's Most Innovative Churches. Ventura, Calif.: Regal Books, 1990.

———, John N. Vaughan, and David J. Seifert. The Complete Book of Church Growth. Wheaton, Ill.: Tyndale House Publishers, Inc., 1981.

Trueheart, Charles. "Welcome to the Next Church." Atlantic Monthly (August 1996): 37–40, 42–44, 46–47, 50, 52–54, 56–58.

Vaughan, John N. Megachurches and America's Cities: How Churches Grow. Grand Rapids, Mich.: Baker Books, 1993.

———. The World's Twenty Largest Churches. Grand Rapids, Mich.: Baker Book House, 1984.

Webber, Robert E. "Church Buildings: Shapes of Worship." Christianity Today (August 7, 1981): 18–20.

———. Worship Old and New: A Biblical, Historical, and Practical Introduction. Rev. ed. Grand Rapids, Mich.: Zondervan Publishing House, 1994.

White, James F. Protestant Worship and Church Architecture: Theological and Historical Considerations. New York: Oxford University Press, 1964.

Williams, Herbert Lee. D. James Kennedy: The Man and His Ministry. Nashville: Thomas Nelson Publishers, 1990.

Williams, Peter W. Houses of God: Region, Religion, and Architecture in the United States. Urbana: University of Illinois Press, 1997.

———. "Religious Architecture and Landscape." In Charles H. Lippy and Peter W. Williams, eds., Encyclopedia of the American Religious Experience: Studies of Traditions and Movements (New York: Charles Scribner's Sons, 1988).

Williamson, Susan. "Planning for Numbers." Texas Architect 47 (March/April 1997): 52–53.

Witvliet, John D. "The Blessing and Bane of the North American Megachurch: Implications for Twenty-First Century Congregational Song." The Hymn 50 (January 1999): 6–14.

Woodson, Carter G. The History of the Negro Church. 1921. Reprt., Washington, D.C.: Associated Publishers, 1945.

Wright, David Gilmore, and Calvin Correll. The Restoration of the Lovely Lane Church, Baltimore City Station: The Mother Church of American Methodism. Baltimore: Trustees of the Methodist Episcopal Church, 1980.

All bold-face page numbers refer to illustrations.

Index

Wagner, C. Peter, 115
Wagoner, Harold E., 108, 109, 237, 275*n1*, 286*n52*
Wanamaker, John, 70, 72, 83, 270*n6*
Warren, Rick, 117, 150
Webber, Robert E., 234
Wesley, John, 17
West Angeles Church of God in Christ, 158, 186, **193**, 285*n41*
White, James F., 108, 109, 275*n1*
White, Stanford, 45
Whitefield, George, 17, 22–23, 38
Williams, Lacy Kirk, 73
Williams, Peter, 7, 155
Williams, Riley F., 104
Williams, Susan, 151
Willow Creek Association, 114

Willow Creek Community Church, 3, 122, 123, 126, 127, 129, **133**, **134**, **135**, 157, 181, 182, 183, **203**, 227, 228, 231, 237, 277*n18*, 278*nn18,19*, 290*n4*, 292*n24*
Wimber, John, 115, 281*n17*
Windsor Village United Methodist Church, 187
Witvliet, John D., 227
Woodlawn Preservation and Investment Corporation, 187, 188
Woodruff, Fuzzy, 91, 93
World Changers Ministries Christian Center, 152, **166**, 282*n23*
Worship: changes in, 2, 89, 226–27; contemporary Christian, 3, 227, 257; Puritan, 7; and rotunda shape, 34; nineteenth-century evangelical, 34, 47–48, 89; in auditorium

churches, 53; of dissenting evangelicals, 89–90; in the "gathered church," 109–10; in megachurches, 132, 226–27, 237, 240, 257, 260; revitalization movement, 226–27, 290*n6*
Wren, Sir Christopher, 10, 35
Wright, Frank Lloyd, 111
Wright, Jeremiah A., Jr. 126, 235–36

Young, Ed, 156–57
Young, Edwin, 150
Young Men's Christian Association, 19, 30, 31, 70, 71

Zimmerman, Philip, 8